EDWARD M. GRAHAM
PAUL R. KRUGMAN

Foreign Direct Investment in the United States

Third Edition

Institute for International Economics
Washington, DC
January 1995

Edward M. Graham, *Senior Fellow*, was Associate Professor in the Fuqua School of Business at Duke University (1988–90), Associate Professor at the University of North Carolina (1983–88); Principal Administrator of the Planning and Evaluation Unit at the OECD (1981–82); International Economist in the Office of International Investment Affairs at the US Treasury (1979–80) and Assistant Professor at the Massachusetts Institute of Technology (1974–78). He is author or coauthor of a number of studies of international investment and technology transfer, including *Foreign Direct Investment in the United States* (second edition 1991).

Paul R. Krugman is Professor of Economics at Stanford University and winner of the 1992 John Bates Clark Medal. He has served as Senior International Economist on the staff of the Council of Economic Advisers and is the author or coauthor of numerous works on international trade and monetary economics, including *Peddling Prosperity: Economic Sense and Nonsense in the Age of Diminished Expectations* (1994), *The Age of Diminished Expectations: US Economic Policy in the 1990s* (rev. ed. 1994), *Has the Adjustment Process Worked?* (1991), *Foreign Direct Investment in the United States* (second edition 1991), and *Rethinking International Trade* (1990).

INSTITUTE FOR INTERNATIONAL ECONOMICS
11 Dupont Circle, NW
Washington, DC 20036-1207
(202) 328-9000   FAX: (202) 328-0900

C. Fred Bergsten, *Director*
Christine F. Lowry, *Director of Publications*

Cover design by Naylor Design, Inc.
Typesetting by AlphaTechnologies/mps
Printing by Kirby Lithographic Co., Inc.

Printed in the United States of America
97 96 95   5 4 3 2

Library of Congress Cataloging-in-Publication Data

Graham, Edward M. (Edward Montgomery), 1944–
    Foreign direct investment in the United States / Edward M. Graham, Paul R. Krugman.—3rd ed.
        p. cm.
    Includes bibliographical references and index.
    1. Investments, Foreign—United States.   I. Krugman, Paul R.   II. Title.
HG4910.G74   1994
332.6'73'0973—dc20
                                                    94-38975
ISBN 0-88132-204-0   CIP

Marketed and Distributed outside the USA and Canada by Longman Group UK Limited, London

To Robin Wells and Mary Graham

Contents

Tables

Figures

Preface

The rapid shift in global economic relationships in recent years is nowhere more apparent than with respect to foreign direct investment (FDI). Until quite recently, most of the analytical and policy concerns on this issue were focused in two directions: on the flow of FDI from the United States into Canada, Europe, and the developing countries, and on the potential global power of the multinational firms themselves. Books with such titles as *Le Défi Americain (The American Challenge)*, *Sovereignty at Bay*, *Global Reach*, and *American Multinationals and American Interests* were widely read and discussed.

In the 1980s, however, the United States became the world's largest host country to FDI as well as the largest home country of multinationals. The rapid rise of Japanese FDI, in particular, opened another front in the debate over that country's role in the world economy and over US–Japan economic relations. Congress began to address the issue through several hotly debated provisions of the Omnibus Trade and Competitiveness Act of 1988, in particular the Exon-Florio amendment, which for the first time in American history set up a mechanism to screen some of the direct investment entering this country.

The initial edition of this study, which appeared in 1989, marked the first attempt at a comprehensive analysis of inward FDI in the United States since the phenomenon became so important to the American economy. It assessed the extent, nature, and causes of FDI and its effect on the economy, political process, and national security of the United States. The book identified specific policy measures, domestic and international, that should and should not be adopted in response. It received extensive critical acclaim, and new legislation in 1990 adopted some of its proposals.

The second edition of the volume in 1991 updated the analysis to include the most recent data available, and expanded its treatment of Japanese investment because of the widespread concerns about that aspect of inward FDI. This third edition further updates the analysis, using some of the data series generated by the 1990 legislation noted above. In addition, the chapters on US policy and the authors' recommendations are extensively revised to reflect legislative initiatives that have appeared during the 1990s and the new focus on foreign direct investment that is emerging in international fora such as the OECD and the APEC.

The study was conducted by Senior Fellow Edward M. Graham and Paul R. Krugman, now at Stanford University and a Visiting Fellow at the Institute. They were ably assisted in preparing the initial edition by a study group of experts on FDI from the US government, the business community, and academia. I would like to add my personal gratitude to that of the authors for the group's assistance.

The Institute for International Economics is a private nonprofit institution for the study and discussion of international economic policy. Its purpose is to analyze important issues in that area and to develop and communicate practical new approaches for dealing with them. The Institute is completely nonpartisan.

The Institute is funded largely by philanthropic foundations. Major institutional grants are now being received from the German Marshall Fund of the United States, which created the Institute with a generous commitment of funds in 1981, and from the Ford Foundation, the William and Flora Hewlett Foundation, the William M. Keck, Jr. Foundation, the Andrew Mellon Foundation, the C. V. Starr Foundation, and the United States–Japan Foundation. A number of other foundations and private corporations also contribute to the highly diversified financial resources of the Institute. The John M. Olin Foundation provided partial funding for the first edition. About 12 percent of the Institute's resources in our latest fiscal year were provided by contributors outside the United States, including about 5 percent from Japan.

The Board of Directors bears overall responsibility for the Institute and gives general guidance and approval to its research program—including identification of topics that are likely to become important to international economic policymakers over the medium run (generally, one to three years), and which thus should be addressed by the Institute. The Director, working closely with the staff and outside Advisory Committee, is responsible for the development of particular projects and makes the final decision to publish an individual study.

The Institute hopes that its studies and other activities will contribute to building a stronger foundation for international economic policy around the world. We invite readers of these publications to let us know how they think we can best accomplish this objective.

C. FRED BERGSTEN
Director
December 1994

Acknowledgments

This study reflects the contributions of many hands other than our own, although we of course bear responsibility for all of the study's failings. The members of the IIE study group on foreign direct investment provided crucial guidance. Officials at the Bureau of Economic Analysis of the US Department of Commerce were extremely helpful with both data and interpretive suggestions, as were officials elsewhere in the Department of Commerce, the Department of the Treasury, the Department of Defense, and the US Congress.

Richard N. Cooper and Rachel McCulloch provided detailed reviews of early drafts of the first edition, which helped us greatly improve the final version. Ted Moran also provided valuable comments. Raymond Vernon provided detailed reviews of the first and second editions, resulting in improvements both times.

We received help from many members of the staff of the Institute for International Economics. Among these, Amelia Porges helped us immensely with legal matters, Michael Treadway provided vital editorial help on all three editions, and J. David Richardson provided numerous suggestions for improvements in the second edition. C. Fred Bergsten provided guidance and assistance throughout the process of preparing all three editions.

Finally, Rose Marie Ham provided extraordinary research assistance for the first edition, Aaron Tam for the second, and Naoko Anzai for the third.

Introduction

The role of foreign firms in the US economy grew rapidly between the late 1970s and the early 1990s. During the twenty years from 1972 to 1992, by a variety of measures, the share of US assets, employment, and production accounted for by US affiliates of foreign firms increased by a factor of between three and five. The most dramatic increase occurred during the six-year period 1985–90, with an equally dramatic slowdown thereafter, continuing right up to the time of this writing (July 1994). As detailed in chapter 1, the increase of the second half of the 1980s was part of a broader trend toward greater participation by foreign firms in the economies of most of the advanced countries of the world.

The growing foreign presence in the United States sparked a flood of popular articles and books, most of them expressing concern, and many alarm.[1] Their authors worried that foreign firms would behave differently from domestic ones in ways that reduced employment, worsened the trade deficit, or inhibited technological progress in America; they warned that too large a foreign presence might compromise national sovereignty or threaten national security. Relatively fewer books and articles were devoted to a defense of foreign investment in the United States, but statements arguing generally in favor of such investment were common, usually proceeding from a general presumption in favor of free markets.[2]

---

1. Recent popular treatments of the subject include Burstein (1988), Frantz and Collins (1989), Glickman and Woodward (1989), Prestowitz (1988), Rohatyn (1989), Spencer (1988), and Tolchin and Tolchin (1988).

2. See, for example, Becker (1989). More balanced discussions that are on the whole favorable to foreign direct investment are those by Peterson (1989) and Morgan Guaranty Trust Company (1989).

Clearly, foreign direct investment (FDI) in the United States had become a major issue. Yet during the late 1980s there was a remarkable absence of serious analytical discussion of the subject. Both critics and defenders of FDI relied primarily on anecdotes and a priori judgments rather than on systematic analysis of the data. To the extent that the debate had a central focus at all, it was on the assessment of the employment impacts of FDI—a question that, we will argue, is misguided and sterile. The original purpose of this study was to fill this gap in the literature. The first edition of this book, which appeared in 1989, presented a more analytical discussion of the growing foreign presence in the US economy than had appeared up to that time. This third edition is an update of the facts and policy analyses presented in that work. Our discussion in this edition, as in the first, focuses on six key questions, our answers to which are summarized here.

- What is the extent of foreign control of US business, and how fast has it grown?

Popular treatments of FDI have sometimes seemed to suggest that a wholesale takeover of US assets is occurring. Since standard statistics indicate that the role of foreign firms, although much larger than it was before the late 1970s, is still modest, the concern is either that the numbers greatly understate the actual foreign role or that the foreign presence is growing so rapidly that it will become very large in the very near future.

Chapter 1 presents and analyzes the most recent US government data on the extent and trend of inward FDI (direct investment entering the United States from abroad, as opposed to direct investment abroad by US firms, or outward FDI). By the end of 1992 foreign-owned firms accounted for about 4 percent of the US economy as a whole (i.e., the value added by these firms was about 4 percent of US national product) and, depending on the measure used, between 11 percent and 19 percent of the US manufacturing sector; by 1993 foreign firms controlled between 16 percent and 23 percent of the US banking industry. Although there are potential errors of measurement in these numbers, in both directions, they are unlikely to be large enough to make much difference. These numbers represent increases in the foreign-controlled share of US assets of about 200 percent for the US economy as a whole and about 250 percent for both the manufacturing and the banking sectors since the mid–1970s. Thus the foreign role in the US economy has indeed grown rapidly and is quite substantial. However, it is still smaller than that in many other advanced countries.

Also worth noting are recent balance of payments statistics that show that, after surging in the late 1980s, FDI inflows into the United States dropped sharply after 1990; indeed, since 1990 inflows of FDI as a share of national income have been well below their levels over the previous 15 years. Thus, the rapid growth in foreign ownership that took place during the second half of the 1980s has not continued.

■ Why has FDI in the United States increased?

Rising concern about the role of foreign firms coincided with the rise of foreign claims on the United States in general, associated with the unprecedented series of US current account deficits after 1981. Thus, much of the popular literature has tied the growth of FDI to the United States' movement toward net debtor status and suggests that increasing foreign control is ultimately tied to low US saving. An alternative view is that the coincidence of current account deficits and the rising levels of FDI during the second half of the 1980s was just that, a coincidence, and that the growing role of foreign firms in the United States has deeper roots in changes in the US role in the world economy. FDI flows in the balance of payments increased sharply beginning late in 1986; some analysts have attributed this development to the decline in the dollar, others to changes in US corporate taxation, or to increased protection, or to the ebb and flow of the business cycle.

Chapter 2 examines the sources of recent growth in FDI in the United States. Explanations of FDI generally fall into one of two categories: cost-of-capital explanations, which tie FDI to international capital flows generally, and industrial-organization explanations, which view FDI as dictated chiefly by corporate strategy rather than by capital movements.

The coincidence of growing inward FDI and US current account deficits after 1981 provides surface plausibility to a cost-of-capital story. However, a closer look at the facts does not support this view. US inward FDI in fact grew quite steadily from the early 1970s through 1990 and indeed grew more rapidly during the period from 1977 to 1981, before the emergence of large US current account deficits, than during the years of peak aggregate capital inflow in the late 1980s. Also, the majority of the increase in foreign holdings in the United States came from European and especially British firms, even though neither Europe as a whole nor the United Kingdom was a large exporter of capital. FDI from Japan, which was a net capital-exporting nation, although of growing importance as the 1980s wore on, still accounted for only a fraction of the story. Examination of individual cases, such as the color television and the automobile industries, confirms that when foreign firms undertake US production it is typically because they have firm-specific assets that give them an advantage in management and technology, not because they have a lower cost of capital. Within the broad industrial-organization story that we believe best explains the general increase of FDI in the United States, shifts in exchange rates, taxation, and protection all probably play important roles in explaining the timing of this investment.

■ What are the economic benefits and costs of a growing foreign presence?

Much of the popular literature has argued that foreign ownership will adversely affect US employment and trade or lead to a shift of good jobs and advanced technology away from the United States. Defenders of FDI suggest that it provides important gains from integration and possibly valuable external economies as well. One issue that has surfaced since the dollar began to fall in early 1985 is whether foreign firms, regardless of their long-run effect on the US economy, are being allowed to buy up US assets at bargain prices—the so-called fire sale issue. This concern was exacerbated by the October 1987 crash of the US stock market and by what was, until the bursting of the "bubble economy" in Japan, a remarkably high level of Japanese stock prices.

The economic impact, positive and negative, of FDI is considered in chapter 3, which argues that most concerns about harmful foreign-firm behavior are not borne out by the experience with FDI so far. US affiliates of foreign firms look quite similar to US firms in the same industries in terms of value added per worker, rates of compensation, and research and development. The only noticeable difference between foreign-owned and domestic firms is that the former do on average import more of their production inputs per worker. We argued in the first edition of this book that this is particularly true of Japanese firms, and this still seems to be the case. This higher propensity to import may be in part a statistical illusion, however, due to misclassifications and biases in the types of activities that foreign firms enter, and even on the most pessimistic assumptions this tendency to import represents a modest cost to the United States. Nonetheless, it has become and may remain a source of considerable tension.

As to the fire sale argument, much of this discussion is conceptually confused. There is little basis for arguing that either the dollar or US assets were undervalued in world markets during the years when inward FDI surged. To the extent that US assets have been sold at prices below their true value, the resulting losses are small even under very pessimistic assumptions.

■ What are the domestic political consequences of FDI?

Concerns have been raised that a large presence of foreign firms will distort the political process in the United States, with foreign interests carrying too much weight in domestic decisions. Defenders of FDI argue that this risk is mild and that other countries have been able to accept substantial amounts of FDI without seriously compromising their sovereignty.

Chapter 4 examines whether foreign firms exert influence on the US political process in ways that ultimately harm the interests of domestic residents. There is some valid logic behind this concern—not in that foreign firms differ qualitatively from other special interests in their behavior, but because any redistribution of income to foreign firms through the political process represents a national loss in a sense that purely internal redistribution does not. In practice, however, the costs and inefficiencies associated with even run-of-the-mill domestic special-interest politics make it difficult to get especially concerned about the additional costs arising from foreign intervention.

■ Does foreign investment threaten national security?

There is concern that the presence of foreign firms, particularly in industries that generate advanced technology, will somehow compromise US security interests; others dismiss this as a minor issue, adequately dealt with under existing rules and regulations.

We discuss the national security implications of FDI in chapter 5. There are some serious problems to be dealt with in this area. The reason is not so much that foreign firms themselves endanger national security as that existing procurement practices and regulations designed to safeguard sensitive US technologies complicate, if not preclude, potentially beneficial contractual arrangements between the Pentagon and foreign-owned firms. As a result, there is a sense in which FDI shrinks the industrial base available for defense contracting. This issue has yet to be fully resolved. It is complicated by the fact that now, at a time when the foreign role in the US economy has grown, the US defense-related sector as a whole is shrinking.

■ What should be done?

A variety of proposals have been offered to deal with the growth of FDI in the United States; these range from benign neglect, through proposals for stiffened reporting requirements, to demands for restrictions and performance requirements on foreign investment. The ultimate purpose of this study is to shed light on the merits of these proposals; in chapter 7 we also offer a few proposals of our own.

The basic thrust of this study is that alarm about the consequences of a growing foreign presence in the US economy is not warranted. The share of the US economy controlled by foreign firms, although it has grown, is not exploding; indeed, at the moment it has stopped growing at all—a point that current US policy does not seem to have fully absorbed. At current levels, the importance of foreign firms in the US economy is less than what has been more or less comfortably accepted in a number of European countries since the early 1970s. And although foreign firms do apparently have a higher import propensity than domestic firms, the more serious charge—that foreign firms keep their high-value-added or more sophisticated activities at home—is not borne out by the evidence. Moreover, should a real threat to national security arise from the attempts of foreign firms to acquire US assets, the US government is well empowered to block such action. Indeed, ambiguities in existing law open the door to wholesale screening of foreign investment and imposition of performance requirements in a manner that would run sharply counter to the traditional US posture of neutrality toward FDI (i.e., general adherence to principles of national treatment for foreign investors).

For these reasons we believe that new measures that would place special burdens on foreign-owned firms that are not placed on domestic firms are not warranted. There are some difficult issues to be addressed in the defense area, but these require domestic reforms that accommodate the fact of FDI, not efforts to subject it to special and discriminatory regulation. Unfortunately, as we detail in chapter 7, US policy has, since the publication of the first edition of this book, shifted rather far in the direction of discrimination against foreign-controlled firms, and measures recently put before Congress would take policy even further in this direction. Perhaps more than anything else, this shift is what motivates this third edition.

Another motivation, we should note, is the availability of new data series that provide us with better as well as newer information than was available for the second edition. The new series were made possible by linking data held by the Bureau of Economic Analysis and the Bureau of the Census in the US Department of Commerce, and by the Bureau of Labor Statistics in the US Department of Labor. The data-linking exercise being conducted by these three agencies was enabled (and mandated) by the Foreign Direct Investment and International Financial Data Improvements Act of 1990, a piece of legislation prompted in part by our first edition (see appendix A). In fact, a casual reader comparing the tables in the first edition of this study with those in this edition might not realize that the data in this book are often of the new and improved variety, because we have tried to keep the tables consistent in format from edition to edition. But readers should take our word for it—the improvements are there!

1

Extent and Trends

Debate over foreign direct investment in the United States begins with a dispute over facts. Critics allege that official US statistics fail to measure the true extent of growing foreign ownership and control of the US economy. In the view of Representative John D. Dingell (R-MI), chairman of the House Energy and Commerce Committee, these statistics are "incomplete, inaccurate . . . [and] virtually useless to the analysis and decision making of policymakers" (Frantz and Collins 1989, ix). A bill proposed in 1988 by Representative John C. Bryant (D-TX)—the so-called Bryant amendment—would have mandated increased public disclosure of financial and operating information by foreign-owned firms. Although it did not become law, the fact that this proposal drew considerable congressional support is an indication of how important—and how inadequate—the measurement of FDI had become in the eyes of many US policymakers. Thus we begin with a discussion of what is known about the extent of FDI and its growth in the United States.

What Is FDI?

The very definition of FDI poses serious problems. What we seek to measure is the extent to which foreign firms and individuals control US production, yet it is not easy to define precisely either the nationality of a firm or what constitutes control.

What Is the Nationality of a Firm?

Foreign direct investment is formally defined as ownership of assets in one country by residents of another for purposes of controlling the use of those assets. In most cases, however, the foreign "resident" is a firm—a legal person but not an actual one. This raises the question of where a firm that produces in more than one country "resides," and indeed whether such a firm can properly be said to have a nationality at all.

It is easy to come up with examples that call the very notion of the nationality of a firm into question. Shell and British Petroleum (BP) are multinational firms with huge stakes in both the United States and Europe. In what realistic sense are they more foreign than Exxon and Mobil, of which exactly the same may be said? True, the central headquarters of Shell and BP are in Europe, whereas those of Exxon and Mobil are in the United States, but it is far from clear that this makes any substantial difference in the ways these firms behave. More generally, if a firm is simply conceived of as an organizational entity that sprawls across national boundaries, it does not make obvious sense to speak of the firm as a resident of any one of the countries in which its operations—including operation of a central headquarters—takes place.

Questioning the meaningfulness of the concept of firm nationality leads naturally to abandonment of the attempt to measure the role of foreign firms in the US economy at all. On an extreme view we should instead simply measure the role of multinational firms, whatever their national origin. By this measure it is not at all clear that the United States is experiencing any noticeable change: if Honda comes to have a larger share of US automobile production, and General Motors a smaller share, this is simply substituting one multinational for another.

In practice we need not give up quite so easily. In our still imperfectly integrated world, firms by and large continue to have different centers of gravity that give them a more or less definable national identity. To call General Motors an American company, and Honda a Japanese one, does some violence to the fact that each is a multinational concern producing in several countries, yet Honda is clearly more Japanese, in terms of the weight of its interests and economic stake, than is General Motors.

The nationality problem becomes most acute in defining the effective nationality of firms originating in small and medium-sized countries. Philips (the European electronics giant), Hoffmann–La Roche, SKF, and Seagram are all firms that originated in such countries (the Netherlands, Switzerland, Sweden, and Canada, respectively) yet produce and sell most of their output elsewhere—in the case of Philips and SKF to such an extent that English rather than Dutch or Swedish is the official corporate language. Since total direct investment by Dutch, Swiss, Swedish, and Canadian firms is a substantial part of FDI in the United States (and UK firms often seem equally anational or binational), there are in fact serious definitional problems with the numbers discussed later in this chapter.

What Constitutes Control?

Direct investment is ownership that carries with it actual control over what is owned; this aspect of control distinguishes direct investment from portfolio investment, which is simply the establishment of a claim on an asset for the purpose of realizing some return. In practice, even if the intent of the investor to assert or not assert control could be objectively determined, there remains the difficulty of determining what share of ownership brings with it actual control.

The US Department of Commerce defines a foreign investment as direct when a single investor has acquired a stake of 10 percent or more in a US firm. That firm is then considered a domestic affiliate of the foreign investor. The 10 percent criterion, although arbitrary, is meant to reflect the idea that a large stockholder will generally have a strong say in the operations of a company even if that stockholder does not have a majority stake. The requirement that the 10 percent be held by a single owner reflects the possibility that a firm may have many small foreign stockholders while remaining effectively under domestic control.

It is easy to see how this working definition could go astray in either direction, by failing to identify control exercised by a group of foreign investors each holding less than a 10 percent stake, or by defining a US firm as foreign controlled when the foreign owner does not exercise real control. The question is whether these potential pitfalls are important in practice. The evidence is strong that they are not.

The potential for understating foreign control comes from the possibility that a firm with many small foreign investors may effectively act in their collective interest even though no one of them has more than a 10 percent share. Suppose, for example, that 15 Japanese residents (individuals or firms) together hold 80 percent of a US firm's shares. Even if these foreign residents do not constitute a preorganized group, management might act in a way that favors the interests of the Japanese stockholders over those of the US stockholders. This would give the foreign shareholders a measure of de facto control even though the US firm would not be recorded as a subsidiary of a Japanese firm.

In practice, this particular measurement problem has been less of a concern in regard to foreign ownership of US businesses than in regard to other kinds of investment. For example, small-scale foreign investments in real estate are sometimes organized through mechanisms that effectively give control to foreign residents without the official statistics reflecting such control. In particular, when foreign investors buy US real estate through a limited partnership where the controlling partners are US residents, the investment is not counted as direct, because the limited partners do not have de jure control. In practice, however, limited partners can have an important say in operations.

Almost certainly, however, such exceptions are not of great economic importance. The potential dollar value of investments that miss being counted in this way is regarded by all of those familiar with the numbers as limited, and in any case such investments are not the ones that have caused FDI in the United States to become a major issue. What we are really interested in are the situations in which US manufacturing firms, banks, and other large institutions are integrated into the control structure of foreign-based multinational firms. These cases require that a single foreign parent establish unambiguous control and are not disguisable.

What about the possibility of overstating FDI? The misclassification of some firms as foreign-controlled when they are de facto US-controlled may be a significant source of overstatement. The main potential problem is that of large investments where the 10 percent criterion is met but where the investor does not attempt to establish operational control. Suppose that a foreign individual or firm purchases 13 percent of a US firm purely as an investment, leaving existing management in charge, the corporate headquarters in the United States, and so on. Counting this as FDI will surely overstate the extent of change in actual operational control.

There are some familiar examples of this problem. The most notable case is that of Du Pont, 22.9 percent of which is owned by the Bronfman family of Canada (the founder-owners of Seagram); as a result, Du Pont is classified as a Canadian firm. Since Du Pont's operations have not been placed under the control of a foreign-based chemical enterprise—and the de facto nationality of the owner is itself arguable, whatever the family's citizenship—this is clearly a misclassification in the sense that foreign interests do not have managerial control of the firm. Indeed, the situation is even more interesting because Du Pont also qualifies as a US parent firm holding controlled affiliates abroad. We are told by the staff of the Bureau of Economic Analysis (BEA) that there are a number of other cases in which the same enterprise is classified both as foreign-owned and as a US parent. (Under confidentiality rules, the BEA cannot reveal who these firms are; we offer Du Pont as an example because it conspicuously meets BEA criteria on the basis of public information.)

However, in the aggregate the danger of overstatement or understatement due to these problems is small. Table 1.1 shows the financial structure of US affiliates of foreign firms in the aggregate for 1991. On average the foreign parent controlled 77.5 percent of the affiliate's equity. Thus, the typical US affiliate of a foreign firm is clearly majority owned, rather than an ambiguous case in which the foreign firm holds a fractional stake. It follows that borderline cases where passive investments by foreigners are classified as FDI must be the exception rather than the rule. Preliminary

Table 1.1 Financing of US affiliates of foreign firms, 1991

Investor	Debt and current liabilities		Equity		Assets	
	Millions of dollars	Percentages of total	Millions of dollars	Percentages of total	Millions of dollars	Percentages of total
Foreign parent	179,866	16.1	289,413	77.5	469,279	31.4
Other foreigners	53,305	4.8	1,330	0.4	54,635	3.7
US persons	887,210	79.2	82,657	22.1	969,867	64.9
Total[a]	1,120,381	100.0	373,400	100.0	1,493,781	100.0

a. Figures may not sum to totals because of rounding.

Source: Bureau of Economic Analysis, "Foreign Direct Investment in the US: Operations of US Affiliates of Foreign Companies" (preliminary 1991 estimate), table C–1.

calculations by the BEA staff suggest that raising the classifying criterion to 20 percent or even 50 percent would have a minor impact on the extent of US business classified as being under foreign control.

The statistical coverage of FDI is known to be imperfect. The BEA acknowledges that there has been some underreporting of FDI, and investigations have been conducted to determine its extent as well as to determine why the underreporting occurred. However, the imperfections are not likely to loom very large. Broadly speaking, US official data on FDI do give an accurate picture of the extent and trend of foreign investments aimed at establishing corporate control. (Appendix A further examines the nature and adequacy of the BEA data.)

The Rise of FDI: Alternative Measures

One commonly used measure of the rate at which foreign control in the US economy is increasing or decreasing is the flow of FDI into the United States as measured in the balance of payments. This inward flow measure combines three elements: purchases of equity, whether they lead to acquisition of a controlling interest or expand the holdings of foreign owners who already hold a controlling interest; retained earnings of foreign-controlled firms; and net lending from parents to subsidiaries. It does not count investment by foreign-controlled firms financed by selling either debt or equity to unrelated parties, foreign or domestic, nor does it allow for increases in the value of existing foreign-controlled assets. Thus, the balance of payments data may understate actual increases in foreign control to a fluctuating degree. Nonetheless, the balance of payments numbers are useful because they become available more quickly than other measures. As we shall see, this is a potentially crucial point.

Figure 1.1 shows flows of FDI into the United States since 1974 using the balance of payments measure. These inward flows are expressed as a share of US GNP. There have been two major surges in this investment. The first occurred from 1978 to 1981, and the second from 1986 to 1990. After 1990 the inflows not only slowed but virtually dried up: FDI inflows in recent years have been smaller as a share of GNP than at any time since the early 1970s.

The effect of FDI inflows (or outflows) is presumably to expand (contract) the share of the US economy that is foreign controlled. Even for a given set of firms identified as foreign controlled, however, there are alternative ways of measuring the size of the foreign stake in the United States. All such measures are subject to criticism, but by looking at several alternatives we are likely to get a reasonably comprehensive view. Table 1.2 shows six indices of the role of foreign firms in the US economy, based on four alternative measures: the stock of FDI as measured by cumulative investments, the assets of US affiliates of foreign firms, the number of workers employed by these affiliates, and the value-added component of the output of these affiliates (figures 1.2 and 1.3 present these same series in graphic form).

The Stock of FDI

The most commonly cited measure of FDI is the balance of payments–based measure of the cumulative stock of FDI in the United States. This is the sum of foreign owners' equity (including retained earnings) on the balance sheets of all firms defined by the BEA as foreign affiliates, plus the sum of net lending to these affiliates from their parents. It is thus a stock figure reflecting the sum of earlier FDI flows. More interesting than the nominal value of this measure is a value that adjusts in some way for inflation and economic growth, to give some idea of the extent of FDI relative to the US economy as a whole. Table 1.2 shows the FDI stock in the United States as a percentage of the total net worth (by book value) of all nonfinancial US corporations. This FDI stock ratio increased by a factor of over four from 1977 to the end of 1992, when it stood at 11.6 percent.[1] The rise in this ratio following 1990 is, however, largely illusory. It came about not because the stock of FDI in the United States grew substantially (we have already seen that it did not), but rather because the denominator—the net worth of all US nonfinancial corporations at book value—fell. This in turn was due to a large drop in the aggregate value of commercial real estate, one of the components of the denominator. If this component were

---

1. Discontinuities in this ratio appear in 1980 and 1987 and are due in part to revisions of the FDI data series following the BEA benchmark surveys in those years (see appendix A).

Figure 1.1 Foreign direct investment flows into the United States, balance of payments basis, 1974–92

percent of GNP (four-quarter moving average)

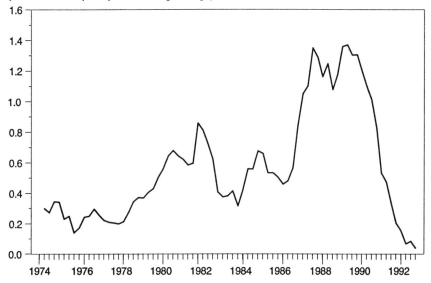

Source: From data in *Survey of Current Business*, various issues.

removed from the denominator, the FDI stock ratio would have been almost constant following 1990.

The FDI stock ratio is useful because it is easily calculated and can be brought quickly up to date, but it is not an adequate measure by itself. In particular, it presents problems of valuation: it is in effect a measure of FDI at historical cost, and thus it neglects capital gains and losses on these investments, which are potentially large. Recent estimates by the BEA, shown in table 1.3, indicate that changes in market prices of assets have large effects on the net US direct investment position. At the end of 1989, FDI in the United States, measured on a historical cost basis, was slightly larger than US direct investment abroad. On a market value basis, however, the inward FDI stock was only 66 percent as large as the outward. By 1992, the combined effects of the collapse of inward investment and a revival of outward investment had reduced the ratio of book values to 0.86; but the ratio of market values had actually risen to 0.89, largely as a result of the rise in US equity prices.

More fundamentally, the FDI stock ratio fails to measure the extent to which foreign claims are leveraged into larger control, both through less-than-100-percent ownership and through borrowing from unrelated parties. As can be seen in table 1.1, the typical US affiliate of a foreign firm is in fact largely financed with credit from US residents, so that the FDI stock ratio could represent a serious understatement of foreign control.

Table 1.2   Alternative measures of the role of foreign direct investment in the US economy, 1977–92 (percentages)

Measure	1977	1978	1979	1980	1981	1982	1983	1984
FDI stock ratio[a]	2.6	2.8	3.0	2.7	3.2	3.5	3.8	4.5
Share of foreign affiliates								
In US mfg. assets[b]	5.2	5.7	6.6	7.2	9.6	9.8	10.1	10.2
In total US employment[c]	1.7	1.9	2.2	2.6	3.0	3.1	3.2	3.3
In US mfg. employment[d]								
By industry of affiliate	3.5	3.9	4.8	5.5	6.5	6.6	7.2	7.1
By industry of sales								
By industry of establishment								
In US GNP[e]	1.7	1.9	2.2	2.6	3.2	3.3	3.3	3.4
In US mfg. value added[f]	3.6	3.9	4.6	5.3	7.2	7.3	7.6	7.9
Memoranda:								
FDI stock (billions of dollars)	51.5	63.5	79.4	83.0	108.7	124.7	137.1	164.6
Total net worth of US nonfinancial corporations (billions of dollars)	1,992.2	2,278.0	2,659.8	3,048.3	3,391.1	3,539.0	3,607.5	3,690.6

a. FDI stock as a percentage of total net worth of US nonfinancial corporations. *Source:* Federal Reserve Board, "Balance Sheets for the U.S. Economy 1945–92," 17 September 1993, 36.

b. Assets of foreign affiliates in manufacturing divided by assets of all US manufacturing corporations, excluding petroleum refining. *Sources:* Affiliates' assets for 1977–86 from BEA, "Foreign Direct Investment in the United States: Operations of U.S. Affiliates of Foreign Companies" (FDIUS:OUSAFC), various years, table B-1; affiliates' assets for 1987–91 from BEA, "U.S. Affiliates of Foreign Companies: Operations in 1991," *Survey of Current Business*, May 1993, and similar articles in previous years; US manufacturing assets from Bureau of the Census and Federal Trade Commission, "Quarterly Financial Report for Manufacturing, Mining, and Trade Corporations," various issues and tables.

c. Employment of foreign affiliates divided by total US employment, excluding banking. *Sources:* affiliates' employment from FDIUS:OUSAFC, various years, table F-1; total US employment from "National Income and Products Accounts" (NIPA), *Survey of Current Business*, various issues and supplementary volume, tables 6-6B and 6.4C). Figure for 1992 is preliminary.

(continued next page)

Assets of Foreign-Controlled US Affiliates

A natural alternative to using the stock of foreign equity as a measure of FDI is to compare the total assets of foreign-controlled firms with those of

Table 1.2 (continued)

Measure	1985	1986	1987	1988	1989	1990	1991	1992
FDI stock ratio[a]	4.9	5.8	6.8	7.8	8.9	9.7	10.7	11.6
Share of foreign affiliates								
In US mfg. assets[b]	10.8	11.4	12.4	14.6	17.6	18.9	19.2	n.a.
In total US employment[c]	3.3	3.4	3.7	4.2	3.8	4.0	4.8	4.6
In US mfg. employment[d]								
By industry of affiliate	7.6	7.5	8.1	9.5	11.0	11.6	11.9	10.8
By industry of sales			7.7	8.9	10.2	11.0	11.6	11.6
By industry of establishment				8.2	n.a.	10.6	n.a.	n.a.
In US GNP[e]	3.4	3.4	3.5	3.9	4.3	4.3	4.5	4.4
In US mfg. value added[f]	7.8	7.9	8.6	9.5	10.9	13.8	14.5	15.0
Memoranda:								
FDI stock (billions of dollars)	184.6	220.4	263.4	314.8	368.9	394.9	418.8	425.6
Total net worth of US nonfinancial corporations (billions of dollars)	3,755.3	3,783.5	3,866.9	4,012.4	4,125.4	4,088.5	3,888.1	3,646.4

d. Employment of foreign manufacturing affiliates divided by total US manufacturing employment (excluding petroleum refining). *Sources:* Industry of affiliates, same as for note c; industry of sales, from *Survey of Current Business*, July, 1994, pg. 161, table 7; industry of establishment data from BEA and Bureau of the Census, "Foreign Direct Investment in the United States: Establishment Data for Manufacturing, 1990, and 1988, table 1.1. See text for definitions of "industry of affiliate," "industry of sales," and "industry of establishment." Figures for 1992 are preliminary.
e. Output of foreign affiliates divided by US GNP. *Sources:* affiliates' output from BEA, "Foreign Direct Investment in the United States: Gross Product of Nonbank U.S. Affiliates of Foreign Companies, 1977–87" and similar article for 1987–90 (FDIUS:GPN), various tables; US GNP from NIPA, *Survey of Current Business*, various years, tables 1-1 and 1-9.
f. Value added of foreign manufacturing affiliates divided by total US manufacturing value added. *Sources:* affiliates' value added from FDIUS:GPN, November 1992, table 1; US value added from NIPA, Gross Domestic Product by Industry, *Survey of Current Business*, May 1993.

the US business sector generally. Unfortunately, total US business assets are dominated by the assets of financial firms, which do not carry with them comparable value added or employment and thus can give a misleading picture of the extent of foreign control. A reasonably valid alternative approach is to look at the assets of foreign-controlled manufacturing

Figure 1.2 Alternative measures of the share of foreign affiliates in the overall US economy, 1977–92

percentages

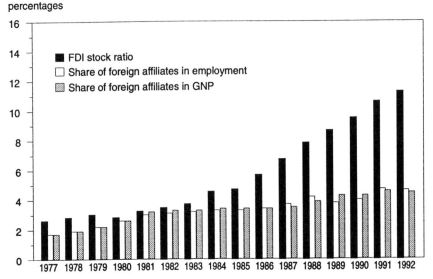

Source: From data in table 1.2.

firms alone relative to those of all US manufacturers. (Petroleum refining, which, like financial services, is highly capital-intensive and has a disproportionate foreign presence, is also excluded from these series.) The asset ratios thus calculated (second line in table 1.2) are substantially above the FDI stock ratio in every year of the period; as we will see shortly, however, this primarily reflects the fact that foreign firms have a larger role in the US manufacturing sector than in the rest of the economy. The other notable difference is that the asset ratio has grown more slowly than the FDI stock ratio, especially since 1981. At the end of 1991 (the most recent year for which data were available at the time of this writing), assets of US affiliates of foreign-controlled firms in the manufacturing sector amounted to 19.2 percent of total US manufacturing assets. Because of the slowdown in inflows of FDI that followed 1990, we doubt that this ratio increased significantly after 1991.

Employment in Foreign-Controlled US Affiliates

An arguably better measure of actual foreign control of the US economy is the share of the US work force employed by foreign-controlled firms. Table 1.2 shows employment in US affiliates of foreign firms as a share of

Figure 1.3 **Alternative measures of the share of foreign affiliates in US manufacturing, 1977–91**

percentages

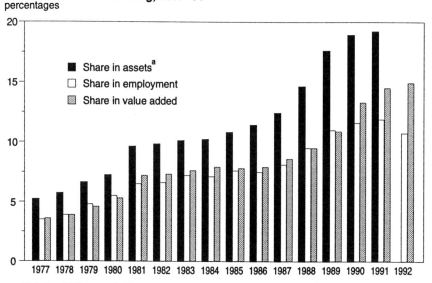

a. Data for 1992 unavailable.

Sources: From data in table 1.2.

total US employment, part-time and full-time, for the economy as a whole and for manufacturing alone (less petroleum refining).[2]

The aggregate employment ratio is substantially lower than the FDI stock ratio throughout the period, reflecting the fact that FDI is more concentrated in the corporate sector of the US economy than in the economy as a whole. The manufacturing employment ratio is roughly equal to the FDI stock ratio by the end of the series, but it starts a little higher and therefore grows more slowly. This manufacturing employment ratio is consistently somewhat smaller than the manufacturing asset share but grows at about the same rate. This would suggest that foreign-controlled

---

2. Beginning in the spring of 1992, the BEA began publishing employment data by two methods, by industry of affiliate and by industry of sales. The aggregate figures are the same, but the classification of employment by industry is affected by which method is used. Classification of employment by industry of affiliate was the only method used by the BEA until 1992; under this method, all employment by a US affiliate of a foreign firm is classified in the primary industry in which the affiliate operates. This creates measurement problems when the affiliate operates, and thus employs workers, in more than one industry. To remedy this, the industry of sales method attempts to disaggregate employment by the industry in which workers actually perform labor services. Although the second method is probably more analytically useful than the first, at present only limited employment data disaggregated by industry of sales are made available by the BEA. Hence, most of our data series are disaggregated by industry of affiliate, but where we have been able to do so, we have also included employment data by industry of sales.

Table 1.3 Foreign direct investment in the United States and US direct investment abroad, by book and market value, 1982–92 (billions of dollars)

Measure	1982	1983	1984	1985	1986	1987	1988	1989	1990	1991	1992[a]
FDI in the United States (inward FDI)											
By book value	124.7	137.1	164.6	184.6	220.4	263.4	314.8	373.8	396.7	414.4	420.0
By market value	133.0	157.5	177.7	227.9	283.2	315.7	391.0	533.5	536.6	673.0	692.3
US direct investment abroad (outward FDI)											
By book value	207.8	207.2	211.5	230.3	259.8	314.3	335.5	370.1	424.1	461.0	486.7
By market value	228.3	273.3	267.6	380.5	519.5	577.6	678.8	807.7	716.4	809.6	776.3
Ratio of inward to outward FDI											
By book value	0.60	0.66	0.78	0.80	0.85	0.84	0.94	1.01	0.94	0.90	0.86
By market value	0.58	0.58	0.66	0.60	0.55	0.55	0.58	0.66	0.75	0.83	0.89

a. Preliminary.

Sources: BEA, "Valuation of U.S. Net International Investment Position," *Survey of Current Business*, May 1991, table 1; "International Investment Position of the United States in 1990," *Survey of Current Business*, June 1993, table 4, and similar articles in *Survey of Current Business*, various June issues.

manufacturing operations in the United States tend to be more capital-intensive than US manufacturing in general.[3] One should note that the growth of the foreign-controlled share of manufacturing employment results both from increases in the number of employees of US affiliates of foreign firms engaged in manufacturing and from a decline in the total US manufacturing work force.[4]

These series highlight the substantially larger role of foreign firms in manufacturing than in the economy generally. They also reveal that the time pattern of growth in the foreign presence is not a simple trend; instead there were two surges, the first beginning in the late 1970s and the second in the mid-1980s, each followed by a deceleration of growth—indeed, by a virtual collapse in growth after 1990.

Value Added by Foreign-Controlled US Affiliates

Yet another alternative measure of the foreign role in the US economy is the value added by US affiliates of foreign firms as a share of value added for the US economy as a whole. Table 1.2 presents data on the share of foreign-controlled firms in value added (GNP) for the overall US economy and in the manufacturing sector alone (again excluding petroleum refining). These ratios look similar to the corresponding employment ratios: in 1990 foreign-controlled firms were estimated to account for 4 percent of US total employment and 4.3 percent of GNP, with substantially higher levels, 11.6 percent of both employment and value added, in manufacturing. The deceleration of growth from 1982 to 1986 that we observed in the employment data is even more marked in these value-added numbers; in the aggregate, growth in the foreign share virtually stopped from 1981 to 1986.

Thus, one major surprise in these data is the episodic nature of the growth of FDI in the United States: by most of our measures, the increase in foreign control has been concentrated in two surges, one that lasted from 1978 until 1981 and a second that lasted from 1986 until 1989.

One reason why the non–balance of payments measures and the FDI stock ratio do not always move together is that some foreign firms have

---

3. As is detailed later in this volume, this is largely the result of industry mix rather than of differences at the level of individual operations; otherwise put, foreign-controlled operations account for a larger percentage of capital-intensive subsectors than of other manufacturing subsectors.

4. The manufacturing employment ratios by industry of sales are somewhat lower than those by industry of affiliate. This occurs largely because certain large US affiliates of foreign firms are engaged both in importing (the industrial category for which is "wholesale trade") and manufacturing. When employment by these affiliates is classified by industry of affiliate, apparently more employees actually engaged in importing are put into the manufacturing category than the other way around. As we shall see, however, the opposite result holds for Japanese-owned affiliates.

been increasing their stake in their own subsidiaries; this shows up in the data as an FDI flow but does not increase the employment or value added by foreign-controlled firms in the US economy. For example, in 1985 Shell acquired the remaining 30.5 percent of its US affiliate, converting it to a wholly owned subsidiary. Similarly, in 1987 BP acquired the remaining 45 percent of its US affiliate. In each case the extent of control by foreign firms, as measured by share of employment or value added, did not change, but the outlay of funds was presumably reported as an FDI flow. (We say "presumably" because, again, the BEA does not release information pertaining to specific firms, but given what we know about BEA procedures, these publicly reported outlays would have been so recorded.)

Another factor explaining this discrepancy is found in the pattern of FDI during the 1986–90 surge, which was biased toward highly capital-intensive activities such as banking and finance, in which employment and value added per unit of capital are low. Banking in particular constitutes an important special case and is treated separately later in this chapter.

One basic message of the data, in any case, seems to be that although there has been a major increase in the role of foreign firms in the US economy, this increase has been poorly correlated with the swings in the current account deficit—slowing as the deficit surged, surging as the deficit declined, and coming to a virtual halt after 1990 despite a persisting current deficit. This observation will prove important in our interpretation of the causes of FDI in chapter 2.

The Slowdown of the Early 1990s

After five years of rapid and uninterrupted growth, the flow of FDI into the United States fell off sharply in 1990. In that year total inflows were slightly over $37 billion, down from over $72 billion in 1989. By 1992 FDI inflows had fallen virtually to zero. As shown in figures 1.4 and 1.5, all of the major countries with a significant FDI presence in the United States sharply reduced their rates of investment after 1989; the decline was very steep for Japan but even steeper for Europe. Obviously a key question is whether this represents a permanent break in trend: was the great FDI surge of the 1980s a one-time event?

We postpone a full discussion of this question until our consideration of the causes of FDI in chapter 2. It is worth pointing out immediately, however, that in some respects the slump in the balance of payments measure of inward FDI may not represent a comparable slowdown in the rate of growth of foreign control of US enterprises. Recall that the balance of payments measure of FDI is the sum of three component flows: net changes in equity in US affiliates by foreign direct investors, the retained earnings of these affiliates, and net lending from the foreign investors to the US affiliates. Only changes in equity, however, are necessarily associated with changes in the extent of foreign control.

Figure 1.4   Foreign direct investment flows into the United States, by source nation, all sectors, 1989–92

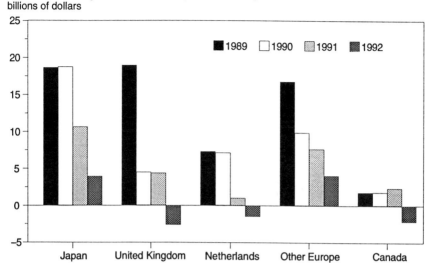

billions of dollars

Source: Bureau of Economic Analysis, *Survey of Current Business*, various issues.

Figures 1.6 and 1.7 separate FDI into these three components. They show that what happened after 1989 was a substantial slowdown but not a collapse of inward equity flows, combined with a very sharp decrease in loans from parents to subsidiaries and an acceleration of reductions in retained earnings. Retained earnings of US affiliates of foreign firms declined because payouts of dividends exceeded earnings. Moreover, there was a net flow of funds from established subsidiaries to their parents (i.e., the sum of net intrafirm borrowing and changes in retained earnings was negative). This in part reflected lower costs of borrowing in the United States and in part the efforts of some investors, particularly certain Japanese ones, to shore up the balance sheets of their home market operations following asset writedowns.

Also, as can be seen in table 1.4, the asset value of US businesses acquired or established by foreign firms declined in 1990, but significant investments continued to be made. To stylize the situation somewhat, after 1990 foreign firms continued to buy US firms, but at a reduced rate; simultaneously they stopped lending to their existing subsidiaries and started borrowing from them instead ("borrowing" here is to be read as the sum of dividend payments and intrafirm borrowing).

The Mechanics of FDI

In principle, growth of the foreign presence in the US economy could take place in either of two ways. Foreign firms could grow through the con-

Figure 1.5   Foreign direct investment flows into the United States by source nation, in manufacturing only, 1989–92

billions of dollars

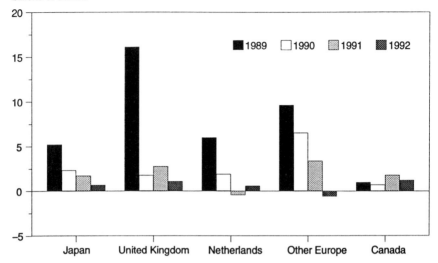

Source: Bureau of Economic Analysis, *Survey of Current Business*, various issues.

struction of new, "greenfield" production facilities in the United States, financed either through establishment of new subsidiaries or through new investment by existing US affiliates of foreign firms. Alternatively, foreign control could grow through acquisition of existing US firms.

Obviously both kinds of growth have been taking place: such ventures as the opening of new Japanese automobile plants in the United States are occurring in tandem with foreign takeovers such as Seagram's acquisition of Tropicana. In quantitative terms, however, acquisitions are clearly the more important source of growth in foreign control. Table 1.5 shows some indicative numbers. The table first compares actual investment outlays by foreign firms to acquire existing business firms in the United States with outlays for the purpose of establishing new subsidiaries. In most years the value of acquisitions has been several times that of new establishments. The table also shows the value of all US enterprises acquired or established by foreign firms; this is a much larger number because it includes noncontrolling claims such as minority shareholdings and debt that is not owed to the parent. This number is considerably larger than total expenditure on new plant and equipment by US affiliates of foreign firms (the next item in table 1.5). If one bears in mind that this is gross rather than net investment, it becomes clear that acquisitions have been the dominant source of growth. One should think of Matsushita's purchase of MCA, not Honda's opening of its Marysville, Ohio, plant, as the characteristic way in which FDI grew in the United States during the 1980s.

Figure 1.6 Foreign direct investment flows into the United States by financial composition, all sectors, 1989–92

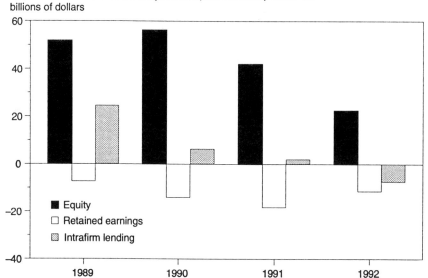

billions of dollars

Source: Bureau of Economic Analysis, *Survey of Current Business,* various issues.

The Role of Japan

For a number of reasons, Japanese direct investment in the United States has attracted special attention. Japanese firms have been the most spectacular competitors to US-based corporations, and there is naturally curiosity and concern about whether they can repeat their successes in the United States. Japan was also the world's principal exporter of portfolio capital in the 1980s—in effect the principal source of financing for the US current account deficit—and some have asked whether rising direct investment from Japan was the result of Japanese investors moving from a passive to an active role. Finally, there is a general sense that Japanese firms may behave differently from other foreign firms, either because of their protected domestic base or because they have a different culture and institutional structure.

We address the question of differences in behavior in later chapters. For now, our major point is that despite the rapidly increasing role of Japanese firms in the US economy during the 1980s as indicated by several measures, this role remained small relative to that of firms from elsewhere, most notably Europe. Table 1.6 shows seven indices of the share of Japanese firms in the overall foreign presence in the United States: their share in the FDI stock, their shares of foreign-held assets in the aggregate and in manufacturing (excluding petroleum refining), their shares of employ-

Figure 1.7 Foreign direct investment flows into the United States by financial composition, manufacturing only, 1989–92

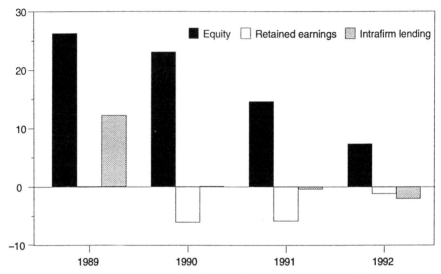

billions of dollars

Source: Bureau of Economic Analysis, *Survey of Current Business*, various issues.

ment by foreign firms in the aggregate and in manufacturing (this last by industry of affiliate, industry of sales, and industry of establishment), and their shares of total value added by foreign firms in the aggregate and in manufacturing. Despite the marked upward trend, Japan remains a relatively small part of the total FDI picture, as measured by its shares of employment and of value added. The large Japanese acquisitions and establishments in 1987–90, shown in table 1.4, increased the Japanese asset share; indeed, assets of firms classified as Japanese-controlled doubled in 1987 alone. These increases, however, took place primarily in financial firms, where large assets carry with them control over only small value added and employment.

The key point is that the rise in FDI in the United States has not been an essentially Japanese phenomenon. One way to make the point is to look at the raw employment numbers. From 1980 to 1990, the number of workers employed by US affiliates of foreign firms increased by 2.7 million, but only 550,000 of these additional employees were in Japanese-controlled firms.

Banking

The banking sector constitutes a special case, in which the numbers look quite different from those for other forms of FDI. The leveling off of the

Table 1.4   Asset value of US business enterprises acquired or established by foreign firms, 1980–92 (billions of dollars)

Year	All industries	Banking and finance	Japan
1980	49.7	29.0	n.a.
1981	87.7	39.3	n.a.
1982	31.9	11.8	1.1
1983	22.3	11.3	0.8
1984	40.5	17.3	7.4
1985	36.1	7.4	2.0
1986	71.8	18.1	11.2
1987	131.1	83.4	75.3
1988	142.6	27.5	29.5
1989	127.5	41.3	43.4
1990	95.0	14.8	30.5
1991	152.1	50.7	11.6
1992[a]	30.9	10.6	5.4

n.a. = not available
a. Preliminary.

Sources: For 1991 and 1992, BEA, "U.S. Businesses Acquired or Established by Foreign Direct Investors in 1992," *Survey of Current Business*, May 1993, tables 7.1, 7.2, and supplementary tables; data for previous years from similar articles in *Survey of Current Business*, various May issues.

foreign role after the early 1980s that is apparent in the aggregate data did not happen in banking, where the share of foreign ownership continued to rise rapidly. Also, Japanese firms dominate FDI in banking, in contrast to manufacturing and other sectors.

Foreign banks can operate in the United States in any of three forms: branches, agencies, and subsidiaries. (In New York State there is a fourth form, investment companies, but these appear to be a minor factor.) The distinctions among these forms of ownership need not concern us here. Table 1.7 shows several measures of the role of foreign banks' branches, agencies, and subsidiaries in the US banking sector. Overall, the foreign role in this sector has grown at about the same rate as in the economy as a whole, but the foreign presence has consistently been much larger than in other sectors. Another special feature of the banking sector is the importance of Japan; whereas in other sectors Japan is generally a relatively minor presence, table 1.8 shows that Japanese banks account for 45 percent of the assets of foreign banks in the United States.

Clearly the banking sector is an exception to several of our generalizations about FDI in the United States. We discuss some of the reasons for this different behavior in chapter 2.

Table 1.5 Sources of growth in foreign control of US firms, 1980–93 (billions of dollars)

	1980	1981	1982	1983	1984	1985	1986	1987	1988	1989	1990	1991	1992	1993
Investment in:														
Acquisitions	9.0	18.2	6.6	4.8	11.8	20.1	31.5	33.9	64.9	59.7	55.3	17.8	10.6	23.1[a]
Establishments	3.2	5.1	4.3	3.2	3.4	3.0	7.7	6.4	7.8	11.5	10.6	7.7	4.7	3.1[a]
Assets of firms established or acquired	49.7	87.7	31.9	22.3	40.5	36.1	71.8	131.1	142.6	127.5	112.0	152.1	35.6	97.1[a]
Investment in new plant and equipment	16.9	26.7	28.1	23.2	25.2	28.9	28.5	33.0	44.3	55.2	69.6	69.8	60.9	n.a.

n.a. = not available

a. Preliminary.

Sources: BEA, "U.S. Businesses Acquired or Established by Foreign Direct Investors in 1993," *Survey of Current Business*, May 1994, table 1 and supplemental tables; similar articles in *Survey of Current Business*, various May issues; and BEA, "Foreign Direct Investment in the United States: Operations of U.S. Affiliates of Foreign Companies," tables D-26 (for 1987–92) and D–29 (other years).

Table 1.6 Alternative measures of the Japanese share in foreign direct investment in the United States, 1977–92
(percentages)

Share in:	1977	1978	1979	1980	1981	1982	1983	1984	1985	1986	1987	1988	1989	1990	1991	1992
Total FDI stock[a]	5.0	6.5	6.4	5.1	6.4	7.8	8.3	9.0	10.5	12.2	13.1	16.2	18.0	21.0	22.4	23.1
Total assets[b]	11.8	12.2	10.6	9.5	8.0	7.5	7.3	8.6	8.7	11.7	21.2	24.1	24.2	24.7	25.1	n.a.
Mfg. assets[c]	4.8	4.8	5.0	4.7	4.0	4.2	4.5	5.8	6.1	5.9	7.0	11.2	12.9	15.2	15.5	n.a.
Total employment[d]	6.3	6.3	6.0	5.7	5.7	5.7	6.4	7.0	7.4	7.5	9.4	11.1	11.7	13.3	14.7	n.a.
Mfg. employment[e]																
By industry of affiliate	3.1	3.4	3.6	3.3	3.7	3.6	4.0	4.7	5.1	5.0	5.6	8.7	10.5	13.3	14.0	n.a.
By industry of sales											7.8	11.7	13.4	15.6	16.5	n.a.
By industry of establishment														14.5	n.a.	n.a.
Total value added[f]	7.1	6.7	6.9	7.0	6.6	7.0	7.4	9.1	10.1	9.7	11.1	12.6	13.9	14.6	n.a.	n.a.
Mfg. value added[f]	3.4	3.7	3.7	3.4	3.5	3.0	3.7	4.6	5.0	5.0	5.8	8.5	9.8	12.7	n.a.	n.a.

Mfg. = manufacturing; n.a. = not available

Sources:
a. BEA, "Foreign Direct Investment in the United States: Detail of Position and Balance of Payments Flows," *Survey of Current Business*, various August issues.
b. BEA, "Foreign Direct Investment in the United States: Operations of U.S. Affiliates for Foreign Companies" (FDIUS:OUSAFC), various issues, table B-3. Figure for 1991 is preliminary.
c. FDIUS:OUSAFC, various issues, tables B-6 (for 1987–91) and B-7 (other years). Figure for 1991 is preliminary.
d. FDIUS:OUSAFC, various issues, table F-2. Figure for 1991 is preliminary.
e. FDIUS:OUSAFC, various issues, tables F-4 and F-11. See text for definitions. Figures for 1991 are preliminary.
f. BEA, "Foreign Direct Investment in the United States: Gross Product of Nonbank U.S. Affiliates of Foreign Companies, 1977–87," table 3, and similar article for 1987–90, tables 1 and 2.

Table 1.7 Assets, loans, and deposits of US financial affiliates of foreign banks and bank holding companies, 1973–93[a]

	Amount (billions of dollars)			Share of total for all US banks (percentages)		
Year	Assets	Loans	Deposits	Assets	Loans	Deposits
1973	32.3	17.6	11.4	3.8	3.7	1.7
1974	46.1	27.0	17.0	4.9	5.1	2.3
1975	52.4	29.9	22.6	5.3	5.7	2.9
1976	61.3	35.4	26.1	5.8	6.4	3.1
1977	76.8	41.5	33.8	6.4	6.6	3.6
1978	109.1	65.3	46.3	8.0	8.8	4.5
1979	149.6	91.9	62.8	9.9	10.9	5.6
1980	200.6	121.4	80.4	11.9	13.4	6.6
1981	250.6	157.7	101.8	13.5	15.4	7.7
1982	299.8	185.2	154.3	14.4	16.3	10.4
1983	328.8	192.4	181.3	14.6	15.6	11.1
1984	394.4	220.1	233.7	15.9	15.1	12.9
1985	440.8	247.4	236.7	16.1	15.4	12.1
1986	524.3	276.9	278.2	17.3	15.6	12.8
1987	592.6	310.9	316.1	19.0	16.6	14.1
1988	650.6	338.8	335.1	19.6	16.9	14.1
1989	735.7	369.8	376.1	20.6	17.2	14.9
1990	791.1	397.9	383.9	21.4	18.0	14.5
1991	860.7	412.3	444.5	22.6	18.9	16.2
1992	869.0	407.5	464.3	22.2	18.9	16.6
1993	852.7	389.3	452.3	21.8	18.0	16.5

a. Data are as of December except for 1993, for which data are as of June. Affiliates include branches, agencies, subsidiary commercial banks, and New York investment companies, but not Edge or Agreement corporations.

Source: Federal Reserve Board, "Structure Data for U.S. Offices of Foreign Banks," October 1993.

Real Estate

Of all the various aspects of FDI in the United States, the ownership of US real estate by foreigners has emerged as one of the most sensitive. Some of this sensitivity has to do with the fact that foreign ownership of US real estate seems to be heavily concentrated in a relatively small number of locations: Hawaii, downtown Los Angeles and Houston, and some other major urban areas. However, emotional articles regarding foreign ownership of urban real estate have appeared in the popular press even in areas

Table 1.8   Assets of US financial affiliates of foreign banks and bank holding companies, by country, 1993[a]

| Country | US banking assets of foreign affiliates | | |
	Billions of dollars	As a percentage of US banking assets held by foreign banks	As a percentage of total US banking assets
Japan	383.5	44.9	9.8
France	84.0	9.8	2.1
Canada	56.7	6.6	1.5
United Kingdom	50.0	5.8	1.3
Switzerland	41.6	4.9	1.1
Italy	38.9	4.6	1.0
Netherlands	36.9	4.3	0.9
Germany	31.9	3.7	0.8
Hong Kong	21.1	2.5	0.5
Korea	10.9	1.3	0.3
Sweden	9.6	1.1	0.2
Spain	9.5	1.1	0.2
Israel	9.4	1.1	0.2
Ireland	7.6	0.9	0.2
Taiwan	7.1	0.8	0.2
Australia	6.5	0.8	0.2
Finland	5.5	0.6	0.1
Belgium	5.4	0.6	0.1
Austria	5.0	0.6	0.1
Mexico	4.4	0.5	0.1
Brazil	4.0	0.5	0.1
Venezuela	2.2	0.3	0.1
Indonesia	2.1	0.2	0.1
All others	20.9	2.4	0.5
Total[b]	854.7	100.0	21.9

a. Data are as of 30 June 1993. Affiliates include agencies, branches, subsidiary commercial banks, New York investment companies and Edge or Agreement Corporations.
b. Figures may not sum to totals because of rounding.

Source: Federal Reserve Board, "Structure Data for U.S. Offices of Foreign Banks by Country of Foreign Bank."

where this ownership does not seem to represent a particularly large percentage of the total; see, for example, a 1989 article in *Boston* magazine (Jahnke 1989).

Another contributing factor is the widespread belief that there is a great deal of unreported foreign ownership of US real estate. This is a difficult question to deal with, for three reasons. First, the BEA readily admits that there may be some underreporting of small holdings of US real estate by nonresident foreigners. If so, it is probably largely a result of ignorance on the part of the investors themselves. For example, a private Japanese citizen who buys a residential property in a major US city to hold as a personal investment may not know that he or she is legally obligated to report the holding to the BEA; indeed, the real estate agent who arranges the purchase may be just as ignorant of this requirement as the client. However, analysts we have interviewed doubt that the aggregate value of real estate held by foreigners that is unreported for this reason amounts to more than 1 percent to 2 percent of the total value of reported foreign real estate holdings. A second factor that complicates measurement in this area was a loophole in US reporting requirements, noted above, that allowed certain limited partnerships created to hold real estate to escape reporting altogether. US officials have closed this loophole, and the total number of cases involved is quite small. A third problem is deliberate evasion of reporting requirements; the best-known cases are those of the family of former Philippine president Ferdinand Marcos and of members of the Medellín (Colombia) cocaine cartel. Again, although the stories are true, their aggregate significance is doubtful.

What is known about foreign real estate holdings in the United States? First, like all other categories of inward FDI, they have grown quite rapidly in recent years. The National Association of Realtors estimates that these holdings more than doubled in value, from $11.4 billion to $24.5 billion, from 1982 to 1987. The BEA, however, reports that total assets held by US affiliates of foreigners classified as being in the real estate industry totaled $67.8 billion at the end of 1986, which is considerably higher than the National Association of Realtors figure. BEA data also indicate that foreign investors owned almost 15 million acres of US land at the end of 1986. As always, the BEA asset figures are stated at book value, and hence it is not quite correct to compare them with the market value of all US real estate at the end of 1986. Also, the BEA asset figures do not include the value of real estate held by foreign-controlled US affiliates not classified as in the real estate industry; these affiliates accounted for over 85 percent of the total foreign ownership of US acreage at the end of 1986.

The 15 million acres owned by foreigners represent less than two-thirds of 1 percent of all the land in the United States, although it is almost surely true that the percentage share of foreign-owned land among high-valued properties (such as urban real estate or high-grade farmland) in the United States is greater. Indeed, given the concentration of foreign holdings in urban land areas, one might suppose that the foreign share of US real estate by value is much higher than the share of acreage. However, the figures that we have been able to obtain do not show this. The Federal Reserve Board estimates that the total value of real estate in the United States at the end of 1987 was $9,489 billion. The National Association of

Realtors figure divided by the Federal Reserve Board figure suggests that, by value, foreigners held only 0.25 percent of US real estate in 1987. When the BEA number is used as the numerator, this ratio rises to 0.7 percent. These percentages clearly are not accurate: the National Association of Realtors figure for market value is surely too low, and the BEA number is misleading for the reasons noted. Nonetheless, even if these numbers are off by as much as a factor of ten, it would appear that foreign holdings of US real estate as a percentage of the total are less than the foreign presence in the economy as a whole. Indeed, the data all suggest that the foreign presence in US real estate is very small.

During the late 1980s the MIT Center for Real Estate Development performed detailed studies of foreign investment in US real estate in six major cities: Los Angeles, Honolulu, Chicago, Phoenix, Atlanta, and Washington (Bacow 1987, 1988). Two points in particular seem worth noting. First, the bulk of foreign acquisitions of real estate in these cities was by passive investors who held the assets as portfolio investments for income and capital appreciation rather than as direct investments. Second, the preference of foreign investors for "showcase" investments tended to give these investments greater visibility than their overall importance warrants. To take the most extreme example, more than two-thirds of the office space in downtown Los Angeles was owned by foreigners in 1990, yet the percentage of foreign-owned office space in the whole of the Los Angeles metropolitan area was quite small.

We do not have good data on recent trends in foreign real estate investment, but anecdotal evidence suggests that the boom in that investment ended after 1989; indeed, there have been a number of conspicuous examples of disinvestment in high-profile urban developments. At least two large office buildings in downtown Los Angeles acquired by Japanese investors during the late 1980s have since reverted to domestic ownership. Like domestic real estate investors, foreign firms suffered from the weak markets of the early 1990s; the financial woes of the most dramatic foreign real estate venture of the 1980s, the 1989 purchase of a 51 percent stake in Rockefeller Center by Mitsubishi Estate Co., have received wide publicity.

FDI in Other Countries

A useful way to assess the growing role of foreign-controlled firms in the US economy is to compare the US experience with FDI with that of other countries. As we noted at the beginning, concerns about FDI are new only in the United States. Other countries, including other advanced countries, have long had a substantial foreign presence. It is arguable that the United States is simply becoming more normal—that it is becoming, like other countries, a host as well as a home for multinational firms.

International comparisons of FDI are difficult because the data are scarce and often noncomparable. Table 1.9 presents some US Department of Commerce (1993) estimates showing shares of foreign-owned firms in manufacturing sales, value added, and employment in France, the United Kingdom, and the United States for 1985 and 1990. These estimates are not perfectly comparable across countries, but they are useful as indicators and tell a suggestive and credible story.

That story is essentially one of convergence. In 1985 the United States had an exceptionally small amount of inward FDI; much of the rise between then and now can be viewed as a shift to a more typical position. Yet despite the rapid growth in the role of foreign firms in the United States, in 1990 such firms were still somewhat less important than in either France or the United Kingdom. The United States is, however, much larger either of these or indeed than any single Western European country, and one would expect a somewhat smaller foreign role as a result. To put it another way, interregional investment that appears as domestic in the United States is recorded as international in Europe. In France about half of the foreign share in sales, employment, and assets consists of firms from other European nations (although France is exceptional in this regard). Thus, the role of foreign firms in the United States, while still less than that in Europe, has converged to a considerable degree toward the European situation.

Although the upward trend in the importance of foreign firms in the United States was more pronounced than elsewhere, it seems also to have been part of a global phenomenon. As direct investment into the United States surged after 1986, it rose considerably in other industrialized nations as well. According to a recent UN *World Investment Report* (United Nations Centre on Transnational Corporations 1993), during the period 1986–91 the United States ranked 10th out of 23 industrialized countries in average FDI inflows as a share of gross domestic capital formation—behind Belgium-Luxembourg, the United Kingdom, the Netherlands, Portugal, Australia, Spain, New Zealand, Greece, and Sweden. Other European countries such as Switzerland and France were close behind the United States. The UN rankings thus provide evidence that the rapid influx of FDI into the United States in the 1980s was part of a larger phenomenon of more intensive FDI activity in most of the developed nations.

If the United States is becoming more or less ordinary with regard to foreign penetration, Japan remains a marked outlier, with a very small foreign presence in its economy compared with other industrial countries. This presumably reflects a long history of Japanese controls over FDI, which have only recently been relaxed, together with the familiar yet elusive cultural and institutional barriers that make access to the Japanese market difficult for exporters and investors alike. Further, the 1991 *World Investment Report* ranked Japan next to last among the industrial nations (ahead of only South Africa, which experienced net foreign disinvestment

Table 1.9 France, United Kingdom, and United States: shares of foreign-owned firms in manufacturing sales, value added, and employment, 1985 and 1990 (percentages)

Country	Sales 1985	Sales 1990	Value added 1985	Value added 1990	Employment 1985	Employment 1990
France	26.7	28.4	25.3	27.1	21.1	23.7
United Kingdom	20.3	24.1	18.7	21.1	14.0	14.9
United States	8.0	16.4	8.3	13.4	8.0	10.8

Source: US Department of Commerce, *Foreign Direct Investment in the United States: An Update* (1994)

in that year) on its measure of FDI as a share of gross domestic capital formation.

Conclusions

Since the mid-1970s there has been a major qualitative change in the role of the United States with respect to multinational enterprise. Instead of being primarily a home country for multinational firms, with little domestic production by foreign firms, the United States is now, like most other advanced countries, both a home and a host to multinationals on a significant scale. The foreign presence still represents a small fraction of overall US output and employment, but it is more prominent in the manufacturing sector and quite considerable in the banking sector.

Three common perceptions about FDI in the United States are not borne out by the data. First, the growing foreign role is not primarily a US-Japan issue. Except in banking, Japanese firms account for only a fraction of both the level of foreign presence and its growth, although they have increased considerably in relative importance.

Second, the data do not suggest that the rate of growth of foreign firms in the US economy accelerated in tandem with the emergence of large US current account deficits after 1981. If anything, most measures suggest a leveling off of FDI after 1981 or 1982, following a surge in the 1977–81 period. FDI did not surge again until 1987–89, and that surge has had more modest effects on the foreign share of the economy than is widely believed.

Third, foreign investors do not own a large fraction of US real estate. By several measures the foreign presence in this sector seems to be significantly lower than in the economy as a whole. This statement remains true even under the assumption that the reported aggregate figures for foreign ownership of US real estate understate the true amount by an order of magnitude.

2

Sources of Growth

The Theory of Foreign Direct Investment

As a starting point for any understanding of the rising role of foreign-controlled firms in the US economy, at least a rough theoretical framework is necessary. Although there is a very large literature on the causes of foreign direct investment, for the purposes of this study many of the issues raised there may be neglected. Instead we focus on a few key points, and in particular on a distinction between two competing classes of explanations.

This distinction may be made with a simplified example. Imagine that an existing US factory could be acquired by either a US-based or a foreign-based firm and that both firms expect this factory to yield a steady annual cash flow in perpetuity (although they may have differing expectations about the size of that steady flow). Why might the foreign firm be willing to pay more for the factory than the domestic firm? There are two possible reasons: either the foreign firm expects the annual cash flow to be larger—that is, the factory will be more profitable in its hands—or it values any given cash flow more highly, because it has a lower cost of capital than the domestic firm. The same logic obviously applies when considering who will build a new factory or expand existing facilities. When foreign rather than domestic firms do so it is either because they expect higher returns or because they require lower returns.

Let us first ask why the factory might be more profitable—earn higher returns—in foreign hands. The bulk of the FDI literature is concerned with this question. There is a presumption that, other things being equal, domestic firms should have an advantage in producing on their home ground. There are then a wide variety of explanations for how this presumed domestic advantage may be offset. The foreign firm may have some firm-specific knowledge or assets that enable it simply to do a better job of managing. The apparently superior production-management skills of Japanese automobile manufacturers are an example. Alternatively, the US factory may be of greater value to the foreign firm because it has a potential role in that firm's global strategy that it does not have for the US firm. For example, if there are strong advantages to vertical integration that only foreign suppliers of upstream inputs can capture, they may value downstream plants in the United States more than their domestic rivals do. Or firms may need to produce in the United States in order to appropriate the gains from their activities elsewhere—in research and development, for example. In general, we may characterize all the reasons why a factory in the United States might be worth more to a foreign-based firm than to a domestic firm as "industrial-organization" explanations of FDI.

On the other hand, foreign firms might be no better than US firms at producing and might receive no other special payoff from controlling US production, yet be willing to pay more for US factories simply because they apply a lower discount rate to expected cash flows. This may be referred to as the "cost-of-capital" explanation of FDI, because it is the cost, or required return, of a firm's capital, that determines the discount rate it applies to the investment projects it considers. To the extent that the cost-of-capital explanation is correct, the motivation for FDI is similar to that for foreign investment in general: it is simply a matter of resources in search of the highest return.

The consensus in the academic literature on FDI since the seminal early work of Hymer (1959) has been that industrial-organization considerations better explain most FDI than do cost-of-capital considerations. (A brief survey of this literature is given in appendix B.) If this is correct, FDI is best seen essentially as a means to extend control for reasons of corporate strategy, rather than as a channel for shifting resources from one country to another. In other words, the "investment" component of FDI is actually the least important part of the story.

Several arguments are typically offered in support of this view. First, foreign investors simply seeking a higher return can achieve that aim through portfolio investments in US securities rather than by the more cumbersome route of corporate direct investment, so that the cost-of-capital view fails to explain why the direct rather than the portfolio route should be chosen. Second, firms engaging in FDI often finance an important share of the investment locally; it is hard to understand why they would do this if a low cost of capital at home were the motivation for investing in the first place. Third, FDI among advanced countries typically proceeds in both directions, sometimes in the same industry. This is difficult to account for if international differences in the cost of capital are the reason for FDI.

For these reasons, the majority of economists studying FDI tend to dismiss cost-of-capital explanations and focus on industrial-organization motivations for the formation and expansion of multinational enterprises. However, the recent experience of the United States has given new life to the cost-of-capital approach, at least in popular discussion. The growing concern about foreign firms in the United States has coincided with the plunge of the United States into net debtor status, and since 1980 the rates of growth of the stock of FDI and of total foreign claims on the United States have been similar. Thus, it is natural to suspect that the growth of FDI in the United States is tied to the same factors that have led to a growth in US indebtedness generally. Furthermore, anecdotes about foreign (especially Japanese) investors have stressed the high prices of foreign (relative to US) stocks and the high values of foreign currencies relative to the dollar, which make US assets seem cheap by foreign standards. This is, in effect, a cost-of-capital argument.

As we have seen, US-Japan FDI flows in the 1980s were indeed largely one way, from Japan to the United States. This lends support to a cost-of-capital argument. Recent empirical work suggests, however, that the difference between US and Japanese capital costs narrowed during the 1980s, and seems to have disappeared altogether (see, e.g., Frankel 1993; Kester and Luehrman 1991). This evidence suggests that cost-of-capital differences are not as powerful an explanation of Japanese FDI as some have suggested.

We do not, however, wish to rule out differing costs of capital as a factor in the FDI story. Instead we offer a more sophisticated cost-of-capital argument for FDI, based on imperfections in capital markets and in corporate organization. Assume that debt is cheaper (requires a lower rate of return) than equity, that firms are constrained to keep their debt-equity ratios below a certain level, and that management regards internally generated funds as cheaper than equity obtained through sale of new shares. Then at least some firms will borrow as much as their constraints allow and invest as much of their internal cash flow as they can while neither issuing new equity nor paying more dividends than necessary to pacify stockholders. The investments of such firms will then be determined by their available cash flows, rather than by comparing the returns on their investments with some market-determined cost of capital.

This approach can help explain some of the seeming paradoxes with the cost-of-capital view. First, firms will prefer to undertake their own foreign investment rather than pay large dividends and allow their stockholders to invest in foreign firms; this explains the choice of direct instead of portfolio investment. Second, the firms may well want to borrow, and if the costs of debt are similar they may borrow in the host country, especially if this is viewed as a way to reduce exchange rate risk. Third, differences across industries together with limits to diversification can explain two-way FDI. In one industry, firms in Europe may have plenty of cash flow but few local investment opportunities, and therefore invest in the United States; in another industry the reverse may be true. The firms could instead try to invest across industries in their home countries, but management often seems to believe that it is easier to invest in a familiar industry abroad than to get into a new one at home.

Intraindustry two-way investment still cannot be explained by this view, but a sophisticated cost-of-capital explanation is at least a contender for explaining a significant fraction of FDI. The important point for the US experience is that the cost-of-capital view offers a possible link between the United States' shift to debtor status and the rise of FDI. If a decline in US saving and a perceived rise in investment opportunities in the United States led to a rise in the domestic cost of capital generally relative to that abroad, the same divergence would presumably occur in the firm-specific costs of capital to US and foreign firms. Thus, foreign firms would be willing to bid more for US assets, and the rise in foreign participation would be linked to the US current account deficit.

Does the distinction between industrial-organization and cost-of-capital stories have any importance for policy? If FDI in the United States is primarily motivated by industrial-organization considerations, its link with the growing foreign debt is largely a coincidence; it might well continue to increase sharply even if the United States were to balance its national accounts. On the other hand, if FDI is linked to capital flows, future FDI flows may depend crucially on the prospects for the US current account.

We defer discussion of the policy implications of these two alternatives until chapter 7, but here we will look at the evidence on the actual behavior of FDI in the United States. We will argue that the evidence, when looked at carefully, suggests that the industrial-organization motivation dominates the cost-of-capital motive. This implies that the apparent coincidence of rising FDI and growing debt in the 1980s is indeed simply a coincidence, and that the future growth of FDI may have little to do with the US balance of payments.

Evidence on FDI in the United States

The basic question in assessing the rise of FDI in the United States is whether this rise is a side effect of the general shift of the United States into net debtor status or whether it represents a longer term trend driven by other factors. The widespread assumption that the debt and growing foreign control are linked comes from the brute fact that since 1980 large increases in FDI and US debt in general have gone together, and from the fact that Japan has simultaneously moved into a position as a large creditor and become a large direct investor in the United States. However, three less obvious facts, in our view, call into question the linkage between capital flows and FDI. First, FDI in the United States has been rising rapidly for an extended period, beginning well before the emergence of large, chronic US current account deficits. Second, for much of that period the driving force behind the growing FDI was not the growth of foreign assets in the United States generally as much as a shift in the composition of foreign claims away from portfolio investments toward FDI. Third, the national composition of FDI in the United States has consistently been one that makes no sense if FDI is viewed chiefly as a particular way of transferring capital between countries.

Figure 2.1 shows the long-term trend of the FDI stock in the United States, measured as a share of GNP. This share rose steadily from the early 1970s until 1990. A simple exponential trend fits the data quite well, and there is no evident acceleration in the rate of growth in the 1980s. Of course, since the base grew over time, the absolute increases in the foreign presence were larger in the late 1980s. What is clear (and was emphasized in the previous chapter), however, is that unlike the net debtor status of the United States, the growth in FDI represented a long-term trend, not a development that appeared after 1981. Within this trend were two surges, one beginning in the late 1970s and continuing into the early 1980s, and the other beginning in the second half of the 1980s, with a period of little or no growth in between. The second surge came to an end in the early 1990s, despite persisting current account deficits; indeed, it is possible that a trend break occurred in 1991, such that the trend that had lasted from roughly 1972 has come to an end, but it is really too early to tell.

The change in the United States' net FDI position is also part of a long-term trend. Figure 2.2 shows one simple measure of this net position, namely, the ratio of the stock of US direct investment abroad to FDI stock in the United States, measured by book value at historical cost from 1972 to 1992. In 1972, of course, the United States was overwhelmingly a home country rather than a host country for multinational enterprises, with an FDI stock abroad six times as large as the foreign stock in the United States. The transformation of this position, with the United States converging toward a more typical advanced-country situation as both home and host, was proceeding steadily even during the 1970s, when the United States on average was running slight surpluses on current account.

The increasing role of the United States as a host country did not for the most part have as its counterpart a general increase in foreign ownership of US assets. Instead, until the surge in foreign portfolio investment after 1981, the chief mechanism of FDI growth was a shift in the composition of foreign claims away from portfolio toward direct investment. Figure 2.3, which graphs the ratio of the FDI stock to total foreign claims on the United States, shows how misleading it can be to look only at the 1980s: the surge of portfolio investment in the early to mid-1980s masked the trend toward increasing FDI as opposed to portfolio investment that marked the late 1970s (and reasserted itself in the late 1980s, when US current accounts were declining). It is difficult to see how to reconcile the

Figure 2.1 Ratio of foreign direct investment stock in the United States to US GNP, 1972–92

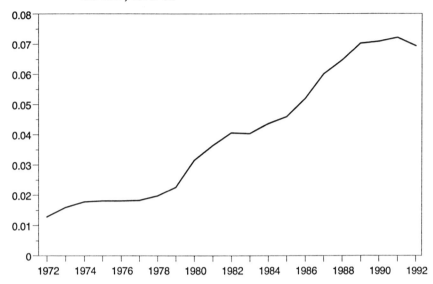

kind of large shifts seen here with a view that FDI is closely tied to capital inflows in general.

Another piece of evidence in favor of an industrial-organization explanation is the large variance of foreign control across sectors of the US economy. Table 2.1 shows how the share of gross product originating from foreign firms varied widely across sectors in 1990. It is hard to see why there should be such large variances if direct investment were simply a by-product of differences in the cost of capital.

Finally, the composition of FDI by nationality of owner is a key piece of evidence in favor of industrial-organization rather than cost-of-capital explanations of FDI. We have already noted that although Japan has been the principal exporter of capital in the world economy in the 1980s, it has accounted overall for only a fraction of the increased foreign presence in the United States. Further, the biggest surge in FDI from Japan occurred during the late 1980s and 1990, a time when Japan's overall current account surplus was shrinking.

Table 2.2 makes the point more generally, by showing the percentage distribution of FDI by parent country for the four countries with the largest stakes in the US economy. What is striking is not only that the United Kingdom, which has not been a large net exporter of capital to the United States in this century, remained the largest foreign direct investor until 1992, but that its share sharply increased from 1980 to 1988 (although it fell steadily thereafter).

What explanation of the growth in FDI is suggested by this evidence? Twenty-five years ago, US-based firms had significant advantages over

Figure 2.2 Ratio of US direct investment stock abroad to foreign direct investment stock in the United States, 1972–92

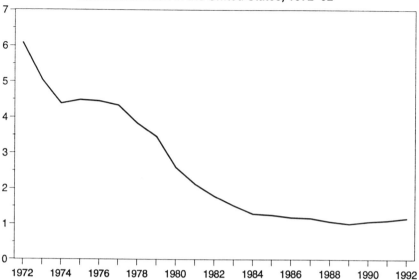

firms from other countries in terms of technology and management skills. These advantages were reflected in a variety of ways: in the United States' position at the top of the product life cycle, in the large US trade surplus in high-technology products, and in the ability of US firms to pay much higher wages than firms elsewhere. This superiority also meant that US-based firms, besides often having an advantage over foreign rivals even in producing abroad, almost always had such an advantage at home. The result was that there was little direct investment by foreigners in the United States.

What happened over the following years was an erosion of that US superiority on all fronts. The reasons for this erosion are the subject of intense debate, but the fact of erosion is not (see, e.g., Krugman 1990). As US economic leadership diminished, US margins in productivity narrowed, the US position as the innovating country in the product life cycle became ambiguous, and the United States became almost as much an importer as an exporter of high-technology goods. It is not surprising in this context that the one-sided relationship between the United States and multinational enterprises should also have changed; instead of US firms having a uniform advantage, there are now many areas in which foreign-based firms have technological or managerial advantages that enable them to produce more effectively even in the United States.

In other words, we regard the data as most consistent with the view that growing inward FDI in the United States has been a part of the general decline of US economic preeminence rather than a by-product of the trade deficits of the 1980s. It is important to be careful in interpreting this view:

Figure 2.3 Ratio of US foreign direct investment stock to total foreign claims on the United States, 1972–92

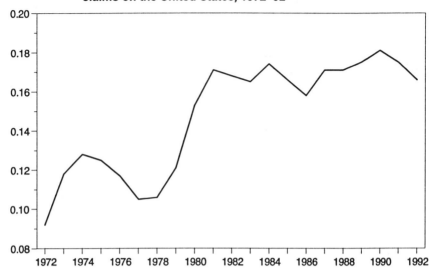

Source: *Survey of Current Business*, various issues.

although FDI here is a symptom of relative US decline, it need not be viewed as a cause. Indeed, as we argue in chapter 3, a good case can be made that inward FDI will help to limit that decline. This explanation of the causes of FDI does not carry with it any immediate policy implications.

As was detailed in the previous chapter, FDI flows into the United States declined markedly during the early 1990s, and this was accompanied by steady increases in outward direct investment from the United States. During the same years, US multinational firms appear to have gained worldwide market share in certain industries, for example, automobiles and electronics. It is probably too early to offer a definitive explanation of these trends (or, indeed, even to identify them as trends—they could be short-run aberrations). Nonetheless, it is interesting to speculate that the erosion of US economic preeminence may have abated and that the re-emergence of the United States as a strong net creditor nation on direct investment account (at historical cost) might signal, for the moment at least, an end to decline. But, again, at the time of this writing it is much too early to attempt to say anything definitive in this regard.

The Role of Financial Markets

We have argued that the rising share of foreign firms in US production may be attributed primarily to shifts in international technology and comparative advantage, and the consequences of those shifts for long-term corporate strategies and advantages, rather than to the differences in costs

Table 2.1 Share of gross product controlled by foreign firms in US manufacturing, 1990 (percentages)

Industry	Share by industry of enterprise	Share by industry of establishment
Food and kindred products	11.5	13.8
Chemicals and allied products	36.2	31.9
Primary metals	19.1	19.3
Fabricated metal products	10.6	7.9
Nonelectrical machinery	8.7	10.3
Electrical and electronic goods	16.3	15.6
Textile products and apparel	4.4	5.3
Lumber, wood, furniture, and fixtures	1.8	1.7[a]
Paper and allied products	6.6	7.9
Printing and publishing	7.6	10.1
Rubber and plastic products	13.4	17.6
Stone, clay, and glass products	23.5	24.8
Transportation equipment	3.5	4.9
Instruments	5.7	11.9
Other manufactured goods	11.8	12.2
Total	11.6	13.4

a. Value added by foreign-owned establishments for furniture and fixtures is suppressed.

Sources: Industry of enterprise data from BEA, "Foreign Direct Investment in the United States: Gross Product of Nonbank U.S. Affiliates of Foreign Companies 1987–90," *Survey of Current Business*, November 1992; industry of establishment data from BEA and Bureau of the Census, *Foreign Direct Investment in the United States: Establishment Data for Manufacturing, 1990*; total US manufacturing data from BEA, "Gross product by Industry, 1977–90," *Survey of Current Business*, May 1993.

of and returns to capital that made the United States an aggregate capital importer in the 1980s. However, popular discussion of FDI—notably the critical discussions by Rohatyn (1989) and others—has focused attention on the role of financial developments. In particular, the combination during the late 1980s of a dollar that was weak by historical standards and a strong Japanese stock market is alleged to have caused a "fire sale" of US assets to foreign firms. By this same account, the slowdown in FDI flows to the United States in 1990 stemmed from a strengthening dollar and a fall in Japanese stock prices.

This argument needs careful discussion. The assertion that the United States impoverished itself by selling assets off cheaply is dealt with at some length in our discussion of the welfare effects of FDI in chapter 3. For now let us simply focus on the question of whether the weak dollar, the strong Japanese stock market, or both can reasonably be invoked as major causes of the surge of FDI from Japan during the 1986–90 period.

Table 2.2 Distribution of foreign direct investment in the United States by country of ultimate beneficial owner, 1980–92 (percentages of total FDI stock)

Country	1980	1981	1982	1983	1984	1985	1986	1987	1988	1989	1990	1991	1992
United Kingdom	16.6	17.2	23.0	24.0	23.3	23.9	25.4	28.7	30.4	28.2	25.0	24.2	22.6
Netherlands	25.0	24.9	21.0	21.3	20.5	19.7	18.5	17.7	15.3	15.1	16.4	14.3	14.6
Japan	6.2	7.1	7.8	8.2	9.7	10.4	12.2	13.1	16.2	18.0	21.0	22.4	23.1
Canada	14.4	11.0	9.3	8.2	9.3	9.1	9.2	10.1	8.4	7.7	7.5	9.0	9.3

Source: BEA, "Foreign Direct Investment in the United States: Detail for Position and Balance of Payments Flows," *Survey of Current Business*, July 1993 (for 1990, 1991, and 1992) and various August issues (other years).

There is an evident correlation between changes in FDI flows into the United States and the movements of the dollar. During the weak-dollar period of the late 1970s and early 1980s there was a first surge of direct investment into the United States. This surge then trailed off as the dollar rose, to be followed by the surge that began in late 1986 as the dollar fell. The weakness of the dollar was commonly cited in the business press as a motive for FDI.

At first sight it seems obvious that a weak dollar makes producing in the United States more attractive, and thus makes acquisition or establishment of new facilities in the United States more attractive as well. However, this proposition neglects the point that the FDI decision always depends on a *comparative* assessment: is this factory worth more to a foreign firm than to a domestic one? A fall in the dollar that raises the expected returns to a US owner by the same amount that it raises the returns to a foreign owner should not lead to net purchases by foreigners.

One must also ask, If US real assets in general have become more attractive to foreign investors, why did the dollar fall? The fall in the dollar must reflect some general downward revision of opinions about the eventual value of claims on the United States. If everyone knew that US assets were undervalued, they would not long stay so cheap.

To establish a link between a weak dollar and increased FDI, then, it is necessary to establish some reason for a differential effect of the dollar's fall on the attractiveness of assets to foreign and domestic firms. There are several possible arguments, which we summarize briefly.

One argument places the emphasis on the changing composition of US output associated with the dollar's decline. That decline, to the extent that it affects US competitiveness, brings about a shift in US output from nontraded sectors like services and retail trade toward tradeable sectors like manufacturing. As we have already noted, FDI in the United States is strongly concentrated in tradeable sectors, presumably because the strategic advantages that make an enterprise in the United States worth more to a foreign firm are much more likely to occur in industries engaged in tradeable production. In particular, half of FDI in the United States is in manufacturing, which accounts for only 20 percent of GNP, and the dollar's decline was associated with a revival of US manufacturing output and investment.

We can now see how a declining dollar could be associated with a rise in the role of FDI: as the economy shifts from production of nontraded to traded goods, it also shifts from activities in which foreign-based multinationals have little role to areas in which they have a much larger role. Consider the following extreme numerical example. Suppose that all foreign subsidiaries are in the tradeable sector, which we take initially to represent 20 percent of GNP. Suppose also that the US current account deficit were to decline by 3 percent of GNP, with all of the improvement taking place through increased production of tradeable goods. Then, even with a constant foreign share of the tradeable sector we would see a 15 percent rise in foreign control of the US economy.

In the case of the United States, where there is a long-run trend toward a rising share of foreign control, changes in the exchange rate may also have an important effect on the timing of increases in foreign ownership. Suppose that foreign firms have a greater advantage over US firms in newly constructed capacity than in existing capacity. Then, in an industry in which foreign firms have a potential advantage, this advantage is likely to go unrealized if there is little capacity expansion. Thus, when the dollar was strong and US tradeable-goods industries were static or shrinking, foreign shares would have been stagnant. Once it became profitable to build new capacity in tradeable-goods industries, however, the foreign share would have surged back to its long-run upward trend. This is, as we have seen, in fact pretty much what happened during the 1980s.

However, given the crucial role played by acquisitions in the growth of foreign control in the United States, this cannot be the full story. A second explanation, emphasized by Froot and Stein (1991), stresses relative wealth effects. The rise of foreign currencies against the dollar raises the book value of foreign firms compared with US firms. To the extent that firms are capital-constrained, their potential borrowing limited by their debt-equity ratios, this rise increases the purchasing power of foreign firms; this may lead a foreign firm to outbid a domestic firm in an acquisition contest even when the expected present value of the target is the same in either firm's hands—to stylize, the foreign firm's pockets have suddenly become deeper.[1]

A variant on the Froot-Stein explanation would emphasize the increased opportunities for managerial empire building that would result from the decline of the dollar. A weak dollar may make it easier for the executives of foreign-owned companies to expand their firms even where such expansion is contrary to the interests of their stockholders.

A third explanation is one that allows for some misplaced concreteness on the part of foreign investors. These investors may focus on the fact that US real assets appear cheap compared with physically equivalent assets abroad and neglect the question of whether the economic returns are really equivalent.

Whatever the role of the dollar in triggering booms and slumps in FDI, it should be borne in mind that these fluctuations took place around a long-term rising trend. The timing of surges in FDI may be attributable at least in part to movements in the dollar, but the decline in the dollar cannot explain the whole long-run upward trend in foreign control that began in the early 1970s and lasted through at least 1990.

---

1. Klein and Rosengren (1994) present analysis that questions the robustness of the Froot and Stein results.

The role of stock market divergences is more difficult to assess, partly because the financial events themselves are so hard to understand. What, for example, caused the incredible surge of Japanese stock prices in the late 1980s?

We can at least offer a hypothetical scenario. Suppose that for some reason there indeed was an irrational "bubble" that caused Japanese stocks to rise to unprecedented heights during the second half of the 1980s. (It is now almost conventional wisdom that the rise that did occur was such a bubble). If Japanese firms realized the bubble for what it was, and if they were willing to issue new equity to take advantage of the high stock prices, this would have in effect lowered their firm-specific costs of capital and allowed them to invest in the United States even if their expected returns were lower than those of US firms. In effect, those who bought overpriced Japanese stocks would have been subsidizing the acquisition of US assets by Japanese firms.

But then a major (and obvious) question would be, Who actually paid the subsidy? As long as the Japanese boom remained a domestic affair, the answer is that the Japanese themselves paid. Only to the extent that US residents bought into overpriced Japanese stocks can we say that the United States gave up its own assets cheaply. (We return to this theme in chapter 3.)

The events of the late 1980s and early 1990s seem to confirm the importance of exchange rates and other financial prices in determining short-run changes in the pace of FDI. During late 1989 and early 1990 both the yen and Japanese stock prices declined sharply. The dollar value of the Nikkei index (the most commonly cited index of Japanese stock prices) fell 30 percent from December 1989 to March 1990. The dollar subsequently appreciated against all major currencies, including the yen, in early 1991. To the extent that financial factors play an important role in FDI, one would expect this decline to be reflected in a corresponding decline in FDI inflows; as we noted in chapter 1, there was indeed a sharp drop in FDI flows into the United States in 1991 that has persisted to the time of this writing. But in the meantime the dollar has now entered another period of weakness, while the Japanese stock market has begun slowly to recover. If financial factors are playing a role, one would expect FDI from Japan now to begin rising once again. But whether this actually will happen, only time will tell.

Taxation

The 1980s were marked by two major changes in US income tax policy: the tax cuts of 1981 and the tax reform of 1986. Although it is natural to suppose that these changes should have had an important effect on FDI in the United States, it is important to be careful in assessing the impact of taxation. FDI is primarily about control rather than movement of capital.

Thus, we need to ask how the tax laws affect the tax burdens on US activities owned by foreign corporations differently from those on operations owned domestically.

An interesting argument, first advanced by Scholes and Wolfson (1988), suggests how changes in the tax law may have contributed to the timing of surges and slumps in FDI. Of the four countries with the largest shares of FDI in the United States, the Netherlands and Canada have "territorial" corporate taxation, which does not attempt to tax the income of subsidiaries abroad, whereas the United Kingdom and Japan—the two largest source countries of FDI in the United States—have "worldwide" systems that do tax subsidiaries but grant a tax credit for taxes paid to host-country governments. Changes in taxation should in principle have a major impact on the investment decisions of firms based in countries with a tax credit system.

Abstracting from the immensely complicated details, a worldwide system works as follows. Subsidiaries of foreign firms pay corporate taxes to the US government just as if they were domestic firms. However, when they repatriate income to their parent company, they are liable to taxation at the home-country rate, with a credit for any taxes paid to the US government. If both the US and the foreign government levied straightforward corporate taxes at the same rate, this system would be neutral in its effect on the ownership of productive assets. A foreign-owned enterprise in the United States would pay normal US taxes; these would then give it a tax credit exactly equal to the tax liability to the home-country government, so that no taxes would be paid abroad. Other things equal, a shift from domestic to foreign ownership would have no effect either on total tax liability or on the distribution of revenues between the US and other governments.

The neutrality of taxation for FDI breaks down, sometimes in surprising ways, when corporate tax regimes differ across countries. Consider, for example, the effect of a reduction in the US corporate tax rate that is not matched by tax cuts abroad. One might expect that this would encourage foreign investment in the United States generally, and that FDI would rise along with the rest. In fact, however, such a cut, while encouraging portfolio investment in the United States, would put foreign-owned firms at a disadvantage relative to domestically owned firms. The domestically owned firms would receive a tax reduction by the full amount of the tax cut. Foreign subsidiaries, however, would find their tax credit reduced, and thus their lower US tax liability would be offset by an increased liability to the home-country government. Other things equal, then, reducing corporate tax rates in the United States would make foreign control of US firms less attractive.

In the 1980s US corporate tax policy shifted twice. In the early 1980s corporate taxation was cut sharply, notably by the introduction of accelerated depreciation. The tax advantages of accelerated depreciation were valuable to US-owned corporations but were probably worth much less to foreign-owned firms, since they were offset by reduced domestic tax credits. Thus, the tax regime for much of the 1980s acted as a substantial disincentive to FDI in the United States from some countries. Conversely, the 1986 tax reform eliminated the special investment incentives and thus the bias against foreign ownership.

In practice, the story is not quite so clear-cut, because of the combined effects of deferral of taxation and mixing of tax credits. Consider a UK firm with a US subsidiary, in a situation in which the United Kingdom has a higher effective corporate tax rate than the United States. The analysis above suggests that a reduction in the US corporate tax rate would provide this firm with no advantages. The UK firm, however, pays taxes only when earnings are repatriated; it therefore has an incentive to defer repatriation, allowing its profits to be taxed at the lower US rate in the meantime; thus, the present value of its tax liability will fall if the US tax rate falls. Also, the firm may be in an excess tax credit position, with no offset to changes in US tax collection at the margin, even though the US tax rate is lower than that in the United Kingdom. This could happen if the firm has other subsidiaries in countries with still-higher tax rates, such as Germany, and must mix the tax credits from these subsidiaries with the credits from US subsidiaries.

Perhaps because of these complications, international cross-sectional evidence does not agree too well with the view that changes in taxation have been of decisive importance for the observed shifts in FDI since 1980. Tax considerations alone would have led one to expect a decline in the relative share of Japan and the United Kingdom and a rise in the relative share of Canada and the Netherlands from 1981 to 1986, followed by a reversal; in fact, no such clear pattern is visible. More elaborate investigation of international FDI flows by Slemrod (1989) also fails to show a strong tax effect on FDI.

Evidence from within the United States, however, does support the idea that taxation might be an important determinant of FDI. Swenson (1990) points out that the effective tax rate on capital varies considerably across US industries. Given this variation, the Scholes-Wolfson model suggests a seemingly paradoxical implication: the share of foreign ownership should be larger in industries with high effective taxation than in industries with low rates. This prediction is borne out by the evidence: Swensen finds a significant positive association between effective tax rates and FDI. Using somewhat different techniques, however, Klein and Rosengren (1991) conclude that no such association exists.

Shifts in taxation thus probably have played a subsidiary role, if any, in determining the ups and downs of FDI over the past decade.

Protection

Case studies of decisions by foreign firms to invest in the United States, especially in manufacturing, often give a key role to actual or possible protectionist measures by the United States. Thus, protection needs to be considered in any explanation of the rise of foreign firms in the United States. As with taxation, however, it is important to be careful in defining the question. We need to ask not whether protection makes it more attractive for a foreign firm to produce in the United States, but whether it makes production by foreign-owned firms more attractive than production by domestic firms.

Consider the effects of a tariff or import quota imposed on some industry. By protecting the industry, the United States can induce a shift of production from foreign locations to domestic. The domestic production could, however, be undertaken by domestic firms—after all, US import quotas on cheese and sugar have not led to the wholesale establishment of foreign-owned dairies and sugar plantations in the United States. To explain why foreign firms establish or expand their US subsidiaries, it is necessary to start with some explanation of why the foreign firms have an advantage over domestic ones to begin with. This firm-specific advantage, rather than the protection, should be regarded as the underlying source of the FDI.

There is nonetheless a sense in which it is probably true that protection has tended to increase the extent of foreign control in the US economy, but the argument is more subtle than is usually appreciated. It is that there is a bias in protection: a domestic industry that appeals for protection is especially likely to be one in which foreign firms have some kind of special advantage. (This is apparent in the case of automobiles and that of color televisions, discussed below.) Thus, protectionism in effect biases the US economy toward producing those goods that foreign firms are better at producing than domestic firms.

An analogy with developing countries may be useful. Protectionism in these countries has often promoted FDI because it pushes their economies into activities in which they do not have comparative advantage, and as a result domestic firms have little aptitude; it is this shift in the mix of production rather than the incentives offered by protection per se that explains the association of protectionism and FDI.

Protectionism, then, plays a key role in the specifics of FDI in some important industries and has had some effect in increasing the overall foreign share in the US economy, but it is not a fundamental explanation of the rising trend.

The Business Cycle

The recession that began in the United States in 1990 and the slump in FDI flows into the United States in the same year are a reminder of the continuing importance of the business cycle as a determinant of all investment decisions, including those that cross borders. However, there is no obvious reason why the business cycle should affect the relative attractiveness of assets to foreign versus domestic investors in any systematic fashion, and thus no reason to expect booms and recessions to have much effect on the *share* of foreign control of the US economy—for example, on decisions to acquire US firms or establish new subsidiaries. As we pointed out in chapter 1, however, the balance of payments measure of FDI includes intrafirm financing (that by parent firms of subsidiaries, or vice versa), and thus is affected to a significant extent by the decisions of *existing* subsidiaries of foreign firms about how much to invest in plant and equipment.

In fact, aggregate FDI flows among the major industrial countries are strongly affected by the business cycle. Figure 2.4 shows the rate of growth of real FDI inflows into the Group of Five (G-5) nations, compared with the real rate of growth of those nations, since 1971. There is an obvious procyclical relationship. Julius (1990) finds that a simple regression of the rate of FDI growth among the G-5 on that of their real GDP indicates an income elasticity of 3.4, suggesting that FDI should normally rise faster than output during periods of economic recovery and fall faster during recessions.

Almost surely the developing recession in the United States was part of the explanation of the fall in FDI after 1989. This conclusion is reinforced by the observation that equity flows into the United States, associated with expansion of foreign control, fell much less than did intrafirm financing flows.

It is important to realize, however, that both quantitatively and empirically the business cycle can explain only a part, and the least interesting part at that, of the surge in FDI in the 1980s. Real inward flows into the United States grew several times as fast during the post-1985 period as one would have predicted from the historical relationship between the growth rate of the US economy and inward FDI. And in any case the business cycle primarily affects the investment decisions of existing US affiliates of foreign firms, rather than the decisions of foreign firms to establish or acquire new affiliates.

Three Case Histories

Color Televisions

The case of color television production in the United States provides a useful illustration of the forces underlying FDI. In many respects this industry is both an early and an extreme example of the role of foreign firms in the United States. Although the United States imports many color televisions, there is still a significant amount of domestic production: more than half of the color sets sold in the United States are at least assembled in the United States. The domestic industry is, however, for the most part foreign controlled. Large-scale acquisition and establishment of US subsidiaries by foreign firms began in the late 1970s; since the sale of General

Figure 2.4 Foreign direct investment inflows and GDP in the Group of Five countries, 1971–91

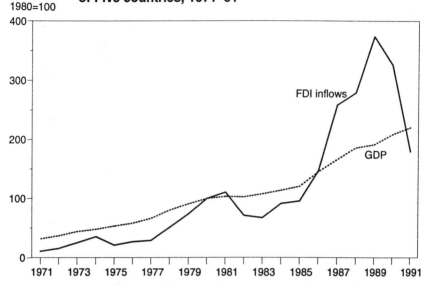

Source: From data in International Monetary Fund, *International Financial Statistics*, various issues.

Electric's television production operations to Thomson, a French group, in 1987, only one major US-based firm, Zenith Electronics Corp., remains in the domestic industry.

The basic story of color television production is quite simple: foreign producers, especially the Japanese, had developed by the mid-1970s both better product designs and better production systems than their US rivals. Japanese televisions were designed with many fewer parts than US sets, allowing greater production efficiency and reliability, both as a direct result of simplicity and because the simpler design lent itself better to automation. Coupled with this design advantage was an emphasis on quality control that both greatly reduced the need for testing and repair before sale and delivered much more reliable sets to consumers. When US television firms appealed for and received protection from their foreign competitors, in the form of a voluntary export restraint (VER) agreement, the foreign firms moved to establish production facilities in the United States as a means of circumventing the new ceilings. The firm-specific assets that had enabled the foreign firms to outperform US firms proved both transferable and appropriable, so that the US firms found themselves crowded out despite protection.

Matsushita Electric's acquisition of a Motorola, Inc., factory in Illinois ex-emplifies how the strong Japanese advantage was transferred to operations in the United States. After the acquisition, productivity increased by 30 percent, and defects were cut to a small fraction of former levels (Lewis 1982).

Ironically, US firms, unable to match Japanese productivity or quality, responded by attempting to compete on the basis of labor costs, shifting to heavy sourcing from developing countries. The result was that, in terms of location of production for the US market, Japanese firms became more American than the US firms. In 1987 Japanese firms produced 6 million color televisions in the United States, whereas only 1.4 million were imported from Japan (although a much higher share of components came from Japan). Meanwhile, Zenith maintained at that time only one television and one picture-tube plant in the United States; the bulk of Zenith's television manufacturing was located in Mexico.

This reversal of roles is interesting for our discussion of the economic consequences of FDI in chapter 3. The important point here is that the advantage of Japanese producers, it is clear, came from superior technology and management techniques that proved transferable to US production. The shift from US to foreign control in this industry had nothing to do with inflows of capital as such.

Automobiles

The growing Japanese presence in the US automobile industry has attracted widespread attention. Honda Motor Company began producing automobiles in the United States in 1982 and has been followed by five other Japanese manufacturers. By 1992 foreign transplants produced 21.8 percent of the automobiles manufactured in the United States (although this number fell slightly in 1993); joint ventures produced another 3.2 percent. The transplant share of value added is considerably smaller, because of a lower domestic content in the Japanese product.

In broad outline, there are strong resemblances between this case and that of color televisions. As with televisions, the initial Japanese move to US production was prompted by a VER agreement. This incentive was reinforced by the rise in value of the yen against the dollar after 1985. However, these incentives to increase production in the United States could have been met by expanded production by US firms, and indeed have been to some extent. The reason why Japanese rather than US firms have been adding US capacity lies in the firm-specific advantages of the Japanese: the now-familiar but still hard-to-emulate differences in organization that make not only plants in Japan but also Japanese-owned plants in the United States more productive than those owned by US firms.

The automotive industry also provides a useful case study of the differences in behavior between foreign and domestic firms, as is discussed in chapter 3.

Banking

As we noted in chapter 1, FDI in the US banking industry differs from FDI in other industries on a number of measures. The foreign presence in this industry, as measured by the share of total US banking assets under foreign control, is much greater than in any other, and the Japanese presence within US banking is much larger. Industrial-organization-based theories of FDI do not seem as robust when applied to this industry as, for example, in the two manufacturing industries described above.

One explanation often given for the large foreign presence in banking is that banks follow their customers abroad. For example, when manufacturing companies headquartered in Japan create subsidiaries in the United States, the Japanese banks with which these companies have their principal relations will establish US operations primarily to service the banking needs of these subsidiaries. Considerable support is given to this view by the fact that business loans are a much higher share of the portfolios of US affiliates of foreign banks than of domestically owned banks (64 percent versus 22 percent in 1991).

One of several competing explanations invokes the need for Japanese banks to create US operations in order to participate in the market for dollar-denominated bankers' acceptances used to finance oil imports. Another explanation sees the large Japanese banking presence as a means to help intermediate Japan's current account surpluses. These surpluses in turn are in large part accounted for by Japan's bilateral trade surplus with the United States. Hence, unlike for other forms of direct participation by foreign investors in the US economy, for Japanese banking there might be a strong direct link with the US current account deficit. Unlike that in other industries, then, the Japanese presence in banking might be better explained by financial market considerations than by industrial-organization considerations.

Until recently, it was widely claimed that Japanese banks had a lower cost of capital than their non-Japanese competitors and that this allowed them to practice predatory pricing to increase market share. The high price-earnings ratios of Japanese banks relative to US banks lent some support to this claim. However, this argument was subject to the same criticisms as the "fire sale" explanation of Japanese FDI in general (discussed earlier in this chapter); and the decline of Japanese stock prices after 1990 has made the point less relevant in any case, even though Japanese companies' price-to-earnings ratios are still on average above those of US firms.

Still another explanation of the strong presence of Japanese banks in foreign markets sees it as a means to circumvent home-market banking regulations and as a reflection of the propensity of these banks to follow one another into new activities (Terrell et al. 1989). These arguments may have some validity, but at present the phenomenon remains something of a mystery.

What about the non-Japanese foreign presence in the banking sector? As table 1.8 showed, the nationals of no country other than Japan hold a particularly large share of US banking assets. While it is possible that financial market considerations are part of the story for these other foreign banks as well, the industrial-organization explanation seems to be equally plausible. That is, the non-Japanese foreign banks might be present in the United States simply to service the needs of US subsidiaries of nonbanking firms headquartered in their home countries.

The Outlook for FDI

The United States has gone in the course of a decade from having a very small foreign economic presence to the point where FDI in the United States, as measured by historical cost, now about equals US direct investment abroad. In 1980 US inward FDI stood at $83.0 billion and outward FDI at $220.2 billion; by the end of 1992 FDI in the United States had grown to $420.0 billion whereas American FDI abroad amounted to $486.7 billion. The natural question is how far this trend will go: how much of the US economy will end up being controlled by foreign-based firms?

Much popular discussion relates the rise in FDI to the dependence of the United States on foreign capital inflows, putting the question in terms of how fast the United States can bring its current account into balance. We have argued, however, that the rise in FDI has little to do with capital inflows; the United States could continue to import capital without further expansion of foreign firms, or (more likely) bring its current account into balance yet find that foreign firms continue to expand, as they did during the 1970s.

We argue that the rise of inward FDI is part of a process by which the United States is becoming a "normal" advanced country in which multinational firms play about the same role as in other industrial countries. There is no longer a presumption that multinationals will be headquartered in the United States. This suggests that FDI will not grow indefinitely, but rather that it will approach a natural limit when foreign firms have expanded into all those sectors in which their specific advantages outweigh the "home court" advantage of US firms.

A useful model for the United States may be the European countries. As we saw in chapter 1, foreign firms still appear to have a somewhat larger role in the economies of the major European nations than in the United States. This role grew during the 1980s in Europe, just as it did in the United States, but the total change in the share of foreign-controlled firms was much less than in the United States, and most of the growth represented extensions into the various national markets of Europe by firms based in other European nations (see Cantwell 1992; Thomsen and Woolcock 1993). Japanese and US direct investment in Europe also increased, but the overall level of control by non-European firms did not grow significantly.[2] A sort of natural limit on the extent of non-European control within the European economy thus seems to have been reached. It is reasonable to suppose that something similar may happen in the United States, so that the European experience provides an upper bound for the extent of possible foreign control of the US economy. Despite fears raised in Europe in the 1960s, Europe does not exactly look like a colonized economy; in particular, the substantial foreign share in the European economy does not prevent Europe from being in turn a substantial direct investor abroad. Especially in light of the downturn in the past several years in FDI flowing into the United States, and the upturn in direct investment flowing out, it appears that much the same statement would also apply to the United States: that fears of foreign control are unwarranted.

Conclusions

The composition and history of growth in FDI in the United States seem inconsistent with a view that such investment is driven by international differences in the cost of capital. Instead, the growth of inward FDI seems best viewed as part of the general decline in US technological and managerial superiority. This means, in particular, that growing foreign investment in the United States has little to do with the US trade deficit and the resulting growth in aggregate foreign claims.

The emphasis placed by some on the role of a low dollar and high stock prices in Japan as explanations of rising FDI in the late 1980s may contain a grain of truth: each could explain some of the increase in the foreign presence. However, the potential role of these explanations is limited, and the major explanation of the rising foreign presence must lie elsewhere.

Changes in taxation might have played some role in determining the timing of FDI in the United States. The system of US corporate taxation from 1981 to 1986 probably discouraged inward FDI, temporarily delaying the underlying upward trend.

Other explanations of the rise in FDI (e.g., that it represents an attempt by foreign firms to overleap US trade barriers) are partial at best: they have explanatory power only when foreign firms possess firm-specific advantages relative to their US rivals. It is the existence of these advantages that must be seen as the major underlying reason for the entry of foreign firms into the US market through the vehicle of FDI.

---

2. On the rise of Japanese FDI in Europe, see Thomsen and Nicolaides (1991) and Mason and Encarnation (1994).

3

Economic Impact

The Gains from FDI

Much of the discussion in recent years of the economic effects of foreign direct investment in the United States has focused on the possible risks and costs. It seems appropriate as a starting point, however, to discuss the potential benefits. After all, direct investment is a form of international integration, and as with more traditional forms of integration such as trade in goods and services or portfolio investment, we may take as a first presumption that direct investment yields gains in efficiency. Only once we have thought about these gains does it make sense to turn to the potential costs.

Broadly, we may divide the potential gains from FDI into two categories. First are the conventional gains from integration: to the extent that FDI in effect facilitates trade in goods and services, it increases the conventional benefits that we normally associate with such trade. Second are the external economies: the benefits that may result from FDI but are not part of the motivation of the firms that engage in it.

Benefits from Increased Integration

The standard analysis of the gains from international trade recognizes three sources for such gains. The first is comparative advantage: countries are different, and trade enables them to specialize and benefit from their differences. The second is increasing returns to scale: trade allows each country to produce a narrower range of goods than it otherwise would, and thereby to achieve a larger and more efficient scale of production. The third is increased competition: trade effectively widens the scope of competition, reducing the monopoly power of large firms.

In the industrial-organization view of FDI that we have argued is the principal explanation of the growth of FDI in the United States, a multinational firm may be thought of as a facilitating device for trade in goods, services, and knowledge. For example, transactions costs may be reduced when international trade takes the form of intrafirm trade rather than arm's-length transactions between unrelated parties. This is because some services, such as the coordination provided by the headquarters, may be difficult to trade on any market but can effectively be exchanged internationally under the umbrella of a multinational firm. Perhaps the best example of how a multinational can facilitate trade is the case of trade in knowledge. Given the well-understood problems of markets in information, a firm may not be able to appropriate enough of the benefits of its own research and development (R&D) through international licensing of its patents to make the R&D worthwhile to begin with. (This can be so even if there would be net benefits to society from the firm undertaking the R&D.) But by producing the relevant goods itself in different countries, the firm creates de facto trade in the results of R&D (i.e., knowledge), providing the inducement to engage in the activity.

To the extent that FDI facilitates trade in goods, services, and knowledge, it magnifies the gains from trade. Countries will be able to specialize more effectively in the production of intangibles such as knowledge as well as of tangible goods, and thus benefit from both comparative advantage and economies of scale. At the same time competition will be increased.

How large are these gains? Unfortunately, there does not seem to be any way to get even an order-of-magnitude estimate. In 1990, for example, about 23 percent of US exports of merchandise were sold and 36 percent of US imports of merchandise were purchased by US affiliates of foreign firms. Slightly more than 40 percent of the exports of these US affiliates were to their foreign parent groups, whereas slightly more than three-quarters of the affiliates' imports were from the foreign parents. However, we do not know how much more costly it would have been to conduct these transactions through other mechanisms. Furthermore, many of the gains from FDI presumably are achieved through exchanges of intangibles, such as knowledge. And in any case, gains from rationalization and increased competition may exceed the direct reduction in the cost of transacting.

The bottom line is that FDI may be expected to bring gains from integration that are qualitatively similar to the conventional gains from trade, but the magnitude of these gains is anyone's guess.

External Benefits

Advocates of more liberal treatment of FDI in developing countries typically argue that such investment brings benefits over and above the usual gains from trade, in the form of valuable spillovers to the domestic economy. The benefits usually cited are the introduction of technology that can be emulated by other firms and the training of workers who may then transfer their skills elsewhere. In each case the point is that the foreign firm is not able to appropriate all the benefits of its activities; some of the benefits "spill over" to the economy at large, without the foreign firm receiving compensation.

Exactly the same arguments can be made for foreign firms in the United States. To the extent that foreign firms introduce new technology that diffuses to other parts of the US economy, FDI brings benefits over and above the usual gains from integration. (Technology here is defined broadly, to include not only science- and engineering-based production innovations but also management methods.) Thus, if US firms, by observing the US affiliates of Japanese firms, learn about just-in-time inventory methods or even about the benefits of listening to their workers, they will derive a benefit that magnifies the US gains from FDI. Similarly, if US workers receive training from affiliates of foreign firms and then bring those skills to new jobs elsewhere in the United States, they and the country will derive benefits from FDI over and above the gains from increased international exchange.

There are tangible examples of such benefits. For example, it appears that domestically owned US automakers have in recent years improved both the quality of their products and the efficiency of their manufacture. Almost without question, some of these advances have resulted from the domestic firms emulating certain practices of their Japanese-owned competitors. The results have been not only an increased share of the domestic market for the US firms but benefits for the consumer as well, as product choice has expanded and costs have been reduced.

Nonetheless, measurement of the external benefits from FDI is even more elusive than of the gains from integration. It is important, however, to bear both types of gains in mind as a corrective to any estimate of costs. There is a tendency to use any departure from perfect markets as a debating point against FDI—that is, to assume that any external effects are likely to represent costs that must be set against the more conventional benefits. In fact, a priori market failures are as likely to lead to too little as to too much FDI, and it is possible to argue at least as strongly for hidden benefits from FDI as for hidden costs.

The Potential Costs of FDI

Most discussion of FDI has been motivated by the fear that such investment carries costs for the United States. A good deal of this fear is of risks to sovereignty or national security. However, we postpone discussion of these issues until chapters 4 and 5 in order to focus first on the more purely economic issues.

In this discussion we also neglect concerns about the general role of multinational firms, domestic as well as foreign, in the US economy. For example, it is sometimes alleged that multinationals, by facilitating international capital movements, weaken the bargaining power of US labor in general. There is a huge literature (but no consensus) on these issues;[1] we choose here to limit our focus to those issues that arise specifically from the role of FDI in the United States.

Economic arguments against FDI may be arrayed on a scale of increasing sophistication. At the crudest level it is charged that FDI will cost jobs or worsen the trade deficit. More sophisticated arguments are that FDI will bias US production and employment toward inappropriate activities, that externality-generating activities such as R&D will be shifted abroad, or that the openness of the United States to FDI puts domestic firms at a strategic disadvantage. We will consider some evidence that bears on these concerns shortly; however, as an initial step we examine the underlying logic.

Employment Effects

Much of the popular debate over the economic effects of FDI has focused on its alleged impact on employment and, in what is usually seen as a related issue, the US trade balance. On one side, enthusiastic advocates of inward FDI point to the large number of employees hired by foreign-owned firms and argue that this represents substantial job creation. On the other side, critics argue that foreign owners tend to obtain more of their production inputs from abroad than do US owners, and that the resulting reduced demand for the products of domestic suppliers both costs the United States jobs and worsens the US trade balance. Responding to this debate, many studies of FDI have tried to measure the direct and indirect effects of such investment on employment. For example, the well-received study by Glickman and Woodward (1989) has as one of its central arguments a debunking of claims of significant job creation by foreign investors; a 1988 US General Accounting Office study of foreign investment in the automobile industry also essentially concerns itself with employment impacts.

We will not follow this route, because we regard an emphasis on job creation or destruction as fundamentally mistaken. The dominance of this issue in public discussion of FDI represents a misunderstanding of the nature of the problem. FDI almost surely has very little net effect on

---

1. The classic statement of the US organized labor movement on this issue is Goldfinger (1971).

overall employment in the United States; this conclusion has nothing to do with the results of calculations of net job effects at the industry or regional level, but rests on the macroeconomic point that employment in the United States is essentially determined by supply, not demand, except in the very short run. This does not mean that there is no potential problem arising from a high propensity of foreign-owned firms to source abroad. The problem, however, concerns the impact of FDI on the long-term value of the dollar and hence on the US terms of trade, rather than the impact on employment.

In the US economy of the late 20th century, creating demand for goods and services is not a problem, because of the active role of the Federal Reserve in monetary policy. Faced with an incipient shortfall of demand, the Federal Reserve can easily cut interest rates, thus offsetting the fall in demand and maintaining the level of employment. The aftermath of the stock market crash in October 1987 demonstrated this role clearly: the Federal Reserve's willingness to offset the crash by reducing interest rates not only averted a major recession but actually kept unemployment on its downward trend.

What constrains the Federal Reserve from driving unemployment down to even lower levels is not any difficulty in creating demand but fear of inflation. It is widely accepted among economists that the US economy has a so-called nonaccelerating-inflation rate of unemployment (NAIRU) below which the unemployment rate cannot be driven without causing inflation to spiral upward; this rate is generally estimated to lie in the 5 percent to 6 percent range. The essential determinant of the unemployment rate is therefore not the level of demand—this is not a given, but a policy variable that the Federal Reserve controls—but the NAIRU, which reflects the structure of the labor market. Unless it affects the NAIRU, FDI will have essentially no effect on total employment.

Suppose, for example, that a wave of FDI into the United States turned out to have a substantial immediate positive effect on demand for US workers. The normal response of the Federal Reserve would be to tighten monetary policy to avoid accelerating inflation, so that any job gains resulting from the investment would be offset by job losses elsewhere. Conversely, a wave of investment that had a negative impact on the demand for labor would be met by looser monetary policy and thus be offset by job gains elsewhere.

The main way in which FDI could affect the NAIRU would be if the shifts in employment associated with foreign investment either aggravated or diminished the mismatch between workers and jobs that is one reason the NAIRU is as high as it is. For example, suppose that workers laid off by the US affiliates of foreign firms were typically either in already depressed regions or in skill categories of which there is an excess supply. Then the NAIRU might increase temporarily as a result of increased foreign ownership. (But even so, over the longer term the NAIRU will return to its original level as the result of labor migration, labor retraining, and younger workers with needed skills entering the labor force while older workers with obsoleted skills retire.) There is also evidently a converse case in which foreign firms effectively lower the NAIRU. The point is that such effects, whatever their direction, are certain to be much smaller than the overall job creation or displacement numbers calculated when looking at the demand side and will generally be unrelated to the typical measures of net employment impact.

This does not mean that studies of the impact of FDI on employment in particular industries or regions are of no interest. For example, it is of considerable interest to learn what the effect of Japanese direct investment will be on employment in the US automobile industry. (Even this is hard to determine, since it is unclear how much of the new Japanese production substitutes for imports and how much for production by domestic firms; see the discussion of trade balance effects below.) However, this effect should not be construed as a measure of the effect of this Japanese investment on US employment as a whole, nor should we imagine that the overall effect of all FDI could be gauged by adding up estimates from a series of industry studies. *The net impact of FDI on US employment is approximately zero*, and the truth of this assertion has nothing to do with job gains and losses estimated at the industry level.

Although FDI has essentially no net impact on employment at the national level, it may have some effect on the regional distribution of that employment. A region that succeeds in attracting foreign greenfield investments may well increase overall employment in the region as a result, in the same way and for the same reason that similar investment by domestic firms may increase overall regional employment. The important point is that such gains in employment come essentially at other regions' expense, and are likely to induce migration into the favored region from the disfavored ones. These considerations do not, of course, prevent state development agencies from seeking to attract foreign investment. (We return to the question of state and local competition for FDI in chapter 6.)

Quality of Employment

We have seen that the argument that FDI can reduce overall employment is not one that makes much economic sense. A different and potentially more valid argument is that FDI could shift the quality of employment in an unfavorable way, reducing the number of "good jobs" and replacing them with "bad jobs."

The idea of good versus bad jobs is one that needs some discussion. In an efficient labor market there would be no such distinction. Skilled workers would be paid more than unskilled, but this would simply reflect their differences in human capital—good workers versus bad workers, not good jobs versus bad jobs. Other things equal, a worker would be paid the same in any sector or activity.

In reality, there are substantial differences across sectors in the wages paid to seemingly equivalent workers. Recent work in labor economics (e.g., Shapiro and Stiglitz 1984) has suggested that these wage differentials may be the result of systematic market failures. These market failures, in turn, may originate in moral hazard problems (e.g., difficulties in determining whether workers are putting in their maximum effort), which are more intense in some industries than in others, requiring that employers offer higher wages as an inducement for effective work. They might also originate in other factors such as market power on the part of unions.

In any case, once there are wage differentials that are based on something besides skill differentials, it becomes possible that international integration—of trade or investment—may perversely make the domestic economy worse off, by shifting workers out of the higher-paying jobs. Suppose, for example, that foreign-based firms prefer for some reason to engage in high-wage activities at home, leaving only low-wage activities to be performed in the United States. Then their establishment of a large stake in the US economy will tend to reduce the number of high-wage jobs here, leaving the United States poorer as a whole.

We should note two points about this kind of argument. First, although the idea that foreign firms will keep the good jobs home strikes a nationalistic chord, it is in fact an empirical question. As we will see shortly, there is no evidence from US data that US affiliates of foreign firms do offer worse jobs than their domestically owned counterparts. Second, the argument is not at bottom a case against allowing FDI, but a case for having an explicit industrial policy to encourage the creation of high-wage jobs in the United States. Anyone strongly worried about the possibility that the United States will not have the right kind of employment should be a domestic industrial activist rather than an opponent of any foreign presence. Robert B. Reich (1990) argues that such an activist might actually seek to encourage FDI in the United States, given the record of foreign firms in the country to date.

Trade Balance Effects

Related to the question of the employment effects of foreign ownership is that of its trade balance effects. It is often alleged that foreign-owned firms have a higher propensity to obtain their production inputs from abroad than do their domestically owned counterparts and that, as a result, increasing foreign ownership worsens the US trade deficit.

In part this issue can be addressed in the same way as the employment issue, by pointing out that macroeconomics, not microeconomics, determines the trade balance. By definition, the US current account deficit is equal to the difference between domestic investment and domestic saving; thus, the deficit fundamentally reflects the United States' low level of national saving. Microeconomic events, including changes in import propensities, cannot affect the trade balance unless they somehow affect saving or investment demand.

The principal mechanism through which the saving-investment identity is reconciled with microeconomic decisions about trade is the exchange rate. Suppose that there were widespread foreign takeovers of US businesses, and that the foreign owners exhibited a much higher propensity to import than US firms. Unless the foreign acquisitions also somehow reduced US saving or increased US real investment, the higher import propensity would be offset by a fall in the value of the dollar that would encourage exports, discourage imports, and leave the overall US trade balance (although not the trade balance in particular industries) unchanged.

Because of the macroeconomic determination of the balance of payments, then, even systematic differences in the trading behavior of domestic and foreign firms will not in general be reflected in the overall US trade balance. However, this does not mean that a high propensity to import on the part of foreign-owned firms is not a cause for concern. The reason for concern is that the offset to such a propensity is a weaker dollar, and the need for a persistently weaker dollar would itself represent a cost to the US economy.

For this reason the trade behavior of foreign-owned firms is an important consideration in assessing the costs and benefits of FDI. As we will see, the available data do indeed suggest that foreign-owned firms have a substantially stronger tendency to source abroad than do domestic firms; thus, there is an argument that an adverse trade impact from inward FDI exists, on the grounds that a growing share of foreign ownership implies the need for a weaker dollar.

Valid as this argument may be, it must be treated carefully. First, even where foreign firms appear to have a higher import propensity than domestic firms, their expansion need not have a negative effect on the trade balance at any given exchange rate. Those direct investments that are essentially creations of marketing arms—which, as we will see, account for a majority of the imports by US affiliates of foreign firms—should not be considered as shifting demand away from US-owned suppliers. These investments merely act as channels of distribution for imports that presumably would have entered the United States even if the large direct investments of the 1980s had not taken place. Also, although greenfield plants that foreign firms add to an industry's capacity may not purchase as much from domestic suppliers as do existing facilities, their finished products may displace imports rather than domestic production and thus reduce overall imports in the industry. For example, a US General Accounting Office study (1988) of Japanese investment in the automobile industry concludes that, in spite of a higher propensity on the part of Japanese-owned automobile plants to import components, such investment will actually reduce imports if as much as 40 percent of those plants' production displaces imports of finished cars instead of sales by US manufacturers.

Second, there is a factual question: do affiliates of foreign firms actually have a higher propensity to import than domestic firms in the same line of business? As we will see later in this chapter, they do appear to have a higher import propensity, but some of this may reflect not so much a difference in behavior as a bias in the type of activity in which foreign firms engage.

Finally, there is the question of magnitudes: to what extent does growing foreign ownership weaken the dollar? We present some estimates later in this chapter that suggest that even on the most pessimistic assumptions the impact of foreign ownership on the equilibrium value of the dollar is quite small.

Our assertion that the direct effects of FDI on jobs and trade are not important will probably not pacify those seeking political action on this front—we will certainly want to look at what these effects are likely to be. It is worth emphasizing, however, that in an assessment of the true costs and benefits of FDI in the United States an evaluation of direct impacts on overall employment and trade is simply not an important part of the story.

R&D and the Headquarters Effect

In discussing the potential benefits of FDI we emphasized the possibility that favorable external economies would result from spillovers of technology from the investing foreign firms. A concern that has been raised in the US context is that FDI might instead tend to reduce such favorable spillovers. The argument runs as follows. Valuable externalities arise from the complex intellectual activities undertaken by firms, especially R&D. Firms, however, like to keep these sophisticated activities near their headquarters. When a firm with foreign headquarters acquires or displaces a US firm in the US market, it is therefore likely to shift the sophisticated activities abroad. The result is that US residents, who were previously able to derive indirect benefit from proximity to these activities, can no longer do so.

This is an economically impeccable argument. The only question is whether it is true. The argument has two parts: the assertion that certain identifiable activities yield valuable externalities, and the assumption that there is a strong "headquarters effect" that leads firms to concentrate these activities in their home country. Both of these are in principle empirical questions.

Unfortunately, the issue of externalities is not one that can be easily tackled in practice. External economies, by definition, do not leave a paper trail of market transactions by which they can be tracked and measured. Assessing the benefits from certain activities is therefore difficult, and this difficulty bedevils not only the assessment of FDI but virtually all discussions of competitiveness and industrial policy. We can add nothing here to that discussion except to note that we share the common prejudice that R&D is an activity that is fairly likely to yield positive externalities, although we cannot even guess at their magnitude.

If we accept that R&D is an item of special concern, we then have a more tractable problem in assessing the second part of the proposition: is there a strong headquarters effect? There has been extensive empirical study of the past behavior of US and European multinationals (see Cantwell 1989). It is true that multinational firms, especially US-based ones (Vernon 1974), have historically tended to locate their R&D activities in their home markets, close to corporate headquarters. Some European-based firms, however, have long tended to place R&D both in the home market and in overseas markets as well. In particular, they have very often located such facilities in the United States in order to be in proximity to the large US research community (see Franko 1976). Firms that are newly multinational still do tend to concentrate R&D at home, but experienced multinationals of all nationalities increasingly tend to place R&D activities in all of the major markets in which they participate (Cantwell 1989). We turn to the evidence on US affiliates of foreign firms later in this chapter.

Strategic Effects

The growth of Japanese investment in the United States has raised the possibility that FDI may be subject to the same kinds of strategic manipulation that recent theory has suggested is possible in international trade.

Recent trade theory has shown that in imperfectly competitive markets it is sometimes possible for government intervention to give domestic firms an advantage that enables them to extract high returns at the expense of foreign rivals. The essence of this theory of "strategic trade policy" runs as follows. Suppose that there is a world market in which, because of some kind of increasing returns, there is room for only a few firms to enter profitably. Then a government, either by offering domestic firms a subsidy or by closing the domestic market to foreign firms, can deter foreign firms from entering, thereby allowing domestic firms the opportunity to earn above-normal profits (see Brander and Spencer 1985 and the survey in Helpman and Krugman 1989).

There is a straightforward parallel in the case of FDI. Suppose that there is an industry in which, because of the economies of scope associated with multinational operation, there is room for only a few multinational firms. Suppose also that Japanese firms are able to operate freely in the United

States, but US firms do not receive national treatment and are unable to operate freely in Japan (as we have seen, Japan is indeed an outlier in terms of having very little inward FDI). Then, other things equal, a Japanese firm will have a strategic advantage over a US-based rival and may end up driving the US firm out of its home market as well as the protected Japanese market. In the same way that strategic trade policy can in principle act as a beggar-thy-neighbor policy that raises national income at foreign expense, so could an asymmetric FDI policy (see Graham 1992).

How seriously should this danger be taken? The strategic trade policy argument has been subject to extensive theoretical criticism, which has established that it is a possibility but by no means a general proposition that aggressive trade policies benefit the aggressor country. Efforts to quantify the potential gains from strategic trade policies indicate that these gains are small (Helpman and Krugman 1989). Since FDI in the United States is still a smaller factor than conventional integration through trade, we may suspect that the results carry over to an even greater extent here. It is hard to believe that the strategic disadvantages of US multinationals are a major drag on the US economy or will be any time soon. Nonetheless, the strategic issue is one worth monitoring in the future, and it gives some priority to US demands for parity of treatment in Japan in particular.

Characteristics of FDI in the United States

Foreign direct investment is no longer a marginal presence in the United States, and the question of how foreign firms will behave in the United States is therefore no longer a purely hypothetical one. We can ask how the many foreign firms already here behave, and we can compare their behavior with that of domestic firms. The largest question mark hangs over Japanese firms. Although Japanese FDI grew more rapidly than the aggregate of FDI during the surge of the late 1980s, it still represents a minority of FDI in the United States. In addition, Japanese FDI is arguably not mature, especially in manufacturing. We will thus want to contrast the behavior of Japanese-owned affiliates with that of foreign affiliates in general, while bearing in mind that eventual Japanese behavior may look quite different.

We want to focus in particular on those features of FDI that may shed some light on its possible negative effects. Does the behavior of US affiliates of foreign firms appear consistent with the kinds of scenarios in which FDI is harmful, or does it look fairly innocent? We consider three features of FDI: the alleged high propensity of foreign-controlled firms to import, due to a preference for foreign suppliers; their alleged tendency to keep the good jobs and the high-value production in their home countries; and the alleged headquarters effect that diminishes the extent of R&D and its favorable spillovers in the United States.

Foreign Trade

Table 3.1 compares the trade behavior from 1986 to 1990 of two kinds of firms in the United States: parent companies of US-based multinationals and US affiliates of foreign firms. The table shows exports and imports per worker for all such firms and for manufacturing firms alone. (The figures for US-based multinationals are our estimates based on BEA data.)

A naïve view would focus only on the "All industries" columns of the table, which show that, per employee, affiliates of foreign firms both imported and exported much more than their US counterparts. However, this would give a misleading impression, because the firms covered by these data include firms that are essentially trading branches—the marketing subsidiaries of Japanese automobile companies, for example. It makes much more sense to focus on the manufacturing sector, where the behavior of foreign and US multinationals is much more similar. Even here, however, the data reveal a significant behavioral difference: the affiliates of foreign firms do show an apparent tendency to export somewhat less and import significantly more than US firms–indeed, about twice as much.

This does not necessarily mean that when a foreign firm takes over a US enterprise it will typically shift to foreign suppliers to the extent that imported inputs increase by 100 percent. First, there remains a classification problem. In the data, an affiliate is classified as being in only one industry. For example, a foreign-owned firm that acts both as a marketing and distribution arm and as a manufacturing arm will be classified either under manufacturing or under wholesale trade. We have already noted that this may lead to some understatement of the size of the foreign role in manufacturing. But it can also lead to some overstatement of import propensities within the manufacturing sector, because it means that even by focusing on manufacturing we have not eliminated the distortions caused by including foreign trading operations in the data. This applies both to the data for US affiliates of foreign firms and to those for US-based multinationals.

In addition, some of the difference surely reflects selection bias in terms of activities within the manufacturing sector. In particular, to the extent that foreign firms that acquire or establish subsidiaries in the United States do so as part of a corporate strategy of forward integration, the particular activities into which foreign firms enter will tend to be import-intensive. In other words, those activities would have a greater-than-average propensity to import inputs even if the firms engaged in those activities were US-owned.

Finally, taking a look at foreign firms at a single point in time may yield a misleading picture. It is often argued that FDI in manufacturing typically begins with assembly operations that have low local content, but that over time there is increased local sourcing; this cycle is clearly apparent in the case of Japanese automobile manufacturing discussed below. Because for-

Table 3.1 Employment and foreign trade of US multinational corporations and US affiliates of foreign firms, 1986–90

	US multinationals		Affiliates of foreign firms	
	All industries	Manufacturing	All industries	Manufacturing
Employment (thousands of workers)				
1986	17,831.8	10,431.0	2,937.9	1,411.6
1987	17,985.8	10,195.9	3,224.3	1,542.6
1988	17,737.6	9,819.9	3,844.2	1,828.6
1989	18,721.0	10,138.4	4,511.5	2,138.6
1990	18,549.9	9,843.8	4,734.5	2,220.7
Exports (millions of dollars)				
1986	162,292	123,046	49,560	12,805
1987	169,239	136,854	48,091	15,487
1988	202,632	164,151	69,541	25,192
1989	223,352	179,885	86,316	31,873
1990	229,427	192,902	92,308	36,069
Imports (millions of dollars)				
1986	139,978	77,892	125,732	20,617
1987	156,748	86,616	143,537	24,546
1988	170,804	104,981	155,533	32,762
1989	181,095	110,425	171,847	40,871
1990	199,969	119,707	182,936	47,171
Exports per worker (thousands of dollars)				
1986	9.10	11.80	16.87	9.07
1987	9.41	13.42	14.92	10.04
1988	11.42	16.72	18.09	13.78
1989	11.93	17.74	19.13	14.90
1990	13.40	19.60	19.50	16.24
Imports per worker (thousands of dollars)				
1986	7.85	7.47	42.80	14.61
1987	8.72	8.50	44.52	15.91
1988	9.63	10.69	40.46	17.92
1989	9.67	10.89	38.09	19.11
1990	11.56	12.16	38.64	21.24

Sources: BEA, "Foreign Direct Investment in the United States: Operations of U.S. Affiliates of Foreign Companies," various years, tables F-1 and G-1, and "U.S. Direct Investment Abroad: Operations of U.S. Parent Companies and Their Foreign Affiliates," various years, tables 57 and 58. According to Bill Zeili of the BEA, to the extent that US parent companies of foreign affiliates are themselves US affiliates of foreign parents, there is duplication in the merchandise trade data from the outward and inward surveys of foreign direct investment.

eign manufacturing in the United States surged during the second half of the 1980s, the data show a disproportionate number of relatively new foreign operations; their current high import propensity may substantially exaggerate the import propensity these same enterprises will have after they mature.

Despite these several reasons to discount the high apparent tendency of foreign-owned firms in the United States to import, we have not been able to recalculate the reported numbers to adjust for these effects. The raw facts do support the stereotype that foreign firms import more, and our guess is that even if all plausible corrections were made, this qualitative difference would remain.

What are the costs to the United States of this higher import propensity? To the extent that the additional imports really represent a net increase—in other words, ignoring the extent to which production by foreign firms may substitute for imports or add to exports—the effect is to require a lower value of the US dollar to achieve any given trade balance. It is possible to estimate an upper bound on this effect by assuming that all of the difference between imports of foreign and domestic manufacturers represents a negative effect on the US trade balance. Then we can use the comparison in table 3.1 to derive the size of the required decline in the dollar.

According to table 3.1, in 1990 the typical foreign manufacturing multinational imported approximately $21,000 worth of materials per worker versus only $12,000 per worker for domestically owned firms. In 1990 there were approximately 2.2 million US residents working for foreign-owned manufacturers. This comparison suggests that if these firms had remained domestically owned, imports in 1990 at any given exchange rate would have been approximately $20 billion lower.

Standard estimates of the effect of the exchange rate on trade suggest that a 1 percent fall in the dollar will reduce the US trade deficit, other things equal, by at least $5 billion (Cline 1989). Thus, *on the worst-case estimate* the total effect of foreign ownership of US manufacturing has been to reduce the equilibrium value of the dollar by about 4 percent. Bearing in mind that there was some foreign ownership in US manufacturing even in the late 1970s, and given the limits to using apparent differences in import propensities as a measure of trade impact, it is unlikely that the growth of foreign ownership of US manufacturing after 1980 reduced the equilibrium value of the dollar in 1990 by this much; more likely, this value has been reduced by no more than 2 percent. Whether the correct value is the smaller or the larger of these two figures, it is likely to be lost in the noise of fluctuations in dollar exchange rates stemming from other causes: for example, in May 1991 alone the dollar rose by over 10 percent against other major currencies, and during July 1994 it fell by close to 10 percent against the yen and the deutsche mark.

Thus, although it is undeniable that foreign-owned firms in the United States have a higher propensity to import than do their US-owned counterparts, this is not a good argument by which to prove substantial economic harm from FDI, politically sensitive though the issue may be. This difference in import behavior is in fact the *only* significant behavioral difference between foreign and US firms that we will find.

Wages and Value Added

Table 3.2 compares compensation per employee and value added per employee across industries for US affiliates of foreign firms against US firms as a whole. The striking and at first surprising result is that both compensation and value added per worker are actually higher for affiliates of foreign firms than for the average US firm. However, a look further down the table reveals that the difference is essentially due to differences in industrial composition. The heavy concentration of FDI in high-wage, capital-intensive industries such as petroleum refining and chemicals raises the average. For manufacturing as a whole, and for individual industries within manufacturing, there is no systematic difference between the foreign and the domestic firms in compensation and value added per employee. It is now possible, in fact, to examine these data for 1988 and 1990 at a very detailed level, using data generated by the data interlink generated jointly by the Bureau of the Census and the Bureau of Economic Analysis in the US Department of Commerce and the Bureau of Labor Statistics in the US Department of Labor (see appendix A). What the data show is that, while the above statements are true in the aggregate, there are exceptions at the level of individual industries. The most notable exception is the automotive sector, where foreign-controlled firms do not on average compensate their employees as well as do US-owned firms. There are doubtless several reasons for this difference, notably the fact that the foreign-controlled operations are newer and employ younger workers on average and tend to be more concentrated in lower wage areas (such as Tennessee and Kentucky, where, incidentally, General Motors sited its new Saturn division). than their US counterparts. Also, the US automotive sector has typically paid wages well in excess of the US average for manufacturing industries—a factor that some analysts believe has contributed to the competitive difficulties of US-owned automobile firms (see Womack et al. 1990). Thus, the foreign firms in this sector may be paying wages that are more in line with worker productivity than are the domestic Big Three.

Overall, then, the data do not provide any support for the view that foreign firms typically keep the good jobs or the high-value-added activities at home. In cases where the foreign-controlled firms do pay lower wages on average than their US-owned counterparts, there are reasons other than home-country bias, such as plant location and vintage, that can account for the differences.

Table 3.2 Value added and compensation per worker in US affiliates of foreign firms and in all US firms, 1990

Industry	US affiliates			All US firms			Value added per worker (thousands of dollars)		Compensation per worker (thousands of dollars)	
	Gross product (millions of dollars)	Employment (thousands)	Compensation (millions of dollars)	Gross product (millions of dollars)	Employment (thousands)	Compensation (millions of dollars)	US affiliates	All US firms	US affiliates	All US firms
All industries	241,182	4,734.5	163,592	5,522,200	118,906	3,297,547	50.9	46.4	34.6	27.7
Mining	4,168	36.0	1,523	98,500	712	32,259	115.8	138.3	42.3	45.3
Petroleum	26,828	149.4	6,457	36,700	155	9,251	179.6	236.8	43.2	59.7
Manufacturing	118,230	2,220.7	88,730	1,018,300	19,207	681,132	53.2	53.0	40.0	35.5
Food and kindred products	10,849	247.3	7,290	94,500	1,666	51,336	43.9	56.7	29.5	30.8
Chemicals and allied products	37,286	512.5	23,817	103,100	1,093	52,283	72.8	94.3	46.5	47.8
Primary and fabricated metals	15,451	255.5	11,157	111,300	2,177	81,137	60.5	51.1	43.7	37.3
Machinery	22,910	509.1	20,965	192,600	3,784	145,004	45.0	50.9	41.2	38.3
Other manufacturing	31,733	696.4	25,502	628,100	10,487	351,372	45.6	59.9	36.6	33.5
Wholesale trade	25,110	429.9	15,795	359,700	6,245	221,619	58.4	57.6	36.7	35.5
Retail trade	16,772	744.7	12,500	515,800	20,273	308,706	22.5	25.4	16.8	15.2
Finance,[a] insurance, and real estate	21,133	230.4	11,469	822,700	4,696	174,128	91.7	175.2	49.8	37.1
Banking	n.a.	n.a.	n.a.	152,000	2,256	69,176	n.a.	67.4	n.a.	30.7
All other industries	28,941	923.3	27,188	2,518,500	65,362	1,801,276	31.3	38.5	29.4	27.6

a. Excluding banking.

Sources: Data on US affiliates from BEA, "Foreign Direct Investment in the United States: Operations of U.S. Affiliates of Foreign Companies, Revised 1990 Estimates," table F-1, and "Foreign Direct Investment in the United States: Gross Product of Nonbank U.S. Affiliates of Foreign Companies, 1987–90, table 1; data for all US firms from "National Income and Product Accounts, *Survey of Current Business*, May 1993, table 9, and August 1993, tables 6.2C and 6.4C.

Research and Development

Table 3.3 compares R&D by all US firms and US affiliates of foreign firms for 1991. For all industries, R&D per worker was actually much higher for US affiliates of foreign firms than for US firms in the aggregate if one counts only company-funded R&D for the latter; if one looks at total R&D expenditures by US firms, the foreign affiliates still look better, but the difference is not as great. The difference between total R&D spending and company-funded R&D spending is largely accounted for by federally funded research performed in the private sector, most of it for defense purposes. One stated goal of the Clinton administration is to redirect much federally funded research away from the defense sector and toward civilian activities. Whether foreign-controlled firms will have access to these redirected funds on a national treatment basis is not yet fully re-solved (see the discussions in chapters 6 and 7).

Whatever the outcome of the current debate over the terms on which foreign-controlled firms will have access to federally sponsored R&D en-deavors, in 1991 US affiliates of foreign firms almost surely did much less federally funded R&D as a proportion of their total R&D than did US firms (alas, figures are not available to prove this). Thus, for that year, the more relevant comparison is total R&D per worker for the US affiliates versus company-funded R&D per worker for all US firms.

However, the favorable figures for the US affiliates again largely reflect differences in industrial composition between foreign-owned enterprise and the national economy. The great bulk of measured private R&D in the United States occurs in the manufacturing sector, which accounted for almost half the employment by foreign firms but less than 20 percent of total US employment. The slightly larger number for the foreign affiliates (when compared with company-funded expenditures by all US firms) may reflect a concentration of these affiliates in high-technology industries rather than a higher propensity of these affiliates to do company-funded R&D than their US-owned counterparts.

Like the data on compensation and value added, the data on R&D do not provide any indication that foreign firms behave differently from US firms in a way that could be viewed as detrimental to the US economy. In particular, there is no sign of a headquarters effect that leads foreign firms to perform *disproportionately* large amounts of R&D at home rather than in the United States. Anecdotal evidence further suggests that many foreign firms indeed significantly expanded their R&D activities in the United States after the collapse of the FDI boom in 1990. For example, at least two large Japanese electronics firms announced expansions of their US R&D facilities in 1991. Nor does the anecdotal evidence support the often-heard contention that R&D by foreign-controlled firms in the United States is skewed toward less challenging applications-oriented tasks rather than more basic research (such as, say, adaptation of products engineered else-

Table 3.3 Research and development by US affiliates of foreign firms, 1991

		US firms	
	Affiliates[a]	Total[b]	Company-funded
All industries			
R&D (millions of dollars)	11,772	135,200	78,050
Employment (thousands of workers)	4,809	94,806	
R&D per worker (thousands of dollars)	2.45	1.43	0.82
Manufacturing			
R&D (millions of dollars)	10,103	105,750	76,150
Employment (thousands of workers)	2,214	18,536	
R&D per worker (thousands of dollars)	4.56	5.71	4.11

a. Data are preliminary.
b. Includes federally funded as well as company-funded expenditures.

Sources: Data for affiliates from BEA, "Foreign Direct Investment in the United States: Operations of U.S. Affiliates of Foreign Companies," 1991 estimates; data for US firms from National Science Foundation, *Science & Engineering Indicators* (Washington: National Science Foundation, 1991).

where to meet US product safety standards); indeed, case evidence suggests that foreign firms have established a number of facilities that conduct basic (i.e., scientific) research. Likewise, although much R&D done in the United States by foreign firms results from acquisitions of preexisting, domestically owned US R&D facilities (and thus do not add to the existing R&D "base"), foreign-controlled firms have also established a considerable number of greenfield R&D facilities. Alas, no comprehensive empirical survey has been done that could be used to determine exactly how much foreign-controlled R&D is applied versus basic, or greenfield versus acquired. However, a 1993 survey of US research facilities under foreign control (Dalton and Serapio 1993) does provide brief descriptions of the activities of about 300 of these facilities. The descriptions do not suggest that the activities of these facilities are skewed to the applied end of the spectrum.

Are Japanese Firms Different?

Our survey of evidence on how foreign firms behave in the United States finds, broadly speaking, that they look a lot like US firms: they are comparable in terms of value added, compensation, and R&D per worker. Except for the ambiguous fact of a greater propensity to import, there is nothing in the evidence to justify concerns about the economic impact of an increased foreign role.

In the public mind, however, there is an important distinction among firms of different nationalities. Many US citizens and policymakers may be willing to accept the idea that UK, Dutch, and Canadian firms act much like American firms, and indeed in many cases they may for all practical purposes *be* American firms. Many concerns about inward FDI, however, are focused on Japanese firms. As we have seen, these firms still account for a fraction of the foreign presence in the United States, and their share is not rising nearly as rapidly as some critics of Japan have claimed. Still, there is a question as to whether the growing Japanese presence is qualitatively different.

Table 3.4 provides information on the industry distribution of the gross product of US affiliates by major investing country in 1991. The data present some problems; in particular, gross product is classified by industry of affiliate rather than industry of sales. (See chapter 1 and appendix A for a description of the difference.) Thus the table suffers somewhat from the fact that although many multinational firms are diversified across several industries, the data for each firm are reported as though all activities were concentrated in what the BEA considers to be the primary industry of that firm. In one case where this leads to a well-known major distortion, we have taken the liberty of rearranging the data: all Japanese data pertaining to motor vehicles are presented under "transportation equipment" (a manufacturing category) rather than "wholesale trade." This rearrangement may exaggerate the Japanese presence in the manufacture of motor vehicles in the United States, but because all of the activities of at least two of the three largest Japanese automotive subsidiaries are reported in the base data under "wholesale trade," the original classification enormously understates this presence.

When one looks at the industry distribution of European and Japanese direct investment in the United States, the most striking observation is how different these distributions are, not just the Japanese from the rest, but all the major countries from each other. For example, within the manufacturing sector, investment by UK firms is spread widely across many industries. Germany, on the other hand, has concentrated its US manufacturing investment heavily in chemicals, an area of traditional German strength, as has the Netherlands. Japan's manufacturing investment is, of course, focused strongly on automobiles.

These compositional differences themselves might be expected to lead to substantial differences in aggregate characteristics of US affiliates of foreign firms with different home bases. For example, one would expect (correctly) to find that German manufacturers in the United States, concentrated as they are in the very capital-intensive chemical industry, have relatively high value added per worker.

The important question is whether there are differences in the behavior of investors from different countries that go beyond these compositional

Table 3.4 Distribution of gross product of US affiliates of foreign firms, by industry and by country of ultimate beneficial owner, 1992 (percentages)

Industry	Japan	Europe	United Kingdom	Netherlands	Germany	France
Petroleum	0	11	n.a.	n.a.	0	n.a.
Manufacturing	53	55	55	34	58	63
Food	2	6	8	4	3	4
Chemicals	3	19	18	15	28	14
Metals	8	4	2	1	1	12
Nonelectrical machinery	7	4	3	11	5	3
Electrical machinery	5	6	2	11	8	10
Transportation equipment	18	2	0	0	1	2
Other manufacturing	9	14	21	3	11	17
Wholesale trade	22	8	6	4	16	8
Retail trade	8	8	4	11	18	5
Finance[a]	3	1	2	0	0	0
Insurance	0	n.a.	4	4	n.a.	n.a.
Real estate	3	2	1	2	1	0
Services	8	8	9	10	2	9
Other	3	6	n.a.	n.a.	n.a.	6
Total	100	100	100	100	100	100

n.a. = not available
a. Does not include banking.

Source: BEA, "Foreign Direct Investment in the United States: Preliminary 1992 Benchmark Results," table M-3.

differences. In particular, do US affiliates of Japanese firms behave differently from—and, as their critics argue, in a more antisocial fashion than—affiliates of other countries?

There are several reasons why one might suspect that Japanese firms would behave differently from other firms with affiliates in the United States. One is the difference in the nature of the home base: Japanese firms appear to be much more sheltered than firms in other industrial nations from foreign competition in their home market (although this may change as Japan liberalizes its markets). Institutionally, Japanese firms are structured very differently from firms elsewhere: their participation in *keiretsu* (groups of closely associated businesses) and their focus on very long-term relations with employees are two of the better known differences. There is also a widespread belief that Japanese firms can be induced through the "invisible handshake" to act in ways that the Japanese government believes serve the Japanese national interest, even when this does not maximize their profits.

The question is whether these fears about differences in Japanese firms' behavior are grounded. Since Japanese FDI represents a much smaller and somewhat more recent sample than overall FDI, the lessons of the Japanese experience are not as solid as those for foreign firms in general. Nonetheless, it is useful to compare the evidence on the behavior of Japanese affiliates with that of affiliates of firms from other nations.

As it happens, performance measures of the firms of the major investing countries show considerable intercountry variation. Table 3.5 shows some summary statistics for manufacturing affiliates of the countries that were the largest sources of direct investment in the United States in 1990. (These data are offered based on two classifications: by industry of affiliate and by industry of establishment; the latter are conceptually better—for example, they are not subject to the problem of misclassification of automotive subsidiaries—but are also less complete). No country seems to stand out as a particularly bad performer by these measures. It is possible to pick out particular data points that seem troubling; for example, manufacturing affiliates of UK firms on average perform less R&D than do subsidiaries from other countries. On the other hand, German affiliates seem to do a lot of R&D. But one would not want to assert on the basis of this information that UK investment is somehow detrimental to the United States and should be subject to special restraint; most likely the seemingly poor UK performance, like the apparently very good German performance, is primarily a compositional effect. That is, the UK average may be low because UK firms are concentrated in relatively labor-intensive, low-technology sectors, not because there exists any closed, conspiratorial British system that keeps the good jobs at home. The point is, instead, how difficult it is to draw conclusions about the desirability of foreign investment by examining aggregate performance.

Table 3.5 Measures of performance of US affiliates of foreign manufacturing firms, by country of origin of parent, 1990
(thousands of dollars)

Country of origin	Value added per worker	Compensation per worker[a]	R&D per worker	Imports per worker	Exports per worker	Employment
By industry of affiliate						
United Kingdom	50.85	35.76	3.53	9.61	10.69	535.2
Germany	56.52	43.55	7.01	26.61	20.91	251.5
Netherlands	47.55	40.52	6.19	20.36	11.23	126.7
France	45.65	43.41	4.20	25.26	27.28	193.5
All Europe	51.45	39.68	5.16	16.65	15.76	1,457.9
Japan	50.73	39.13	4.41	47.44	17.87	296.3
All countries	53.24	39.96	5.19	21.24	16.24	2,220.7
Memorandum: all US manufacturing	53.02	35.57	n.a.	n.a.	n.a.	19,207.0
By industry of establishment						
United Kingdom	88.3	30.0	n.a.	n.a.	n.a.	456.6
Germany	89.3	33.5	n.a.	n.a.	n.a.	229.0
Netherlands	94.4	31.7	n.a.	n.a.	n.a.	123.4
France	86.3	31.8	n.a.	n.a.	n.a.	178.3
All Europe	89.0	31.3	n.a.	n.a.	n.a.	1,297.4
Japan	78.3	32.2	n.a.	n.a.	n.a.	291.4
All countries	88.5	31.7	n.a.	n.a.	n.a.	2,004.2
Memorandum: all US manufacturing	70.4	n.a.	n.a.	n.a.	n.a.	18,840.0

a. Compensation figures do not include benefits, which are approximately 19 percent of total employee compensation of foreign-owned establishments.

Sources: Data by industry of affiliate from BEA, "Foreign Direct Investment in the United States: Operations of U.S. Affiliates of Foreign Companies, Revised 1990 Estimates," and "Foreign Direct Investment in the United States: Gross Product of Nonbank U.S. Affiliates of Foreign Direct Investors, 1987–90," *Survey of Current Business*, November 1992; data by industry of establishment from BEA and Bureau of the Census, "Foreign Direct Investment in the United States: Establishment Data for Manufacturing, 1990."

Nonetheless, one major difference between Japanese and other foreign firms is worth noting, namely, a higher Japanese import propensity. In 1990, Japanese affiliates imported 2.2 times as much per worker as did the average foreign-controlled affiliate. Why should this be the case? There may be a national bias involved: Japanese firms may be under pressure at home to continue relying on domestic suppliers, or may simply not trust US suppliers, to a greater extent than other foreign investors. However, we speculate that the main reason is related to the mismeasurement of marketing firms as manufacturers and the selection bias that leads foreign firms to enter the US disproportionately in activities that make use of imported inputs; these factors may be at work in Japanese FDI, which is also newer and less mature, to a greater degree than among foreign investors as a whole. Numerous studies of the behavior of multinational firms indicate that as these firms become more experienced in the conduct of international operations they tend to increase the local content of the output of their overseas subsidiaries (see, e.g., Vernon 1966). Because Japanese firms are typically quite inexperienced in the role of foreign direct investors, it is reasonable to expect them to increase the domestic content of their US subsidiaries' output as they gain experience.

The example of Japanese investment in the US automobile industry usefully illustrates this point. This investment began with assembly plants, which initially relied heavily on traditional suppliers: the automobiles assembled by Honda and Nissan in the United States initially had domestic contents of only 30 percent and 47 percent, respectively, compared with more than 90 percent in automobiles produced by US manufacturers. Over time, however, relationships have been established with US suppliers, and Japanese suppliers have moved to the United States, allowing a rising domestic content. In 1987 Honda and Nissan reported local content of 60 percent and 63 percent, respectively, and both expected to have 75 percent local content or more by the early 1990s (US General Accounting Office 1988). Some evidence suggests that the reported percentages were inflated by reporting some components as 100 percent US-made that in fact contained imported subcomponents; some analysts believe that the correct figure is about 50 percent. Even so, there is no doubt that local content is increasing, and it will probably increase further with time.

The case of color televisions, discussed in chapter 2, is another useful example. US firms responded to the Japanese entry into this market with heavy overseas sourcing, even as Japanese firms increased their US production; in the face of the technological superiority of the Japanese manufacturers, the US firms attempted to compete on the basis of low labor costs. The result was that, by the mid-1980s, the television sets sold in the United States by the remaining US firms had less American content than did those made by the Japanese competition.

Both automobiles and color televisions almost surely represent desirable investments by the Japanese in the United States, in the sense that the investors created greenfield manufacturing operations embodying advanced process technologies and management techniques to build high-quality products. These two industries in fact are very good examples of the "industrial-organization" explanation of FDI, discussed in the previous chapter: overseas-based firms successfully competing in the US market by transferring organization-specific intangible assets to their US operations. Emmott (1994) notes that further exploitation of these assets will drive these firms to increase their local content; without local sources of inputs, he argues, these firms will not be able fully to utilize their proven skills at just-in-time management of their activities.

However, not all Japanese investment in the United States fits the industrial-organization explanation quite so well. Emmott (1994) argues, from a series of case studies, that some of the highly publicized takeovers of US firms by Japanese firms resulted in the Japanese entering new lines of business in which they had little expertise or experience. Some of these acquisitions have already gone sour, and more, in Emmott's view, are likely to do so.

In any case, the idea that Japanese firms keep sophisticated, high-value activities at home is simply not borne out by the data. Nor, in the end, would we expect it to be. If Japanese firms are to succeed in the United States, they must use their intangible assets to advantage, and this means transferring high-value activities to their US operations. Where Japanese investors are unwilling (or simply unable) to do so, they are likely to see their investments fail to generate satisfactory returns.

The "Fire Sale" Issue

Our survey of the evidence does not in general support claims that foreign firms will behave differently from US firms in ways that are detrimental to the US economy. However, another argument against inward FDI that must be considered is one identified with Mundell (1987) and Rohatyn (1989), among others, namely, that foreign firms acquired a large stake in the US economy at an excessively low price because of the low value of the dollar during the late 1980s. The argument that the United States held a "fire sale" of its assets has struck a chord with many, raising worries that the United States has mortgaged its future by accepting FDI to finance its current account deficits.

For the fire sale argument to be valid, two things must be true. First, the dollar must in fact be undervalued, in the sense that the market is making a mistake and that there will be large capital gains for those who buy US assets now. Second, the undervaluation of the dollar must be leading US residents to make some kind of exchange at unfavorable terms of trade.

The proposition that the dollar was grossly undervalued in the late 1980s was stated by Rohatyn and others without much attempt at justification. To assert this proposition requires that one dismiss several counterarguments. The first is that the market did not agree; if it had, the dollar would not have been where it was. The second is that the claim of massive dollar undervaluation was not supported by simple indices of US competitive position, which generally showed the US relative cost and price position in 1989 to have been about where it was in 1980. The third is that econometric studies of international trade adjustment have almost universally concluded that the level of the dollar in 1989 was too high to induce a closing of international current account imbalances. This result was supported by the stalling of US trade balance improvement in mid-1989, before the onset of the 1990 recession caused the imbalance to improve. Finally, there is the fact that at the time of this writing (mid-1994) the dollar was at roughly the same level overall as it was in the late 1980s, and weaker against the yen and the mark, suggesting that foreigners who bought US assets at that time were not getting an unusually good deal.

Suppose for the sake of argument, however, that in fact the dollar was (and remains) greatly undervalued against the yen. This would still not be enough to establish that a fire sale of US assets has taken place. One must examine both sides of the transaction: when foreigners invest in the United States, what are US residents getting in return? It is the terms of trade on this exchange, not the exchange rate, that measures the price that the United States is getting for its assets.

Foreign nations can pay for US assets either by shipping us goods and services or by selling us assets in return. In fact they have done both: while the United States has run large current account deficits, and thus has been a heavy net importer of capital, US outward investment has continued.

Have the terms on which US assets have been exchanged for foreign goods and services been so unusually poor as to constitute a fire sale? The prices of imports into the United States relative to the prices of domestic goods have not been historically high in recent years; indeed, relative import prices stayed surprisingly low during the late 1980s despite the decline in the dollar (Hooper and Mann 1987). Nor were US assets unusually cheap in 1989 relative to the domestic price level; the stock market remained high by the traditional indices despite the October 1987 crash. Thus, there is no argument to be made that the exchange of assets for goods represented a bad deal for the United States. In other words, that part of the gross increase in foreign assets in the United States that was paid for by the US current account deficit must be considered exempt from the fire sale argument.

The fire sale argument only makes sense, then, to the extent that foreigners were able to persuade US residents to give up undervalued US assets in return for foreign assets. To put it another way, the fire sale argument may be reduced to the argument that the United States has a predictable capital loss on its own overseas investment. In 1989, the peak year for FDI inflows into the United States, foreign assets in the United States increased by $208 billion; only $105 billion of this increase was matched by private US acquisitions of assets abroad. The fire sale argument applies, if at all, to the possibility of a capital loss on that $105 billion.

Further, not all of that US capital outflow can be reasonably proposed, even for the sake of argument, to have been subject to a predictable capital loss. As noted above, only for Japan is there a strong—and still highly disputable—case to be made for serious dollar undervaluation. Thus, the potential fire sale loss should be restricted to capital losses on US investment in Japan. In 1989 US private investors placed $14 billion in Japan. Suppose that the dollar were "really" worth 180 yen; then there would have been a predictable capital loss of about 30 percent on a purchase of yen-denominated assets. This implies that the fire sale component to foreign investment in the United States was about $4.2 billion in 1989. Notice that this applies to foreign investment generally, and not specifically to direct investment; it makes no real difference to the cost whether the foreigners are buying firms or Treasury bills.

On the most pessimistic reasonable assumptions, then, which we do not share, the cost to the United States of the fire sale due to a weak dollar amounted to $4.2 billion in 1989, or less than 0.1 percent of GDP. This is not a trivial sum, although it is a hypothetical and speculative one. It certainly falls far short of justifying the apocalyptic rhetoric of Rohatyn, in particular.

Transfer Pricing and Tax Avoidance

In the early 1990s a number of articles appeared in the popular press alleging that US affiliates of foreign firms were paying less tax, relative to the size of their operations, than were domestically owned firms. The charge was made that the foreign-controlled firms were manipulating transfer prices (the prices paid for goods and services exchanged between operations within a firm) to shift profits out of the United States and thereby avoid payment of US taxes on those profits. These allegations led to investigations by the Internal Revenue Service (IRS) of the transfer pricing practices of foreign-controlled firms (we report on these shortly) and a campaign pledge by then–presidential candidate Bill Clinton to crack down on transfer pricing abuses and raise an extra $45 billion in taxes over four years from firms engaging in such practices.

Perhaps the first thing to be said is that transfer price abuse is only one possible reason for the relatively low taxes paid by foreign-controlled firms. Recent work by Long and Ravenscroft (1994), for example, suggests that another possible reason is the large amount of debt that foreign investors took on to acquire US-based firms. If the debt is held by the US subsidiary, the interest paid on it can be deducted from operating income and thus reduce total tax liabilities.

However, some transfer pricing abuse has undoubtedly occurred. If such behavior is widespread it could represent an important additional cost of FDI to the United States. To see how this avoidance of taxation might work in a simplified hypothetical case, suppose that a foreign-controlled firm makes and sells in the United States a car consisting of an engine that is imported from the parent company, other parts made domestically, and labor. Assume that the affiliate in the United States pays the standard world price for the engine of $4,000, that the total of the other parts and labor is $6,000, and that the car sells for $12,000 at wholesale. There will thus be a $2,000 profit on every car sold, which the affiliate reports to the IRS. But now suppose that the manufacturer, wishing to avoid US taxation, charges its US affiliate a price of $6,000 for the engine. The US affiliate will now report no profit on each car sold, and therefore pay no taxes on that profit, but the overseas affiliate that shipped the engine will report to the authorities in its country an additional $2,000 in profit for every engine shipped.

An IRS study on transfer pricing and tax avoidance was released in April 1992. The IRS examined more than 1,300 foreign-owned corporations, or 3 percent of the approximately 45,000 such firms operating in the United States. Comparing the rate of return on assets of US and foreign-owned companies, the IRS found that the foreign businesses consistently reported significantly less profit than US firms. The study attributed some of the disparity to exchange rate fluctuations and higher startup costs for foreign firms than for domestic ones. But it concluded that "Income shifting may be at least partially responsible for the remaining gap between the taxable incomes of domestic and foreign companies." The report did not try to estimate the size of the underpayment.

In at least one case a US affiliate of a foreign firm has been charged substantial penalties for underpayment of taxes. In November 1993 the IRS ruled that Nissan Motor Company had set transfer prices on passenger cars and trucks imported by its US subsidiary in California at much higher levels than appropriate, and had thus reported lower income in the United States than it should have. Nissan paid nearly ¥17 billion (about $150 million at then-current exchange rates) in penalties but continued to maintain that its prices were appropriate; the National Tax Agency of Japan agreed to refund Nissan the ¥17 billion to avoid double taxation.

One reason to suspect that underreporting of US income by Japanese-owned firms is not widespread is that corporate tax rates are actually much lower in the United States than in Japan, so that one would expect profit-maximizing firms to use transfer pricing to shift profits *into* the United States rather than out of it. Indeed, the Japanese National Tax Agency is reported to be considering penalties on firms that shift profits to the United States.

Whatever the extent of tax avoidance by foreign-owned firms, the policy implications are clear. When violations of US law occur, the violators should be prosecuted to the full extent of the law. If irregularities have occurred somewhere in those gray areas where interpretations of the law and regulations might reasonably differ, the IRS should clarify its regulations in a manner that favors the US national interest. Gray areas do frequently arise, largely because in practice it is not always a straightforward matter to determine the "correct" transfer price for an imported component.

Moreover, domestically owned multinational firms have essentially the same opportunities and incentives as foreign firms to engage in transfer price manipulation as their foreign-owned counterparts. Hence the expansion of FDI in the United States appears to add no significant new dimension to the problem, although it may increase the number of potential malfeasors.

Conclusions

A careful assessment of the evidence on FDI in the United States does not justify great concern about its effects. Foreign firms in general do not shift high-value or high-compensation activities to their home countries, nor do they perform less R&D in the United States than their US counterparts. Their only discernible difference is a higher propensity to import, which may represent a difference in behavior but may instead represent a selection bias in the activities in which foreign firms engage. There is little evidence to suggest that affiliates of foreign firms make less of a contribution to the US economy than do US-owned firms in the same industry.

Japanese firms show surprisingly little difference in their behavior from other foreign firms. Their value added and compensation per worker are similar to those of other foreign firms, as is their R&D effort in the United States. The only difference is an apparent propensity to import that is even higher than that of the average foreign affiliate, and this likewise may be the result of selection bias.

The frequently heard argument that foreign firms are buying into the US economy too cheaply does not stand up under careful analysis. If it makes any sense at all, it represents a quite limited cost rather than a wholesale sellout of US assets at fire sale prices.

Finally, although there may be instances in which foreign firms are depriving the US Treasury of tax revenues by means of illegal transfer price manipulations, there is little evidence that this is a major issue. There does, however, seem to be a considerable gray area in the tax code allowing scope for potential abuse by all multinational firms with US tax liabilities, irrespective of their nationality.

4

Political Effects

Up to this point we have focused on the purely economic consequences of foreign direct investment in the United States. But many of the concerns regarding growing inward FDI are political concerns: the worry that a substantial presence of foreign-owned firms will distort the domestic political process.

The question of the political role of foreign-owned firms operating in the United States is sometimes seen as part of a broader issue, that of foreign influence on US policy generally; that is, it is seen in the context of foreign lobbying over US trade policy, government-to-government negotiations, and so on. We have considerable sympathy with this view and will come back to some of the linkages in chapter 7. For now, however, we want to focus on the issues raised specifically by foreign ownership of US firms.

Even with this limitation, the political economy of FDI is a large subject, and one that is less well structured than the economics of FDI proper. We will not endeavor to provide anything like a complete survey of the political aspects of international investment; such a survey would be outside both our competence and the reasonable bounds of this study. Instead we offer an economist's-eye view of the problem, concentrating on three key points that seem to us crucial.

The first point is, strictly speaking, an economic rather than a political observation: when there is substantial foreign ownership of domestic factors of production, the evaluation of economic policies from a national point of view may be quite different from what it would be otherwise. Policies such as provision of subsidies or protection may have the effect of redistributing income to these foreign-owned factors, and thus will be more costly to the nation, perhaps by a large margin, than they would be in the absence of foreign ownership. This has become a relevant issue in the Clinton administration, for example, because of efforts to redirect government-sponsored research from defense-related sectors toward civilian ones. A hotly debated issue is what role foreign-controlled firms will have in new programs created by this redeployment. The specifics of this debate are covered in the following two chapters; here we focus on general issues.

The second point is that the foreign owners of domestic factors, like owners of any factors, will try to influence the domestic political process to adopt policies that they like. If successful, they will redistribute income away from domestic residents toward foreign ones, whereas successful manipulation of the political process by domestic actors only redistributes income among domestic residents. This is the sense in which foreign influence on the political process may be a source of greater concern than influence by domestic special-interest groups.

Is this greater concern really justified? The third point is that foreign influence only adds another imperfection to a political system that is already highly imperfect. Indeed, even without the involvement of foreign multinationals, the US political system quite often implements policies that transfer rents to foreigners (an example is the extensive reliance on export restraints administered by foreign governments to protect domestic industries) or otherwise impose large net losses on domestic residents. Thus, fears about foreign influence may be contrasting a worst-case scenario with an idealized depiction of actual US policymaking.

The Economics of Foreign-Owned Factors

The standard cost-benefit analysis used in public finance and international trade policy alike draws a sharp distinction between the redistributive effects of policies and their efficiency effects. While everyone knows that the distributive effects of a policy are often politically decisive, the economic analysis of policies usually focuses on the efficiency gains and losses instead.

Consider, to take a concrete example, the case of a tariff. Suppose that a country imposes a tariff on a good that it can import from the rest of the world at a fixed price. Then the tariff affects the real incomes of three domestic groups: consumers, producers, and the government. Consumers lose from the higher import price, producers gain from the higher domestic price, and the government collects some tariff revenue. It is a standard exercise to show that because the tariff distorts production and consumption decisions, the losses to consumers exceed the gains to producers and the government, so that there is a net loss to the economy as a whole. However, this net loss is ordinarily much smaller than the cost to consumers, most of which is offset by gains to the government or to producers.

The usual working assumption in cost-benefit analysis is that all such redistributions taken together net out. Everyone is a producer of something and a consumer of something else, so that what one individual loses as a consumer he or she gains back as a producer; in any case income redistribution is accomplished to at least some degree by existing taxation and social insurance policies. So, as a first approximation, it is usual to argue that the economist's job is to focus on the costs and benefits that are not pure redistributions from one group to another. In the case of a tariff, this means that the cost is measured by the net loss that results from production and consumption distortions. One then compares this net loss with whatever objective the tariff is supposed to serve and asks whether the benefits in fact exceed the costs.

Obviously this is not even a caricature of the actual political process by which US trade policy is made. Leaving that issue for later discussion, however, we may ask how the picture changes if there is foreign ownership of some part of domestic industry. The answer is that from a national point of view redistributions cannot be netted out, since those benefiting from (or hurt by) them may be foreign rather than domestic residents.

This point may be made most strongly if we imagine that the industry is entirely foreign owned. Then, from the domestic point of view, the entire producer gain represents a net cost; the national cost of the tariff becomes the consumer cost less any government revenue. If foreigners own only a share of the industry, only part of the producer gain will represent a national loss, but the principle is the same.

For moderate tariff rates the efficiency effects of a tariff are typically small relative to its redistributive effects. This means that in any industry where foreign firms control a substantial part of production, the redistributive effects of policy toward or away from these firms will typically be a more important issue for national welfare than the efficiency gains or losses with which economists are usually preoccupied.

From a world point of view matters look quite different: gains to foreign-owned firms still represent a redistribution rather than a loss. To the extent that a country is a home country as well as a host country for multinational firms, it may prefer rules of the game that prevent countries from worrying too much about international redistributive effects, even if these rules constrain its own actions. This is a point that we will return to; meanwhile let us note three implications of the redistributive effects of policies on foreign-owned factors.

First, the cost (or possibly the benefit) of a policy to the country implementing it may be much larger because of foreign ownership of factors of production than it would be otherwise. A tariff or a subsidy to an industry will impose higher national costs if the benefits go largely to foreigners rather than to domestic firms and workers. Conversely, some policies, such as deregulation of a largely foreign-owned industry, or import liberalization where the affected domestic producers are foreign owned, may in effect legally expropriate foreign holdings, producing national gains over and above any efficiency consequences.

Second, foreign capital inflows may exacerbate the consequences of distortionary policies. For example, a tariff that protects capital-intensive sectors will create high returns for investors in these sectors. If foreign capital moves in as a consequence, the foreign investors may well receive earnings that exceed the true contribution their capital has made to national product, leaving the country worse off (see Brecher and Díaz-Alejandro 1977 for a demonstration of this in a standard trade model).

Third, to the extent that foreign owners of factors of production can influence the domestic political process in their favor, the net national costs will tend to be larger than if domestic firms do the same. The reason is not that foreigners behave any differently, but simply that they and not domestic residents appropriate the gains. If a US firm is able to engineer tariff protection for itself, much of the cost to consumers represents an internal redistribution within the United States; if a foreign firm does the same, the redistribution represents a decline in US national income.

The important point, then, is that the economic impact of political activity by foreign-owned firms will be somewhat different from that of similar activity by domestically owned firms. This will be true even if the firms otherwise behave similarly, which is what we would expect.

Political Influence of Foreign-Owned Firms

In much of the world, multinational firms are viewed as possessing political power disproportionate to that of domestic interest groups. This view is fed by the size of large multinationals relative to indigenous firms in small countries, and by the view that firms from advanced countries are in some degree agents of their powerful home governments (or vice versa).

It is questionable whether this view of multinationals as uniquely powerful and dangerous makes much sense even in small countries. For the United States it is clearly unreasonable to think of foreign-owned firms as qualitatively different political actors from those already on the scene. The United States already has large firms, trade associations, unions, and the like attempting to influence policy. Some foreign firms in the United States compare in scale with their domestic counterparts; only a few are massively larger. Likewise, the US government is not going to become a minor player compared with other advanced-country governments anytime in the near future.

The point, then, is not that foreign-owned firms will play a different political game from domestic interest groups, but that the game will have different outcomes. That is, the concern will be that foreign firms will at least sometimes succeed in influencing the political process in ways that redistribute income away from the United States.

How might the political process be influenced? Foreign firms do not, of course, vote. However, they may influence decision making either directly, through the use of resources to influence voting and legislation, or indirectly, by using their bargaining power to extract special treatment.

There is no generally accepted formal model of the ways in which financial resources may be used to influence political outcomes, even though the existence of the phenomenon is hardly controversial. Aside from straightforward corruption on the part of appointed or elected officials, such expenditures can affect political outcomes primarily because of the public-goods aspects of the political process. Voters do not have much individual incentive to act politically on or even to become informed about issues that have only a small per capita impact, even if in the aggregate these issues matter a great deal. Therefore, an interested party that can mobilize a small group of activists, provide campaign funds to certain key officials seeking reelection, or offer highly visible benefits to some voters may be able to get a policy enacted that is not in the interest of the majority of voters. It is a commonplace that small, well-organized groups often get public policies enacted that benefit them at substantial but thinly spread cost to the general public; the examples range from sugar producers to thrift institutions.

This commonplace applies to interest groups in general, not foreign investors in particular. Foreign firms are not likely to play this game any better than domestic groups—indeed they will normally be at some disadvantage, both because of lack of familiarity with the rules and because they encounter some hostility precisely because they are foreign. When they do play the game successfully, however, they redistribute income out of the country instead of simply within it.

A more easily modeled example of political influence is the way in which a firm may induce governments to compete for a desirable investment. Suppose that a foreign firm has decided to build a facility in the United States that, it is believed, will yield valuable external benefits to the region in which it is located. Suppose also that the foreign firm regards a number of US locations as roughly equally suitable. Then the candidate states and localities may well compete to attract the foreign firm, with tax breaks, provision of infrastructure, and perhaps outright subsidy. The effect of this competition will be to dissipate any national gains from the spillovers, transferring them to the foreign firm instead.

Expensive competition among states and localities to attract foreign firms has become a real issue in recent years. For example, the Mazda Motor Corp. assembly plant in Flat Rock, Michigan, was lured by a 14-year waiver of property taxes, and the Toyota Motor Corp. plant in Kentucky by state provision of free land, $47 million in new roads, and $65 million in employee training programs (Jackson 1987). Some have argued that such interstate competition is more intense for foreign investments than for similar investments by domestic firms, because the foreign investments are more visible and attract more media attention, and hence generate more political points for politicians who succeed in luring them. Whether or not foreign firms actually do better than domestic firms in such bidding wars, those wars are more costly to the United States as a whole than similar bidding for a domestic firm's presence.

Thus, political influence by foreign firms can in principle be a source of economic costs to the United States. The questions that remain are how important those costs are and how much difference foreign influence really makes to the costs imposed by other self-punishing policies.

There is no overall measure of the expenditure of foreign firms on political influence in the United States. In any case, we do not have a standard of comparison: measures of the total political expenditures of domestic interest groups are likewise unavailable. There does not seem to be any reason to suppose that foreign firms are more devoted to the purchase of influence than domestic residents; at a guess, a true accounting would show a foreign share in political spending that is not out of line with the foreign share in total US assets or value added.

How Much Does It Matter?

We have identified some reasons why domestic policies that redistribute income to foreign-owned firms will have a larger cost from a US point of view than similar policies that benefit only domestic firms, and we have briefly discussed the channels of political influence that may lead to policies that redistribute income out of the country. The key question, however, is how much those losses matter. Should we expect the political system to yield outcomes that are significantly worse, from the point of view of domestic residents, than before foreign firms became an important part of the economy?

It is crucial not to start from an idealized conception of policy in the absence of foreign firms. Ideally, economic policy is carried out in such a way as to minimize deadweight costs—those costs, such as inefficiencies or transfers to foreigners, that hurt one group without benefiting another group within the country. If policy were efficient in this sense, then adding foreign owners of factors of production to the process would fundamentally alter it, because only then would the struggle over distribution have as a possible outcome a reduction in national income.

In practice, however, US economic policies already often impose large, unnecessary deadweight costs, whether because of distortion of incentives or because the policy ends up redistributing income out of the country even when foreign firms have no say in the matter. Given that the existing process produces such self-punishing results, one should not overstress the extra concern that arises from the presence of foreign-owned firms.

Two familiar examples may make the point. The first is the case of US trade policy toward automobiles. During the 1980s US affiliates of Japanese firms built operations in the United States, to the extent that they now constitute a substantial (albeit still a minority) fraction of the domestic automobile industry. These affiliates will presumably attempt to affect the domestic political process in their favor. However, it is difficult to imagine that they would induce a more self-punishing policy toward the automobile industry than that actually pursued by the United States during the 1980s. US automotive protection during the early part of that decade was in principle aimed at protecting employment; the textbook answer would have been to subsidize that employment directly or, if a trade remedy were deemed necessary, impose a tariff. Instead, the United States adopted a form of trade restraint in which Japanese producers ostensibly voluntarily (but in fact under the threat of more stringent US action) limited the number of cars they would sell in the US market. This policy based on voluntary export restraints (VERs) distorted consumer choice, reduced competition in the domestic industry (because the policy imposed a fixed quantitative restriction), and actually transferred the quota rents to the Japanese producers—unlike under a tariff, they retained the full amount of the higher prices resulting from the artificial scarcity of their products on the US market. Thus, much of the consumer cost of the VERs leaked away either into inefficiency or as benefits to foreigners rather than being transferred to domestic producers (who did receive some benefit from the higher industry-wide prices) or the government. Had some of the US industry been foreign-owned at that point, the costs would have been even larger—they would have reaped some of the gains that went to the domestic producers—but the policy might not have been the same.[1]

The second example is that of regulation in banking and finance, a sector where Japanese banks have been playing a large role. It is certainly possible that at some future date Japanese financial institutions in the United States will lobby successfully for some change in regulation that benefits them at the expense of US residents in general. However, it is hard to imagine that any such change could be as costly to US residents as the misregulation of the wholly domestic thrift industry, where the combination of deregulation and deposit insurance has led to massive misallocation of resources, only some of which has shown up as gains to thrift owners.

---

1. Hufbauer and Elliott (1994) estimate that had a 1992 proposal to cap the total market share of Japanese automobile firms in the United States gone into effect, the total cost to consumers would have been over $1.74 billion, and that only slightly more than a fourth of this (about $0.46 billion) would have been captured by the domestic firms. Most of the difference would have been captured by the Japanese as rents ($1.24 billion) with the residual (under $0.04 billion) being efficiency loss.

In general, US microeconomic policy, like that of virtually all countries, is full of examples of policies that redistribute income very inefficiently, imposing large net costs either through distortion of economic decisions or through losses to foreigners. We need only note that of the four major industries that have received import protection from the United States during the 1980s (automobiles, steel, textiles and apparel, and sugar), *all* have been protected through arrangements that transfer what might have been tariff revenue to foreigners.

The reasons for this apparent preference for inefficient policies probably lie in the same factors that allow interest groups to affect the political process in the first place: the free-rider problem of getting voters mobilized and the cost of information. An interest group may prefer an inefficient policy such as a VER to an efficient one such as a direct subsidy, even though the VER imposes higher costs on the general public, because those costs are less visible.

The question of how to reform the political process so as to minimize this kind of costly distortion—and the question of how much inefficiency is an inevitable part of any political process—lie far beyond the scope of this study. Our point is simply that a realistic view of how public policies are set should discourage our attributing a special character to political activity by foreign firms. This is not to deny that there is a real issue at stake: a foreign firm that is able to influence national policy in its own interest is somewhat more likely to have a negative effect on national welfare, other things equal, than a domestic firm exerting similar influence. However, in practice national welfare is reduced by successful attempts to influence policies by any special interest, foreign or domestic. In the real, imperfect policy environment, in which bad decisions are made and lived with all the time, adding some foreign influence represents only a minor change.

International Rules of the Game

We pointed out earlier in this chapter that the redistributive effects of policies when there are foreign-owned factors of production look quite different from a world point of view than from the point of view of a single country. A policy that redistributes income toward foreign-owned factors is a cost from the national but not from the global point of view, and correspondingly, a policy that reduces foreign firms' income benefits the home country but not the world.

This immediately tells us that, for the world as a whole to be better off, international investment must take place under some explicit or implicit rules of the game that limit the extent to which countries can take a parochial view that regards income earned by foreigners as a pure loss. In general, world income will be maximized when factors of production are treated the same whatever their ownership, and in particular when multinational firms are treated in the same way as domestic firms.

This view has in fact been the standard US position, dating from a time when the United States was much more likely to be on the receiving than the giving end of policies against foreign firms. The traditional US position is one that advocates right of establishment together with national treatment; that is, a firm from one country should have the unimpeded ability to establish subsidiaries in other countries, and once established, these subsidiaries should receive the same treatment as domestic firms. Together, these rights would in effect establish neutrality of policy with respect to the nationality of a firm's owners.

This position was a natural one for the United States to take when it played a one-sided role as a home rather than a host for multinationals; the advantage to the United States of a code of behavior that allowed its own firms free operation abroad was obvious. However, there are still advantages to such a code even in the more symmetric situation of today. First, the United States is still a major home for multinationals, and it would lose as much as it gained if there were widespread adoption of nationalistic policies aimed against foreign firms. Second, although it may be advantageous to pursue economic policies that reduce the earnings of foreign firms ex post, once those firms are already established, a country would like to assure investors ex ante that this will not happen, so as to attract further beneficial capital inflows. An international code that ensures national treatment is one way to make such an assurance credible.

We discuss the possible outline of such an international code in chapter 7. Here we simply emphasize that the political economy of FDI cannot be addressed purely as a matter of unilateral US policy.

5

National Security Concerns

Of the issues posed by the operations of foreign-based multinationals in the United States, those relating to national security are among the most difficult. Whereas many of the purely economic implications of foreign direct investment are no more serious than the routine problems that occur in virtually all areas of economic policy, in the national security arena special problems arise from conflicts between the objectives of different nations. And, as we argue later in this chapter, the special nature of these problems has not become less acute with the disintegration of the former Soviet Union and the end of the cold war; indeed in some instances they have become even more pressing.

There are two quite different situations in which the national security implications of FDI can become an issue. One is that of potential or actual military conflict between the host country and the home country of a multinational enterprise. FDI has been a problem in such circumstances in the past but, we will argue, seems unlikely to be a major problem in the foreseeable future. The other situation is where the foreign affiliate's home country is a friendly nation but foreign ownership is deemed nonetheless to impair the host nation's defense capability.

We examine each of these situations in this chapter. We conclude the chapter by outlining a few other issues regarding FDI and national security that we see as relevant to US policy concerns but that are not yet wholly resolved. Our policy recommendations relating to national security and FDI are found in chapter 7.

FDI and National Security in Time of War or National Emergency

The threat of FDI to a host country's national security becomes most acute when the host finds itself at war or in a state of national emergency, which we define as circumstances that could lead imminently to war. We concentrate in this chapter on the case in which a parent firm based in the country with which the host nation is at war or about to go to war already controls a subsidiary in the host nation. We defer discussion of the security implications of the imminent takeover of domestically controlled firms by foreign firms until chapter 6, where we discuss the 1988 Exon-Florio amendment to the Omnibus Trade and Competitiveness Act and the subsequent history of this act.

When analyzing the national security implications of FDI it is helpful to have a sense of the present political geography of FDI in the United States. Table 5.1 shows the aggregate stocks of FDI held in the United States as of 1990 by countries in the following categories: members of the North Atlantic Treaty Organization (NATO); non-NATO Western European allies and members of other multilateral military alliances with the United States; former Eastern bloc nations (those that were until recently under the military domination of the former Soviet Union); Middle Eastern nations (except Israel); and all others. The table shows that the vast bulk of FDI in the United States is held by nations in the first two categories, which consist of those nations that have been allies of the United States for the last half century or so; few persons would seriously view any of these as likely military opponents in the foreseeable future—in spite of potboilers such as Lester Thurow's *Head to Head*.

Indeed, the nations that might be considered potential US military adversaries in 1994 are among those in the third, fourth, and fifth categories. We are not claiming that these countries actually are adversaries, or even that all of the countries in these categories are potential adversaries. The former Eastern bloc, until recently the principal potential enemy, has disintegrated, and the nations that once comprised this bloc are transforming themselves with varying degrees of success into open, market-driven economies. There is no doubt some risk of recidivism, especially in Russia, but for the moment these nations pose no direct military threat to the United States. The Middle Eastern states include some decidedly unfriendly to the United States but hardly constitute a monolithic threat—the United States in 1991, and again in 1994, sent forces to the Middle East with the announced intent of protecting one Arab nation from the aggression of another. In any case the bulk of the FDI stock held by countries in these three categories is accounted for by Switzerland and the Netherlands Antilles—both most unlikely military threats to the United States. All of the nations in these three categories combined account for only a very small portion—less than 2 percent—of the total FDI in the United States.

Table 5.1 Foreign direct investment in the United States by security relationship to the United States of country of ultimate beneficial owner, 1993

Security status	Direct investment position (billions of dollars)	Percentage of total FDI
NATO members	275,545	62
Japan	96,213	22
Israel	1,712	0
Taiwan, Korea, Australia, New Zealand	9,449	2
Subtotal: countries that are allies of the United States	384,912	86
Eastern European countries (including former Soviet Union)	**	0
Middle East other than Israel	3,315	1
All others	57,041	13
Subtotal: countries not allies of the United States	60,356	14
Total	445,268	100

** including in "all others"; total is less than $500 million.

Source: From "Foreign Direct Investment Position in the United States: Detail for Historic Cost Position and Related Capital and Income Flows, 1993", Table 10.3, *Survey of Current Business*, volume 74, no. 8 (August 1994)

Even though very little FDI in the United States comes from nations that could be labeled even potential enemies, it is nevertheless worthwhile to examine the issue of actual or possible military conflict between the home and host nations of a multinational firm. The national security issues pertaining to FDI are at their starkest under circumstances of actual conflict and are to a great extent the same issues that are raised under less extreme circumstances, for example when tensions exist between the home and the host country that are unlikely to lead to war but nonetheless cause relations between the two to sour.

Relations between the United States and France during the late 1960s provide an example. At that time there was considerable tension between the two countries, even though relations never remotely approached a state of open conflict. One reason for the tension was the United States' effort to use French subsidiaries of US-based multinational enterprises to further US policy objectives, which at that time were often in conflict with French objectives. In particular, the United States instructed these subsidiaries to withhold technology from the French military as a means to pressure France to be more supportive of US policy in Vietnam. Consequently, during that period the French seriously questioned whether it was appropriate for local subsidiaries of US-based firms to be closely involved with the French national defense effort, and indeed the French government took steps to create independent sources of certain products and technologies that were then heavily dominated by US producers. (See Moran 1990 for details of this period.)

Today no such level of tension exists between the United States and any of the countries that are major homes to multinationals with FDI in the United States; nonetheless, some tension between the United States and certain of these home countries does exist, and the possibility is always there that it will increase. We therefore examine three questions pertaining to FDI in times of military conflict or national emergency that could lead to military conflict, and we ask what, if any, lessons can be drawn for the contemporary situation of the United States.

The first question is whether the overseas subsidiaries of multinational enterprises based in an unfriendly nation will tend to act as a "fifth column" on behalf of the home country. That is, will the subsidiary act as an agent of the home country to reduce the war preparedness of the host country?

Second, will the breaking of managerial links between the parent firm and the subsidiary in time of actual war damage the ability of the subsidiary to contribute to the war effort of the host country? This question is intimately linked to the fifth-column issue, and so to some extent we discuss the two questions concurrently.

Third, is the United States well or at least adequately protected against the eventuality that foreign-controlled subsidiaries might act as fifth columns or otherwise jeopardize the national security in time of war or imminent war?

Foreign Affiliates as a Fifth Column

Possible fifth-column activities of multinational firms include not only overt espionage and other unfriendly acts, but also certain less obviously hostile acts. For example, the subsidiary might leak sensitive but nonclassified information to the parent in circumstances short of war, before links between subsidiary and parent are broken. Such leakage, although harmful to the host country, would fall short of outright espionage. The subsidiary could also act as a "passive" fifth column simply by not producing war matériel at rates or of the quality of which it is capable.

It is difficult to generalize about the prevalence of fifth-column behavior on the part of foreign-owned subsidiaries. A few historical examples serve to illustrate that the outcome can go either way: there have been cases in which subsidiaries have indeed behaved as agents of their home governments in times of conflict, and there have been cases that offer little evidence of such behavior. One point that does emerge, however, is that fifth-column-like behavior by local subsidiaries is more likely in circumstances that fall short of actual war than during war itself.

During World War II, for example, the Ford Motor Company owned subsidiaries in countries on both sides of the conflict, including Belgium, Canada, Denmark, France, Germany, and the United Kingdom. Examination of the conduct of the subsidiaries' operations during the war indicates that each attempted to act as a good citizen of the nation in which it was located (Wilkins and Hill 1964; see also Vernon 1971). Good behavior might have been expected of Ford of Great Britain, but Ford of Germany also made contributions to the war effort on the German side, as, under some duress, did the subsidiaries located in the occupied areas.

The Ford subsidiary in Germany was nationalized during the war, but management, consisting mostly of German nationals, was left largely in place. The nationalized enterprise produced trucks for the German military. The total number of vehicles produced by Ford in Germany during the war was modest (around 80,000), and levels of production in the Cologne vehicle assembly plant were half of prewar levels. According to Walter Hayes, a former Ford vice chairman for Europe, the quality of the trucks was not high.[1] Part of the reason was that before the war Ford of Germany had been mainly an assembly operation, relying on parts supplied from outside Germany itself. Early on, the major source of supplies had been the United States, but during the 1920s the subsidiary began to use parts supplied from the United Kingdom. During the mid-1930s, under considerable pressure from the Nazi government, the firm began using parts supplied by non-Ford German suppliers. However, Ford of Germany executives were able to persuade Nazi officials that in order to expand exports from the Cologne facility it would be necessary to use parts that were interchangeable with those used outside of Germany. This limited the use of German-produced components. After the conquest of Belgium and France in the first year of World War II, the German operation increasingly relied on parts supplied by Ford's Belgian and French subsidiaries. Workers in these subsidiaries reportedly were able to sabotage some shipments to the German subsidiary, often simply by slowing down production, and at least one high-level manager of Ford's Belgian subsidiary was active in the resistance movement.

Was the contribution of Ford of Germany to the German war effort reduced because the firm was playing the role of a fifth column or because of other factors? According to Hayes, "Ford Cologne was neither an effective collaborator nor a fifth columnist, but just a branch operation cut off from headquarters."[2] As we argue in the next section, a subsidiary cut off from its parent organization during time of war is likely not to be as effective a contributor to the war effort of the host nation as it would be if

---

1. Letter from Walter Hayes to John T. Eby, 14 July 1989.

2. *Ibid.*

the links were maintained. And it is clear that those links will be broken if the host nation is at war with the home nation.

Could Ford have contributed more substantially to the German war effort? Germany's weaponry during World War II was technically good; indeed, in the view of some (but not all) military analysts, most German weaponry was superior to that of the Allies (see, e.g., Hastings 1984). Almost without question, however, Germany was somewhat behind the United States and the United Kingdom in the development of mass production techniques. In fact, one firm-specific advantage that had allowed Ford to enter Europe, including Germany, as a direct investor competing against local automotive firms was its mass production technology (Dunning 1958; Wilkins 1970, 1974). On several occasions during the 1930s Adolf Hitler expressed admiration for Ford's production technology, and the Nazi government resisted pressures mounted by indigenous automobile manufacturers to have the Ford operation declared persona non grata (Wilkins and Hill 1964). Interestingly, similar pressure was not applied against Opel AG, the General Motors–controlled subsidiary that was Germany's leading producer of automobiles and trucks.

Ford of Germany attempted to meet the goals set for it by the Nazi government, although under orders from Henry Ford II it resisted pressure to manufacture goods that were clearly military in nature. This resistance did not extend to such dual-use goods as heavy trucks. Had Ford been an integrated operation within Germany, it probably could have applied its technologies to help break wartime production bottlenecks in the manufacture of trucks, of which the Germans were chronically short. Thus, one lesson of this episode is that nonintegrated assembly operations when separated from their traditional suppliers and their parent organizations are of considerably less value to a host nation's defense than are fully integrated operations.

In any case, there is no indication that Ford in Germany acted as a fifth column on behalf of the Allies. Rather, the evidence suggests that Ford's German subsidiary behaved as a good if somewhat ineffectual local corporate citizen. Ford subsidiaries in Belgium and France were another matter, but they, after all, were operated by local nationals in occupied territory. (For more information on the operations of Ford during World War II see Wilkins and Hill 1964.)

In other cases, however, multinational enterprises have clearly used their subsidiaries to impair the military efforts of a host nation. There is evidence that US-based multinational oil companies actively worked with the US Department of State during the late 1930s and early 1940s to prevent Japan from building up petroleum reserves. However, the early moves in this direction were initiated by certain of the oil companies themselves, to prevent the Japanese from discriminating against foreign-controlled petroleum companies and developing a locally controlled refining industry, and were actually resisted by the US government. In particular, in 1934 Stanvac, a joint venture between Standard Oil Company of New Jersey (now Exxon Corp.) and SOCONY Vacuum Oil Company (now Mobil Corp.), joined with The Texas Company (Texaco) and Royal Dutch/Shell (the latter then as now controlled jointly by Dutch and British interests) in an attempt to organize a boycott of shipments of US and Indonesian crude oil to Japanese-controlled refiners. The boycott failed when other oil companies failed to join in and the State Department indicated it would not support the boycott. Secretary of State Cordell Hull indicated at the time that he did not want a further deterioration in US-Japan relations (Hull 1948).

In 1935, during negotiations with their Japanese competitors, Stanvac and Texaco offered to give the Japanese research results on the hydrogenation process for coal gasification; these results could have had military implications. The State Department knew of the offer but took no active steps to block it. Only in 1938, when US-Japanese relations had further deteriorated, did the State Department begin to apply pressure on the oil companies to stall Japan's development of its petroleum industry. Even so, US refined oil product sales to Japan actually rose each year from 1933 to 1940, with the exception of 1938 (Wilkins 1974; Hull 1948; US House of Representatives Committee on Strategic and Military Affairs 1939; US Senate Special Committee Investigating Petroleum Resources 1946).

There have been other cases in which the conduct of multinationals has reduced the military preparedness of a nation even when there seems to have been no active attempt by a hostile government to achieve this outcome. For example, beginning in 1929 Standard Oil of New Jersey entered into a series of agreements with the German chemical firm IG Farben, which resulted in Standard Oil stopping its efforts to develop a synthetic rubber and IG Farben stopping its efforts to gasify coal. The intent of the agreement was to reduce the potential for competition between the two firms within continental Europe and elsewhere. In short, it was a cartel agreement designed to keep each firm out of the other's markets as defined both by industry and by location (US Senate Committee on Military Affairs 1944; Haber 1971). As it happened, however, rubber was in short supply on the Allied side during World War II and petroleum products were scarce on the Axis side. The interfirm agreement thus probably damaged the war effort on both sides, although which was the net loser is difficult to say.

Conspiracy between multinationals and their home-country governments does not always hurt the host nation. When the home and the host nations are on friendly terms, such conspiracy may benefit the host. After the outbreak of hostilities between Germany and the United Kingdom in 1939, the United States at first remained neutral but favored the British in many ways. One of these was to encourage US-based multinationals to convert their UK subsidiaries to the production of war-related goods. If this required something more than an arm's-length involvement of the parent organization in the management of the subsidiary, in a manner that could be considered inappropriate for nationals of a neutral nation, the US government simply looked the other way (Wilkins 1974). The UK and Canadian subsidiaries of Ford made substantial contributions to the Allied war effort; for example, the UK subsidiary produced over twice as many trucks as its German counterpart as well as 14,000 Bren gun carriers and tens of thousands of engines to be used in non-Ford vehicles and fighter planes (Wilkins and Hill 1964). All of this production commenced well before the US entry into the war on 7 December 1941.

These examples provide anecdotal evidence that the subsidiaries of multinationals may indeed sometimes act as fifth columns in host nations on behalf of their home nations under circumstances of hostility between these nations, and that the most likely time for such action is the period immediately preceding the outbreak of war. After war breaks out, links between the subsidiary and the parent are usually broken, although there might still be some communication by way of neutral nations. In all probability the subsidiary would come under direct control of the host government. Under these circumstances it is unlikely that the subsidiary could continue to act as a fifth column, although our example of Ford in World War II Europe indicates that even this is not invariably true: the seditious activities of its affiliates in German-occupied Belgium and France apparently had some effect.

These examples also show that a local subsidiary of a foreign-controlled multinational will not necessarily act as a fifth column even in circumstances leading to war. Numerous subsidiaries of US firms other than Ford operated in Germany during the 1930s, and we can find neither evidence that any of these attempted to restrain Germany's preparations for war nor evidence that the US government attempted to pressure them to do so. Had there been such pressure, it is not clear what would have come of it. By 1940 the management of most subsidiaries of US multinationals in continental Europe consisted almost entirely of nationals of the host countries.

Likewise, subsidiaries of German companies operated in the United States in the 1930s, and there is little evidence to suggest that they in any way attempted to retard the (rather minimal) US war preparations in the years immediately preceding the Japanese attack on Pearl Harbor. After the United States declared war against both Germany and Japan in late 1941, both the subsidiaries of German firms operating in the United States and those of US firms operating in Axis and occupied nations came under national control under relevant national statutes (for the United States, the Trading with the Enemy Act; see chapter 6). There is no evidence that these subsidiaries attempted to act in the interests of the home country against the host country in which they were domiciled. Any damage that might have been done, rather, was the effect of the breaking of links between the parent organizations and the subsidiaries.

The Effect of Breaking Parent-Subsidiary Links

Thus it is reasonable to explore whether, even if subsidiaries do not engage in overt fifth-column behavior, there is some danger that severing the managerial links between parent and subsidiary will impair the latter's ability to produce goods and services needed in time of war. Again history provides no unequivocal answer, although there indeed are examples where such disruption did impair the ability of an individual subsidiary to function. Ford of Germany, as we have already seen, did not function at its prewar levels during World War II after links with its parent and affiliated organizations were severed.

An example from earlier in this century is in some ways more relevant to present concerns. In the first decades of the century, multinational firms based in Germany controlled much of the technology associated with the then-infant chemical industry (Haber 1971). These technologies included the manufacture of high explosives. High explosives indeed might be considered as the most important "dual-use" technology—a technology having key military and civilian applications—of its time, because the manufacturing processes for high explosives were quite similar to those for producing such new products as synthetic fertilizers and synthetic leather.

Following the United States' entry into World War I the assets of US subsidiaries of the German chemical companies were sequestered under the Trading with the Enemy Act (formally the Act of October 6, 1917); after the war these assets were sold to US firms under provisions of the Treaty of Versailles. This treaty also called for German-held technologies to be transferred to the Allies. Several sources indicate that the US firms (principally Du Pont) were at first unable to utilize the technologies and eventually had to seek technical assistance in Germany (see, e.g., Zilg 1974).

Was the war effort substantially hurt by the evident fact that US and other Allied firms did not have access to German technicians during the war? One cannot help but surmise that it was, although there is scant surviving evidence on which to base a firm judgment. If there were adverse effects, these were partly offset by the fact that German firms had licensed certain of their high-explosives-related technologies to UK firms before the onset of the war (Haber 1971). It is clear, however, that chemical firms in the Allied nations did not have access to certain specific technologies that were available to the Germans (and, perhaps more important, the Allies lacked specific technological know-how) and that, at the beginning of the war at least, the quality of German high explosives exceeded that of the Allies.

One very important question, however, is whether the Allies would have had access to the relevant technologies and know-how had there never been any German direct investment in the chemical industry in Allied territory in the first place. For the answer to be yes, it would have been necessary for US or Allied firms to have developed on their own technologies equivalent to those developed by the German firms. Would they have done so? It is far from certain that they would have. A plausible alternative scenario is that, absent technology transfer from Germany to the United States and other Allied nations that accompanied German direct investment, the "technological base" of the Allied chemical producers would have been less than it was. Thus, it is possible that Allied readiness for war would have been reduced, not enhanced, had there been no German direct investment in this industry.

What are the implications for modern times of these anecdotes? Do they provide any guidance for US policies regarding contemporary dual-use technologies such as flat panel displays?

One can interpret the case of the chemical industry in World War I to support the contemporary argument that know-how regarding militarily vital technologies should reside in the home economy, in the hands of domestically owned firms, even at the price of some economic inefficiency. The implication would be that the United States should have fostered the domestic development of leading-edge chemical technology during the period before World War II and should be fostering the development of the modern counterparts of such technology now. We discuss this issue further in the next section. But the lesson from the case can also be read much more narrowly: the United States should never become dependent upon one foreign country that monopolizes a key technology, especially if that country could someday prove hostile. And if a militarily vital technology were monopolized by a non-US firm based in such a nation, one policy response would be to require that firm, as a condition for access to the US market, to license the technology to US firms. During World War I, the United States might indeed have been better prepared if, prior to the war, German firms had licensed technologies to US firms.

Business firms, however, tend to resist licensing their newest and best technologies to potential rivals, even under government pressure. Often what gets licensed is not the newest and best technology but technology that is no longer at the leading edge.

Another response could be actually to require direct investment in the United States as a condition for access to the US market. After all, if the United States depends upon the foreign firm for this technology, it is better to maximize rather than minimize the stake of that firm in the US market.[3] Indeed, FDI could be one means of ensuring that the United States continues to have at least some access to the technology should relations with the firm's home nation go sour. For example, as previously noted, even if the United States was not able to exploit the full potential of the German-

---

3. Much the same point is made in the opening pages of an unpublished report of the Defense Science Board; an unauthorized text of this report is found in Spencer (1991).

owned chemical plants seized during World War I, it is not by any means clear that the United States would have been better off without German direct investment in this industry. In fact, the very opposite might have been true. It is clear, however, that the United States would have been better off had there been more transfer of technology from the German parents to the US subsidiaries, including transfer of know-how.

Thus, a further possible measure, for very sensitive technologies that are under foreign control, would be to set as conditions of access to the US market both that FDI be "integrated" (i.e., that all inputs required for the operation, including R&D inputs, be located on US soil) and that the US subsidiary employ substantial numbers of US nationals in managerial and technical capacities. Such a condition would constitute a performance requirement, something to which we are in general opposed. It is easy to invoke national security to support any number of requirements that in the end have more to do with protecting vested interests than with any real national security needs. However, in certain exceptional cases national security considerations could argue compellingly for such a requirement. The best solution, we feel, would be an international accord on direct investment that would generally forbid performance requirements but would contain an escape clause spelling out as explicitly as possible the circumstances under which national security could be invoked by a host nation to legitimize performance requirements. Chapters 6 and 7 discuss the issue of performance requirements further.

Safeguards Against Fifth-Column Activity

In time of war or events that could lead to war, is the United States adequately protected from fifth-column activities of US subsidiaries of firms controlled by enemy nationals or other conduct that could be detrimental to US security interests?

Provisions of the Defense Production Act

Under the Defense Production Act of 1950, provisions pertaining to defense priorities and allocations apply to all firms doing business within the jurisdiction of the US government, including firms under foreign ownership or control. Under current procedures (described in Office of Industrial Resource Allocation 1984), priorities are invoked by the issuance of what are termed "rated orders" for goods required by the military. (The 1991 bill for renewal of the act contains an amendment that would put services under the priorities system as well.) A rated order must be accepted by a supplier, unless an exception is granted by the Office of Industrial Resource Allocation within the US Commerce Department. Production of the good or service must be scheduled so as to meet required delivery dates. The supplier must use rated orders when obtaining inputs from subcontractors necessary to meet the original rated order. If the good is in short supply, in the sense that standing orders for the good (or other goods that require use of the same production facilities) placed via non-rated orders would preclude fulfillment of the order by the required delivery dates, the supplier must give priority to the rated order so that the required delivery date is met (in other words, defense requirements go to the head of the line).

The importance of these provisions of the Defense Production Act for our purposes is that even US subsidiaries of firms controlled by potentially hostile foreign powers can be required to produce and deliver goods and services needed by the military according to a prioritized schedule. Of course, it is possible that such a subsidiary might take action to stall delivery. But, as we shall see below, the president of the United States has other means to deal with such actions.

An important point is that the priorities and allocations procedures under the Defense Production Act do not necessarily apply to suppliers operating outside US government jurisdiction. This is an argument for encouraging direct investment in the United States by foreign firms in high-technology industries. We return to this point in chapter 7.

Emergency Powers

Assuming that the US government can identify potential fifth columns in wartime, it does have considerable powers to prevent them from taking actions that could be detrimental to the national security. The main powers reside with the president under the Trading With the Enemy Act (TWEA). Under this act, in time of war the president can take any of a number of measures affecting transactions between subsidiaries of foreign-controlled multinationals and their parents. In particular, under Section 5(b) of the act, the president may "investigate, regulate, direct and compel, nullify, void, prevent or prohibit, any acquisition, holding, withholding, use, transfer, withdrawal, transportation, importation or exportation of, or dealing in, or exercising any right, power, or privilege with respect to, or transactions involving, any property in which any foreign country or any national thereof has any interest . . . ."

This and other provisions of the act give the president very broad but quite ambiguous powers to act against foreign interests (see, e.g., Jackson 1977). It is clear that the original intent of Congress was to limit application of these provisions to entities controlled by nationals of countries with which the United States was at war. However, the original language of the TWEA also enabled its invocation whenever the president declared a national emergency. This was done on several occasions, beginning with President Franklin D. Roosevelt's declaration of a national emergency in 1933. Then and later, provisions of the TWEA were used against foreign firms based in nations with which the United States was not at war or even in a state of hostility.

In 1976, concern about potential abuses of the TWEA prompted Congress to pass the International Emergency Economic Powers Act (IEEPA), which restricted somewhat the powers of the president to deal with a national emergency when the United States is not at war. Whereas under section 5(b) of the TWEA the president could sequester and (as the courts interpreted the law) take title to the US assets of enemy nationals during a national emergency as well as in time of war, under the IEEPA the president, in time of national emergency short of declared war, can seize foreign-owned assets but cannot take title to them. Thus, under such circumstances the president cannot permanently nationalize a US subsidiary of a foreign firm. The president can, however, block the assets of the subsidiary and freeze the ability of the subsidiary to do business in the United States. This authority was used following Iraq's invasion of Kuwait to freeze the assets of all firms in the United States owned or controlled by the governments of Iraq and Kuwait, including a number of firms that were not directly owned by the Iraqi government or Iraqi nationals but were nonetheless declared "special designated nationals" (SDNs) of Iraq (see statement by R. Richard Newcomb in US House Committee on Banking, Finance, and Urban Affairs 1991).

Most of the other powers of the president to act against foreign-controlled entities in the United States are carried over from the TWEA into the IEEPA. These powers are quite extensive; for example, the president can block or regulate trade between foreign-controlled subsidiaries and their parent organizations. During the conflict with Iraq, Iraqi-controlled firms and SDNs in the United States were forbidden to do business of any sort. These prohibitions were invoked in part under the IEEPA and in part under the economic sanctions relating to the United Nations Participation Act.

To invoke the IEEPA, the president must declare a national emergency under procedures of the National Emergencies Act of 1975. The national emergency expires automatically at the end of one year but can be extended by the president. The clear intent of Congress was that national emergencies would be rare events (see Carter 1988). However, the IEEPA has been invoked seven times under declared national emergencies from its passage through August 1990; three of these invocations came after 1985. In the views of some analysts, some of these invocations have bordered on the frivolous (see, e.g., Hufbauer et al. 1990; Carter 1988).

The most recent invocation as of this writing, however, was anything but frivolous. On 9 August 1991 President George Bush acted under authority of the IEEPA to freeze all Kuwaiti and Iraqi assets within the jurisdiction of the United States or under the control of US persons. The major actions taken against Iraqi firms, summarized above, were taken largely to fulfill the UN-imposed economic sanctions against Iraq. Kuwaiti assets included at least one major US firm under control of Kuwaiti citizens, Santa Fe Industries. Such firms and other activities under Kuwaiti control were granted a series of special licenses to continue their normal activities after it was officially determined that these transactions were not inconsistent with the objectives of the sanctions and did not confer any realizable benefit on the government of Iraq. A few such licenses were also granted to activities under Iraqi control after the same determination was made and where freezing of the activities would have caused unnecessary and irreparable harm to the interests of innocent third parties (e.g., most Iraqi oil already in transit on the date that sanctions went into effect was allowed to proceed to its original destinations, but payment for the oil went into frozen accounts).

Identifying Potential Fifth Columns

It has been asked whether in a declared national emergency the president could even identify those assets in the United States that are foreign-controlled. The United States does not require registration of FDI except for statistical purposes, and under present law the information collected is not open to officials outside of the relevant agencies, even in time of national emergency. Much has been made of this point, and in 1988 a bill was introduced in the House of Representatives that would have required registration of FDI in the United States and disclosure of certain information about its ownership. This bill, called the Bryant amendment after its sponsor Representative John C. Bryant (D-TX), was not passed, but there is still some sentiment within Congress to enact similar legislation.

From a national security perspective the argument over registration requirements for FDI is something of a red herring. What really matters is that relevant officials have knowledge of *all* foreign-controlled suppliers of goods and services important to the national security, whether those suppliers are US subsidiaries or the overseas operations of foreign firms. In other words, the Defense Department should also know the identity of its foreign sources that do *not* have US subsidiaries. Indeed, dependence upon an overseas source of supply for a militarily critical good is clearly a greater problem than dependence upon a domestic source of supply that is foreign-owned. The present state of the Defense Department's knowledge of who these suppliers are is not, according to some specialists we have consulted, as good as it might be. It has been recommended that the Defense Department take steps to improve its knowledge about which of its vendors and suppliers are ultimately foreign-controlled. In 1988, for example, the report of the Undersecretary of Defense for Acquisition and the report of the Defense Science Board both recommended that prime contractors be required to report on their foreign-sourced components.

Our best information, based on interviews with several Defense Department officials, is that these recommendations have not been fully implemented. However, there is little to suggest that the holes in the Defense Department's knowledge principally involve foreign-controlled domestic suppliers. Rather, the holes seem to lie to a greater extent among firms actually located abroad that serve as subcontractors to domestic defense contractors. The nationality of most first-tier subcontractors is known, but information on that of lower-tier subcontractors has not been gathered systematically.

Information on foreign-controlled firms that are primary contractors to the Pentagon is, in principle at least, immediately available to relevant Defense Department officials. As is detailed in the next section, foreign-controlled firms that are primary contractors to the Defense Department are subject to special regulations that require disclosure of ownership. Thus, any gap in information involves not these direct defense contractors but foreign suppliers of dual-use technologies to the primary contractors. We heartily agree that the Pentagon should know the identity of its major suppliers of dual-use technologies and related goods and services and should know whether these suppliers are under foreign control. However, this does not mean that every foreign subsidiary in the United States should be required to register with the Pentagon. Not all of these subsidiaries are suppliers of dual-use technologies, and not all foreign-controlled suppliers of these technologies are US subsidiaries of foreign firms.

Our discussion thus far has focused on foreign-controlled suppliers to the US military. Is there anything to fear from fifth-column-like action on the part of US subsidiaries of foreign firms that are not engaged in activities of military significance? We would argue that in general there is not. These subsidiaries do not have access to information that is sensitive from a security perspective, except perhaps to certain types of economic and commercial information that would be readily available to a foreign power through any of a number of alternative channels. If these subsidiaries nonetheless were deemed to pose a threat, could they be identified? We feel that they could: emergency legislation could be passed allowing their identity to be obtained from the records of the Bureau of Economic Analysis, for example.

We conclude that the US government in principle should have little problem in identifying potential fifth columns during time of actual war or circumstances leading to war, even without the imposition of new registration and reporting requirements for all foreign direct investors. Indeed, legislation targeted on gathering information about US subsidiaries controlled by foreign interests could miss the important point that the foreign sources on which the United States depends for militarily sensitive goods and technology are not limited to these subsidiaries. We do not claim that the information presently available to the Defense Department about these sources is adequate, and new legislation authorizing the Pentagon to obtain additional information about suppliers of dual-use technologies may prove necessary. But this is not the same as new registration and reporting requirements for foreign direct investors.

Other Aspects

Despite the extensive powers granted to the executive branch by the TWEA and the IEEPA, there are a number of aspects of the potential fifth-column problem that the US government can do little about. One is the fact that foreign-controlled subsidiaries invariably create domestic constituencies that could influence US policy in favor of the home nation of the subsidiary. One such constituency consists of US nationals employed by subsidiaries. The political influence of these constituencies could conceivably constrain the policy choices available to the US government in times of imminent conflict with that home nation. Actions taken by members of such constituencies need not be overtly hostile to national interests in order to put those interests in jeopardy—for example, workers employed by a foreign subsidiary might oppose government emergency action against their employer simply out of a desire to protect their jobs. We call this potential problem that of the "inadvertent fifth column."

It is truly difficult to assess the threat that the inadvertent fifth column poses. Our own feeling is that at present the threat is not great. One reason is that, in a national emergency, the president can seize the assets of a foreign-controlled subsidiary and protect the jobs of the affected workers. It is likely that assurances that their jobs would indeed be protected would dissuade the workers from taking actions contrary to the national interest. Another reason is that, although there is little question that European or Japanese direct investment creates at least a potential pro-European or pro-Japanese lobby in the United States, we do not think it probable that the home governments would try to use those lobbies in ways that are truly detrimental to US national security. Indeed, any such effort would likely provoke a counterreaction and generate strong antiforeign sentiment. Home governments are sensitive to this possibility.

A second potentially dangerous aspect of FDI that the US government can do little directly about is the impact on US defense capabilities if a US subsidiary's links with its parent organization are severed. That impact would be most severe if the United States depended upon the subsidiary as a major or sole source of supply for a militarily critical item or technology. In most other circumstances the impact would likely not be great. To take an improbable example, if the United States were ever again to go to war with Japan, it would not greatly matter if Nissan's US truck facility, cut off from its parent, could not produce military vehicles efficiently; other suppliers could meet the need for such vehicles—within the United States are a number of integrated truck manufacturers, most of them domestically owned. If, in contrast, the US military relied on a domestic affiliate of a Japanese producer as a sole supplier of a microchip needed for the functioning of one of its "smart" weapons, and this microchip could not be produced if the affiliate were to be cut off from its parent, it would be a different matter. Again, however, the United States would be better off in this situation than if the US affiliate and the military relied on imports from the Japanese producer itself. It is likely that in an emergency the United States could have the affiliate up and running considerably faster than a domestic supplier could be created from scratch.

Clearly, however, the United States must know what capabilities it will need in time of conflict and take steps to ensure that those capabilities are in place. This again implies that the United States should never be dependent upon a foreign nation, even through local subsidiaries of firms based in that nation, for a commodity or technology that the foreign nation is in a position to monopolize. We comment on this further later in this chapter and in chapter 7.

One final aspect of the potential fifth column issue is that US subsidiaries controlled by foreign companies might leak information about technologies that national security dictates should remain in the United States. This matter is discussed in greater detail in the next section of this chapter; in general, however, we find that the United States is well placed to ensure that technological and other information vital to the national defense that originates within the United States itself is not placed in enemy hands by the managers of foreign-controlled subsidiaries. Access to truly secret information is limited to persons with appropriate security clearances, and these clearances generally are not given to non-US managers of foreign-controlled firms except under tightly controlled circumstances. Alas, the John Walker case, in which a spy ring made up of US citizens sold US Navy secrets to the Soviet Union, and the Richard Ames case, where a senior employee of the Central Intelligence Agency—again a US citizen—compromised US intelligence agents in the field, illustrate that there is no fail-safe way to protect such information when those who have clearance to receive it choose to work for the enemy. We simply note here that no foreign firm operating in the United States is known ever to have compromised US security on anything like the scale of the Walker or Ames cases.

FDI by Friendly Powers

The leakage issue concerns only technology developed in the United States. Today, however, the United States is only one of several nations capable of innovating technologies of military significance. Does this fact increase the vulnerability of the United States, and if so, what role do multinationals based in countries friendly to the United States play in the overall picture?

As table 5.1 showed, the vast bulk of FDI in the United States originates from foreign firms whose home countries are either military allies or other advanced democracies that are hard to conceive of as military adversaries. Thus, the main national security issue in practice is one of policy toward these friendly multinationals. Stated in extreme form the question is, To what extent should US policy assume that domestic US subsidiaries of friendly foreign investors are, for security purposes, just like domestically owned firms, and to what extent should it be assumed that they are potential enemy agents? It is clear that policy should not swing to either of these extremes, but what intermediate assumption is the appropriate one? We address this question by asking two related ones:

- Are there activities in the United States that should *never* come under foreign control, even if the foreign investor in question is from a friendly nation? That is, are there activities so sensitive that it should be assumed that any foreign control creates a potential fifth column, in the broad sense we have defined it?

- Does foreign ownership by friendly nations threaten the US defense industrial base? That is, does it somehow reduce the resources on which the United States can rely to develop its defensive capability?

We shall address each of these questions in turn. But it is important first to note that proscribing foreign participation in defense activities and constructing safeguards against loss of militarily vital activities can reduce the ability of the United States to avail itself of foreign technologies of potential use in defense. Thus we should ask not just whether US proscriptions and safeguards are sufficient, but whether any of them could have a deterrent effect on foreigners who might be otherwise willing to bring into the United States technologies or activities that could be important to US security. This is not a trivial point; it would be sad and ironic if US policies designed to maintain the defense industrial base instead consigned the United States to technological inferiority by keeping advanced foreign technologies out.

Proscribing Foreign Control

We claim no expertise in determining which specific activities, if any, the national interest requires be performed by domestically controlled firms. It is clear, however, that both the US government and the general public regard it as essential that direct provision of certain key military supplies be done by such firms. Few Americans would feel comfortable if, for example, foreign interests gained control of one of the large defense-contracting aerospace firms such as General Dynamics, Lockheed, or Northrop. For example, the bid by the French firm Thomson-CSF to acquire the missiles division of LTV Aerospace and Defense Company in 1992 was withdrawn in the face of serious concerns expressed in Congress over a major defense contractor coming under foreign control, even though LTV was in a state of bankruptcy and the Thomson-CSF bid represented an opportunity to turn the missiles division around. Yet no existing law or policy states explicitly which activities, or which firms, must for security reasons remain under domestic control.

Although there is no law specifically forbidding a foreign takeover of one of the major defense-contracting firms, the 1988 Exon-Florio amendment (discussed in the next chapter) does serve as a major deterrent to any such effort. It is safe to say that a foreign attempt to buy out Boeing would lead to an Exon-Florio investigation, and that by far the most probable outcome would be blockage of the takeover. The Thomson-CSF bid for the LTV missile division might not have survived an Exon-Florio review, and the expectation of blockage was almost surely a major factor behind the bid being withdrawn. Indeed, this bid led to changes in the law that will make it more difficult for foreign investors under foreign government control to take over defense contractors; these changes are detailed in the following chapter.

The end of the cold war has in many ways intensified rather than defused the issue of what activities should not come under foreign control. The reason for this intensification is that the US defense sector as a whole, which grew relative to the size of the economy during the 1980s, is now shrinking and likely to continue to shrink. This shrinkage has put pressure on major firms in the industry to rationalize their operations, often by selling major portions of their business or by merging with other firms. Some of the best opportunities for rationalization lie in teaming up with foreign, especially European, firms. However, virtually simultaneously with the downsizing of the defense industry has come a hardening in official policies regarding foreign ownership, as signaled by the LTV-Thomson case.

Although the Exon-Florio amendment is the first US law that takes a step toward declaring that there are activities that the United States does not wish to see come under foreign control, it still does little to indicate exactly what these activities are. Indeed, Exon-Florio establishes only very general grounds on which a foreign takeover of a US firm can be blocked, unless (under the new provisions) the foreign entity is under foreign government control. It is left largely to the discretion of the president to determine how to interpret these grounds in specific cases.

Even so, the unwritten rule is that major firms engaged in large-scale defense contracting must be US-owned. There are exceptions to this generality, but these involve Canadian and UK firms that have a long and proven record as suppliers to the Defense Department. This does not mean, of course, that other foreign firms are completely excluded from military contracting for the United States. When foreign-owned firms provide military supplies, however, they do so under special and restrictive rules described below. As is also detailed below, these rules appear to have been tightened under the Clinton administration, and indeed the unwritten rule of US ownership seems to be more zealously enforced under the current administration than under its immediate Republican predecessors.

There has been some concern about whether the rules under which foreign firms can supply military hardware adequately protect military technologies necessary to US security. In fact, however, the rules are at least as strict and often stricter than those applying to domestic firms, so that it is arguable that the *domestic* firms pose a greater security risk. Typically a foreign-owned US subsidiary doing classified work must put greater distance between itself and its owners than a domestically owned subsidiary must put between itself and its owners. If one assumes that each set of owners is equally likely to be a source of leakage, it is then the domestically owned subsidiary that puts the nation at greater risk.

In the absence of an explicit understanding of exactly what defense-related activities should remain under domestic control, decisions with respect to maintenance of a domestically controlled industrial base tend to be made on an ad hoc basis. Although the United States under the Carter, Reagan, and Bush administrations eschewed any formal government industrial policy, ad hoc decisions in this area, by favoring the preservation of certain US industries, can sum up to a de facto industrial policy that makes little sense as a whole (see, e.g., Magaziner and Reich 1982). The Clinton administration, in contrast, has been willing to tinker with industrial policy, although to date this has been on a rather small scale.

What criteria should determine whether a given activity should be placed on the must-maintain-domestic-control list? Obviously, one criterion would be military importance. That in turn depends both upon how important the output of that activity is to the waging of a military conflict and upon whether there are effective substitutes for that output. Thus, production of jet fighter airplanes is a very important military activity, whereas production of eggs is not. An army has to eat, but there are many substitutes for eggs; on the other hand there is no effective substitute for a state-of-the-art jet fighter.

Additional criteria would be the number of alternative sources of supply and the lead time required to develop new sources (see Moran 1990). A key characteristic of advanced jet fighters is that not just anyone can make them; in fact, the number of firms worldwide that can make advanced fighters or their key components is very small. It also requires a very long lead time for a firm that is new to military aviation to develop the capabilities needed to manufacture the most advanced jet aircraft. In contrast, although there is no military substitute for clothing manufactured from textiles—it would be impractical to send soldiers into the battlefield wearing furs—there are literally thousands of alternative suppliers, and it requires very little lead time for a new entrant to become established in this industry. (There are, however, a few highly specialized textile products used by the military for which the number of suppliers is small.) Thus we suspect that it would be considered vital that the capability to produce advanced jet fighters remain under domestic control, whereas we doubt that the same could be said for most textiles and clothing.

Maintaining the Defense Industrial Base

There has been much talk during the past ten years about erosion of the US defense industrial base. Although the term means somewhat different things to different people, among national defense specialists there does seem to be something of a consensus that the "defense industrial base" consists largely of the high-technology industries. There are those who would include a number of low-technology industries in the definition, but this is a minority view held largely by spokespersons for particular low-technology industries that face foreign competition. Thus, the question of the impact of FDI on the defense industrial base comes down to whether FDI threatens to reduce the United States' strengths in the high-technology industries.

Having interviewed a number of defense specialists, we are convinced that there has been some erosion of the defense industrial base, especially within the electronics sector. But has inward FDI been a cause of this erosion or merely a symptom of it? We find that most specialists believe the latter. According to them, FDI is not a primary cause of the uncontestable decline of the once-dominant international position of domestically controlled US producers of advanced electronics. Rather, US subsidiaries of foreign firms have displaced market share once held by domestically controlled firms in this sector because the domestic firms failed to keep pace in increasing efficiency and developing new product technology, not because the US subsidiaries behaved in a predatory manner.

Not all specialists agree with this assessment, to be sure. There are those who would point to the acquisition of small US high-technology firms by foreign investors as one way by which the United States has been stripped of the new technologies needed to maintain the competitiveness of its domestically controlled high-technology firms. The story usually told is one in which the foreign investor buys the firm, transfers the technology overseas, and leaves nothing but a hollowed-out shell.

Although most experts believe that some hollowing out has occurred, we find that only a minority believe that it is a leading cause of US decline in the electronics or other industries. However, there is a remarkable dearth of hard evidence on this subject; what evidence has been brought to bear is largely anecdotal. Only very recently have a number of more systematic studies addressed this issue directly or indirectly, and their conclusions are not yet available.

We will not explore in any depth the reasons for the erosion of the defense industrial base apart from FDI. One of the reasons that has been mentioned is the failure of domestic firms to maintain the rates of capital expenditure needed to preserve a low-cost position in the production of such critical goods as semiconductor memory chips, which tend to be subject to dynamic scale economies (learning curves). Another reason cited is the failure of the United States to arrive at a consensus with respect to product standards, so that production runs can be made large enough to achieve these dynamic scale economies. Specialists indicate to us that the blame for this failure lies with both the industries themselves and the US government. In particular there has been little effort within the Defense Department and other relevant agencies to set common product specifications and, importantly, to attempt to make these consistent with standards in civilian markets for dual-use goods. A third reason—and one that reinforces the point just made—is the government's failure to recognize that nonmilitary uses of some high-technology goods (e.g., semiconductors) today account for almost 95 percent of worldwide sales of those goods. That is a vastly different situation from that of 25 years ago. One consequence is that whereas a quarter of a century ago the leading edge of these technologies tended to be driven by military applications, today this leading edge most often is driven by nonmilitary applications.

If FDI is not the cause of the decline of US-controlled high-technology firms, is there any other basis for the claim that inward FDI has eroded the defense industrial base? We believe that there is.

If there were a clean dividing line between military and civilian technology, then the requirement that key defense activities remain in domestic hands would pose no particular problem: the United States could have a wholly domestic defense industrial base while allowing free right of establishment by foreigners everywhere else. Unfortunately, this is not the case. Not only are many important technologies dual-use technologies, developed for and applied to both civilian and military uses, but, as noted above, the output of goods for civilian uses is in some key sectors (e.g., electronics) much greater than that for military uses. This poses a potential problem. Consider the hypothetical but not entirely implausible scenario in which Japanese firms come to dominate the production of civilian semiconductors in the United States, there are significant economies of scope arising from joint production of military and civilian semiconductors, and the US military considers it unwise to purchase key semiconductors from foreign-controlled suppliers. These products would thus fall into the category for which domestic control is deemed necessary, yet it would be unlikely that any domestic firm could produce state-of-the-art semiconductors solely for the defense market at prices even remotely competitive with the Japanese; in effect, the growth of foreign ownership would effectively have eroded the industrial base for defense. Unlike the purely economic effects considered in chapter 3, this erosion would have nothing to do with loss of external economies. It results simply from the combination of dual-use technologies and a reliance on US-owned suppliers.

One answer to this problem would be to find a secure way to allow defense contracting with foreign-owned firms, as indeed most countries now do. Semiconductors simply would be taken off of the list of activities for which domestic control was deemed necessary. Under the current rules of Department of Defense contracting, however, a foreign-owned subsidiary can be a contractor only if it meets certain stringent requirements: either the subsidiary must be granted a special security arrangement (SSA), or its equity must be placed into a nonvoting trust. Under a nonvoting trust arrangement the foreign owners relinquish the voting rights of their equity in the subsidiary. The board of directors and top management of the subsidiary must also consist of US citizens. Effectively, then, the foreign owners of the subsidiary become passive investors. Virtually the only choice they have with respect to the subsidiary is whether to continue to own it. Since control is the essential objective and defining feature of FDI, this means that the foreign firm must in effect convert its direct investment into a portfolio investment in order to engage in US defense contracting. An SSA offers more flexible (and milder) but still stringent criteria.

Following the attempted takeover of the missile division of LTV Aerospace and Defense Company (described above), the Defense Department announced that most firms under foreign ownership, control, or influence that were engaged in defense contracting would be subject to the more stringent nonvoting trust arrangements rather than the more flexible SSAs. This policy was subsequently formally scrapped after objections that it would deter desired foreign investments in the defense sector, but claims are made that the new policy is still being applied de facto by the Clinton administration.

The preference for US-owned firms tends to limit the willingness of the Defense Department to employ foreign-owned firms as suppliers; in any case the restrictions placed on foreign firms tend to discourage these firms from seeking defense business. The result is that the defense industrial base can be said to be eroded to some extent when foreign firms acquire or replace US firms in activities that have military significance. This is a real issue and poses a problem for advocates of unrestricted FDI. But it also raises the issue of whether or not the rules under which foreign-controlled firms can participate in defense contracting should be revised. These rules were largely written at a time when the United States dominated the innovation of militarily significant technologies, including dual-use technologies, and were designed to keep sensitive technologies from leaking out of the United States. It is entirely possible now that they are doing as good a job at keeping important dual-use technologies out of the United States as at keeping US-developed technologies in.

A second issue arises when, in contrast, a foreign-owned firm participates in an important defense contract and, for some reason, the home government of the parent firm decides it wants the parent to pull out. Could this hurt the US defense effort?

An incident that occurred in 1983 illustrates both of these issues. Responding to the concerns of Socialist members of the Japanese parliament, the Japanese Ministry of International Trade and Industry (MITI) reportedly ordered Kyocera Corporation, a Japanese producer of high-technology ceramic products, not to participate in contracts to supply ceramic nose cones to the US Tomahawk missile program. Kyocera at that time was supplying nose cones through its US subsidiary Dexcel. Kyocera was also under pressure from the Defense Department to place the defense-related activities of Dexcel in a nonvoting trust. The outcome was that Dexcel was sold to US interests. Kyocera is acknowledged to be among the technologically most advanced firms in the ceramics industry, and it can be argued that its withdrawal from this area of US defense contracting hurt the defense effort.

It is important, however, not to stress these issues unduly. First, the range of sectors in which dual-use technologies pose a problem is sometimes overstated, especially because national security is too often used as an excuse for special-interest politics. Numerous US industries have mounted campaigns against foreign competition in their domestic markets, claiming among other things that national security requires that domestic capacity in their industry be maintained at present levels. Trade policymakers have learned to look with a healthy skepticism on such claims, and they should cultivate a similar skepticism toward claims in the investment area. In fact, since cutoff of supply is even less likely when the suppliers are foreign-owned subsidiaries in the United States rather than foreign suppliers overseas, one should be more, not less, suspicious of national security arguments in such cases.

Second, to some degree the erosion of the US defense industrial base is a self-inflicted problem. Essentially, US military procurement is still governed by the assumption that US-based firms can supply all the necessary technology. Even under an optimistic prognosis for the US economy, however, Americans can expect from now on to live in a more symmetric world, in which foreign firms frequently will have technology superior to anything available in the United States. In such a world an insistence on using only technologies developed by US firms will actually impair national security to the extent that it prevents the military from taking advantage of the best technology available.

In recent years the Pentagon has largely adjusted to this reality, albeit in some instances perhaps somewhat unwittingly, in its treatment of indirect suppliers. Major defense contractors routinely subcontract for subsystems or source critical components from foreign suppliers, and the Pentagon accepts this. What could stand some rethinking are policies regarding foreign-controlled firms as direct suppliers.

Some Unresolved Issues

A number of issues related to foreign control of defense-related activities remain murky and must be studied further before useful policy recommendations can emerge. Among these issues are certain dangers that can arise from increased dependence on foreign-controlled firms for defense contracting, and whether hollowing out of US firms acquired by foreign interests poses a serious threat to national security.

We have suggested throughout this chapter that it will be necessary in the future for the United States to depend more, rather than less, on foreign sources for key dual-use technologies and that, if this is so, it is better to have domestic subsidiaries of the relevant firms do the work than to leave it to overseas operations. Two dangers to this policy suggest themselves, however. First, foreign firms cannot always be trusted to transfer their newest and best technologies to their US subsidiaries. Second, the subsidiaries themselves cannot always be trusted not to leak sensitive information gleaned in their defense-related work to their parent organizations, which in turn cannot always be trusted not to leak this information to hostile powers.

Whether, for example, Japanese multinational firms hold back their newest and best technologies from their US subsidiaries is a testable proposition, provided that the relevant firms cooperate. We believe that there is so much at stake that the relevant firms should be willing to cooperate, and it could be presumed that those unwilling to do so are indeed guilty of holding back. In chapter 3 it was noted that the available evidence does not strongly support the hypothesis that multinationals locate R&D activities exclusively near their headquarters; this argues against the proposition that foreign parent firms withhold technology from their US subsidiaries. (Indeed, in many cases the subsidiaries actually develop technologies that benefit the parent firms; examples include the breakthroughs in superconductor technology by the International Business Machines Corp. laboratory in Switzerland and the development of important new pharmaceutical products by Hoffmann–La Roche, Inc., the New Jersey subsidiary of the Roche Group.) However, these conclusions were based on aggregated data. Evidence at a much more disaggregated level is needed.

Likewise, more needs to be known about whether US subsidiaries of foreign firms (or, indeed, foreign firms without such subsidiaries) actually maintain the secrecy of sensitive information made available to them. There clearly have been some cases where secrecy has been breached; an incident involving Toshiba Corporation's (reportedly inadvertent) sale of a controlled US submarine technology to the Soviet Union is often mentioned in this regard. But are these incidents rare exceptions to a good record, or is there widespread leakage of sensitive information? An objective study of this issue would serve US policy interests.

In interviews we conducted with US government specialists in the area of defense contracting, we heard it alleged more than once that, during the 1980s, some foreign-owned contractors holding effective monopoly positions in the high-technology products they supplied to the US government had both withheld their best technology and inappropriately transferred technology to the Soviet Union. These reports, if true, provide evidence that concerns over increased US reliance on foreign-based defense suppliers are not without foundation. We do not think it wise for the United States to be at the mercy of any firm that monopolizes a product that is key to the defense effort, whether that firm is domestically controlled or foreign-controlled. Indeed the United States has antitrust laws on the books that are supposed to protect the US consumer from monopolies in any sector, whether of military relevance or not.

We have already noted that there is a divergence of opinion among specialists with respect to whether hollowing out poses a threat to US national security, and that there is a dearth of hard evidence to bring to bear on this subject. Further study of the hollowing-out phenomenon therefore seems warranted. Indeed, proper administration of the Exon-Florio amendment as discussed in chapters 6 and 7 would seem to us to mandate that this study be accorded a high priority.

6

Current US Policy

The preceding chapters have surveyed the trends in foreign direct investment in the United States and analyzed some of their features. In chapter 7 we draw on this analysis to evaluate a variety of recommendations for US policy regarding FDI. A few key principles underlie current US policy as it has evolved over several decades; those principles remain essentially in place despite significant changes as a result of the 1988 trade act and subsequent developments. However, there does seem to be a drift in US policy, as embodied in certain legislative proposals, away from these principles. In this chapter we review present US policy toward FDI and compare it with the policies of other advanced nations.

Like most aspects of US policy, policy toward FDI needs to be understood at several levels. The first is the explicit policy enunciated and implemented by the federal government. The second is the implicit policy of the federal government toward foreign firms; this policy is evidenced in a variety of ways, not least by the precedents the government sets and the relationships it forms with other nations through its policy toward *outward* investment; these carry considerable weight because the United States is the world's largest home for multinationals as well as its largest host. Finally, an important part of policy that affects foreign firms operating in the United States is set not at the federal level but by states and localities. We therefore describe three kinds of policy: federal policy aimed directly at foreign firms, the important complementary policy toward US direct investment abroad, and policy made at the state and local level.

Federal Policy

Policy Toward Inward FDI

Philosophically, since at least the Carter administration US policy toward foreign firms operating in the United States has attempted to be neutral, without bias either in favor of or against foreign ownership of US productive assets. This general intention toward neutrality has been affirmed repeatedly by statements of recent administrations under both major political parties, notably in a 1977 declaration by the Carter administration and a 1983 statement by the Reagan administration. The 1983 statement was interpreted by some observers as more favorable to inward investment than the 1977 declaration, because it indicated that this investment was "welcome" if it came in response to market forces. However, since the United States never contemplated actually favoring foreign firms over domestic, this difference in language did not represent any change in the basic philosophy of neutrality.

A truly neutral policy toward FDI necessarily involves adherence to two principles. The first is right of establishment: foreign firms should face no obstacles in creating or expanding US operations that are not also faced by domestic firms. The second is national treatment: a foreign firm already operating in the United States should not face greater burdens as a result of government action or policy than domestic firms, nor should it receive special privileges that domestic firms do not. Broadly speaking, US policy toward foreign firms has been fairly close to neutral in this sense.[1] The main deviations from neutrality that are in place derive from a variety of special restrictions that are justified at least in principle on national security grounds. A number of legislative proposals, however, would replace national treatment in a number of domains with conditional national treatment, an issue to which we turn shortly.

Until 1988, federal restrictions on FDI applied essentially to those industries subject to federal regulation. In a few federally regulated industries FDI is simply proscribed. Many of these proscriptions were put in place during the late 19th and early 20th centuries; a history of these is contained in Wilkins (1989). These industries include production and utilization of nuclear energy and most domestic maritime transport as regulated under

---

1. A number of guides to investment in the United States (see, e.g., Industry Canada 1994) list US antitrust and securities laws and regulations as barriers to entry, but these laws and regulations apply equally to domestic and foreign investors. However, some laws and regulations that apply, in a manner consistent with national treatment principles, to domestic and foreign-controlled firms alike might nonetheless discriminate in a de facto sense against the latter (and, indeed, in some cases were designed to do so). An example is a requirement under the 1993 Transportation Appropriations Act that all automobiles sold in the United States, beginning with the 1994 model year, display the percentage of "US content" in their manufacture.

the Jones Act. In some other federally regulated industries limitations are imposed on FDI. In broadcasting and telecommunications, for example, foreign-controlled enterprises may not own more than 20 percent of a company with a broadcasting or common-carrier license, unless the Federal Communications Commission grants an exception. In the domestic air transport sector, no more than 25 percent of the voting shares of a domestic carrier may be owned by foreigners, and foreign interests may not exercise control over a domestic carrier. However, the 1993 approval by the US Department of Transportation of an arrangement by which British Airways acquired effective control of USAir Group has suggested that official policies may in some instances be relaxed in practice. There are also certain specific ventures, such as the Communications Satellite Corporation (COMSAT), in which foreign participation is limited or proscribed. In recent years there has been something of a trend toward liberalizing these restrictions; for example, in 1991 the US Department of Transportation proposed an easing of restrictions on foreign ownership of domestic airlines.

In some industries the principle of neutrality is superseded by that of reciprocity, whereby a foreign firm in the United States is accorded treatment equivalent to that which US firms receive in the firm's home country. Foreign or foreign-controlled companies may not, for example, acquire rights-of-way for gas pipelines across federal lands or leases for mining certain minerals and fuels on those lands if the foreign investor's home country denies similar rights to US citizens or US-controlled corporations.

There are also some US industries, such as hydroelectric power generation and fishing in certain areas, in which only certain legal forms of foreign ownership are allowed; for example, foreign-owned subsidiaries created under US law may be permitted whereas branches are proscribed. Foreign-owned firms participating in these industries can also be subject to US regulations such as the requirement that vessels flying the US flag be used.

Finally, although foreign-controlled domestic firms (and in some cases the foreign parents themselves) may participate in defense contracting work in the United States, these firms are subject to some special conditions (described in chapter 5) if they work on classified projects.

There are clear signs that the trend toward official promotion of certain high-technology industries in the United States will involve a de facto policy of discrimination against foreign firms (Warner and Rugman 1994). The first of these was Sematech, the federally supported research consortium in the semiconductor industry, which includes no foreign-owned firms. In principle, Sematech's membership structure represents a choice on the part of the member firms rather than a federal policy of exclusion. In practice, however, the exclusion has surely also reflected the preferences of the US Department of Defense, which funds the consortium.

Later, more overt examples of such discrimination are contained in a number of laws passed by Congress during the past several years (as well as in a number of bills currently being considered by Congress) that place (or would place) restrictions on the eligibility of foreign-controlled firms operating in the United States for federal funding for research and development. In many cases the restrictions are imposed only if the home country of the firm fails to meet certain reciprocity tests, and thus it is in this domain that concern about conditional national treatment is highest.

Laws already in place include the Energy Policy Act of 1992, which allows a foreign-controlled firm to be eligible to participate in federal programs under titles XX through XXIII (which involve mostly programs for research, development, and commercialization of new energy-related technologies) only if certain reciprocity tests are met. For example, US firms must be afforded "comparable" participation in similar programs in the home country, US firms must have right of establishment in that country, and the intellectual property laws of the home country must offer "adequate and effective protection" for US firms. Also, the US Department of Energy, before allowing a foreign-controlled firm to participate in one of these programs, must determine that such participation is in the economic interest of the United States. Similar requirements must be met before a foreign-controlled firm can participate in the US Department of Commerce's Advanced Technology Program (ATP). As originally established under the 1988 trade act, this program imposed no restrictions on foreign participation, but in 1991 the American Technology Preeminence Act amended its provisions to include reciprocity requirements. Similar requirements must be met before a foreign-controlled firm may participate in certain projects related to defense conversion, as specified in the 1993 Defense Appropriations Act. Responsibility for certification of eligibility for both the ATP and the defense conversion projects is given to the Secretary of Commerce. The National Cooperative Productions Act, which grants certain exemptions to US antitrust laws to some manufacturing and R&D joint ventures, was amended in 1993 to include reciprocity requirements for participating foreign-owned companies, most notably that the company's home country must grant national treatment to US firms. However, such treatment is assumed to exist if the home country participates in an international treaty requiring national treatment for US investors. Amendments passed in 1993 to the Stevenson-Wydler Technology Innovation Act of 1980 require that foreign-controlled firms participating in collaborative R&D arrangements with US national laboratories be from countries that allow US firms access to similar programs in those countries.

Reciprocity measures were also contemplated in a number of bills before the 103rd Congress, including the Aeronautical Technology Consortium Act, the National Environmental Technology Act, the National Competitiveness Act, the Defense Authorization Legislation, the Hydrogen Future Act, the National Aeronautics and Space Administration Authorization Act, and the Omnibus Space Commercialization Act. (These are listed in chronological order by date of introduction.) The most controversial of these were the Manton and Collins amendments to the proposed National Competitiveness Act (the House and Senate versions are H.R. 820 and S. 4, respectively). The act itself would have amended and greatly expanded a number of existing acts, including the Stevenson-Wydler Act and the provisions of the 1988 trade act relating to the National Institute for Standards and Technology (provisions that established the ATP) mentioned above. The National Competitiveness Act would have authorized a wide range of government-funded or government-organized consortia in R&D and in the commercialization of advanced technologies.

Under the amendment offered by Representative Thomas J. Manton (D-NY), participation in these consortia would be limited to "US companies." A foreign-controlled company could qualify as a US company if reciprocity standards were met; specifically, the amendment would require that the Secretary of Commerce find that the country of the parent company both provides US companies with "comparable" opportunities and offers them "access to resources and information equivalent to the opportunities offered under this legislation," and has an "open and transparent standards-setting process." Under the amendment offered by Representative Michael Collins (R-GA), the US government would be prohibited from providing any direct financial aid to anyone not a US citizen, national, or legal alien.

Critics of these amendments fear that the Manton amendment not only violates national treatment standards but sets reciprocity standards that would be difficult for most countries, even those that themselves adhere to national treatment standards, to meet. The Collins amendment could, under some interpretations, prevent any foreign-owned or foreign-controlled company from participating in the relevant programs, no matter how well the reciprocity standards were met. The two bills were passed in their respective houses during the 103rd Congress, but an impasse was reached in conference during the Congress's final days over their reconciliation. The impasse largely centered on the Manton amendment, which was vigorously opposed by a number of key senators. As a consequence, the National Competitiveness Act failed to be enacted. Whether a similar measure will be introduced in the 104th Congress is not known at this writing (in November 1994).

In addition to these laws and proposed laws, there are some other aspects of current US policies that some analysts claim are implicitly in violation of national treatment principles. The partnership between the US government and the US automobile industry to develop a new generation of fuel-efficient automobiles is cited as one example, because although there is no explicit exclusion, policy seems to be to exclude foreign-owned firms from this partnership. Whether the de facto working of the partnership violates national treatment principles is thus difficult to determine, and indeed resolution of issues such as this is one matter that could usefully be taken on by an international investment dispute settlement mechanism, discussed in the next chapter.

Restrictive Powers of the President

National treatment issues notwithstanding, the major recent change in federal policy toward FDI has been the extension of federal ability to restrict such investment in areas beyond the federally regulated industries. The Omnibus Trade and Competitiveness Act of 1988 included a provision (section 721, better known as the Exon-Florio amendment after its sponsors Senator J. James Exon [D-NE] and Representative James J. Florio [D-NJ]) that gave the president power to block mergers, acquisitions, or takeovers of US persons by foreign interests when such actions are deemed a threat to national security. The Exon-Florio authority lapsed for technical reasons in the fall of 1990, but it was reinstituted in August 1991 and made a permanent part of US law. The authority was subsequently amended by a provision in the Defense Authorization Act for fiscal year 1993 and procedurally altered by an executive order in September 1993.

The original version of the amendment offered by Congressman Florio in the 1980s would have allowed blockage of FDI for a wider variety of reasons than national security narrowly defined. In particular, it would have allowed the president to block any takeover that threatened the "essential commerce" of the United States. The amendment would also have placed the Secretary of Commerce in charge of the working-level implementation of the new authority; sponsors of the measure hoped that the Department of Commerce would take an activist role in this implementation. The Reagan administration initially opposed any new authority whatsoever. But when it became clear that sentiment in Congress was strong for some version of the Florio measure, the administration accepted a compromise measure engineered by Senator Exon wherein the essential commerce language was dropped and the choice of implementing agency was left up to the president.

Thus, under the version of the amendment that became law, the power to block a transaction could be exercised only if "the President finds that (1) there is credible evidence that leads the President to believe that the foreign interest exercising control might take action that threatens to impair the national security and (2) provisions of the law other than [the Exon-Florio amendment and the International Emergency Economic Powers Act] . . . do not in the President's judgement provide adequate and appropriate authority for the President to protect the national security . . . ."

The Exon-Florio measure, although enacted as part of the 1988 trade act, technically was an amendment to the Defense Production Act, an impermanent statute requiring periodic reauthorization by Congress.[2] Exon-Florio was clearly intended to become permanent law, but members of Congress and their staff involved in its drafting probably considered its placement in the Defense Production Act a safe choice, because never in its history had the legislation been allowed to lapse for any significant period. Nevertheless, in the closing hours of the 101st Congress during the fall of 1990, the Defense Production Act did lapse, and with it the Exon-Florio measure. The authority was not renewed for almost a year, but when it was, in August 1991, it was made permanent.

The Exon-Florio amendment represents a significant extension of the authority of the federal government to block foreign investment in the United States. At least in principle, the possible grounds for blocking FDI are still narrowly limited to national security, but some critics of the amendment argue that an administration inclined to restrict FDI could do so through a liberal interpretation of the national security clause.

Under regulations issued in November 1991 and still in effect as of this writing, the operating authority to implement Exon-Florio rests not with the Department of Commerce but in the hands of the Committee on Foreign Investment in the United States (CFIUS), an interagency committee chaired by the Secretary of the Treasury and consisting of representatives from the departments of State, Defense, Commerce, and Justice as well as from the Office of Management and Budget, the Office of the US Trade Representative, and the Council of Economic Advisers. Three additional members were added by executive order in September 1993, representing the Office of Science and Technology Policy, the National Security Council, and the recently created National Economic Council.[3] The CFIUS itself antedates Exon-Florio: it was originally established in the 1970s to monitor foreign investment in the United States. Until enactment of the Exon-Florio amendment it had no formal power to recommend that the president intervene in investment transactions, although it had investigated a number of foreign acquisitions of US firms. In at least one such case a proposed deal was withdrawn, and in two others certain "assurances" were sought by the CFIUS and accepted by the foreign investor.

Under the 1991 regulations the CFIUS undertakes investigations of those cases where it sees fit, and reports its findings and recommendations to the president. Cases of potential concern may be notified to the CFIUS by any direct party to the transaction or by a CFIUS member. Other parties (e.g., individual shareholders) may call a transaction to the attention of the

---

2. The legislative history of the Exon-Florio amendment is presented in Graham and Ebert (1991).

3. Technically, the representative of each agency on the CFIUS is the head of that agency.

CFIUS, but this does not constitute a formal notification. The decision to notify the CFIUS of a transaction is thus basically at the discretion of the relevant parties and certain government agencies. However, if the former fail to notify the CFIUS, and no CFIUS member makes a notification, the CFIUS may review the transaction at virtually any time it chooses, subject to procedures discussed below; if the CFIUS then recommends divestment, and the president concurs, the divestment may be mandated retroactively. For these reasons, legal counsel to parties to any transaction that might be deemed subject to review under Exon-Florio have routinely advised their clients to notify the CFIUS voluntarily before closing the deal.

A CFIUS member must, however, give notice of a transaction within three years of the transaction's completion in order to trigger a preliminary review. After that period, "only transactions that appear to raise national security concerns can be reviewed and investigated, pursuant to a request of the Chairman of the Committee, in consultation with other members of the Committee" (US Department of the Treasury 1991).

The regulations list three types of transactions that are subject to the provisions of the amendment (US Department of the Treasury 1991, 58781):

A. The acquisition of a person by
   1. The purchase of its voting securities,
   2. The conversion of its convertible voting securities,
   3. The acquisition of its convertible voting securities if that involves the acquisition of control, or
   4. The acquisition and the voting of proxies, if that involves the acquisition of control.

B. The acquisition of a business, including any acquisition of production or research and development facilities operated prior to the acquisition as part of a business, if there will likely be a substantial use of
   1. The technology of that business, excluding technical information generally accompanying the sale of equipment, or
   2. Personnel previously employed by that business.

C. A consolidation.

Exon-Florio does not cover greenfield investments, nor are portfolio investments and certain others covered where the foreign investor does not acquire managerial control of a US business. Also, Exon-Florio does not apply to the sale to a foreign person of a US-owned business if that business is located entirely outside of the United States.

The regulations set out detailed procedures (including informational requirements) for official notification of a transaction by a party to the transaction or by a member of the CFIUS.

Upon acceptance by the staff chairman (currently, the Director of the Office of International Investment in the Treasury Department) of formal notification, the CFIUS has 30 days to decide whether it will review the case. At least three of the committee's members must seek to have the case reviewed in order for the review to be launched. If the CFIUS decides against review, the transaction is deemed not to be blockable for reasons of national security, and the matter is ended as far as the CFIUS is concerned (unless it should later become apparent that the decision was based upon falsified information or misrepresentation). If the CFIUS does decide to review the case, it has 45 days to recommend to the president whether or not the transaction should be blocked or, if no unanimous decision can be reached, to submit to the president a statement of opposing views. Upon receipt of the CFIUS's recommendation, the president must decide within 15 days whether or not to proceed with the block. The president has final authority on the matter; the CFIUS only recommends.

Under the regulations, the CFIUS is obliged to take a broad interpretation of what activities and industries are of relevance to the national security. No activity or industry is automatically excluded from the committee's purview, and no precise definition of "national security" is offered. The first CFIUS investigation under Exon-Florio, conducted in late 1988 and early 1989, was that of the proposed takeover of the silicon wafer division of the Monsanto Company by Hüls AG, a German chemical firm. Monsanto was the last remaining US producer of these wafers apart from certain captive operations of vertically integrated US firms. According to press reports, some (but not all) members of the CFIUS felt that the takeover should be blocked to preserve independent US production of these goods and services. It was also reported that the CFIUS negotiated with the transacting parties and that in the end Hüls agreed, as part of a quid pro quo, that it would maintain US production of silicon wafers and continue relevant research and development on US soil in return for CFIUS approval. CFIUS proceedings are not made public, and therefore we cannot verify these reports. If such a quid pro quo was in fact agreed, it would constitute a de facto performance requirement (performance requirements are discussed later in this chapter and in chapter 7). Whatever actually happened, President Bush decided not to intervene in the merger.

Up to the time of this writing (mid-1994), the CFIUS has received over 750 notifications of transactions, which have led to a total of 15 investigations that went beyond the initial 30-day review period into the more exhaustive 45-day phase. Of these, one resulted in a unanimous CFIUS decision to block the transaction (with concurrence by the president); this was the proposed acquisition of the Mamco Manufacturing Company, a supplier to major aerospace firms, by the China National Aero-Technology Import and Export Corporation. In five cases the original proposal for takeover was withdrawn. In one of these (the proposed acquisition of US machine tool maker Moore by the Japanese firm FANUC) the withdrawal took place after the formal lapse of Exon-Florio authority. It is widely rumored that the Japanese government pressured FANUC to withdraw its takeover offer in the storm of widespread congressional criticism of the deal. In another case that ended in withdrawal, the takeover of the US firm General Ceramics by the Japanese firm Tokuyama Soda, the structure of the original deal would almost surely have raised major concerns leading to a recommendation for blockage. Therefore the deal was restructured and renotified, and it was ultimately approved. The third withdrawal involved a hostile takeover of Norton Company, a US abrasives manufacturer, by the British firm BTR; Norton was eventually taken over in a "white knight" deal by the French firm Compagnie de Saint-Gobain. The fourth case of withdrawal of a takeover offer involved the effort of India's Lalbhai Group to take over the US firm Tachonics. The fifth was Thomson-CSF's bid for the missile division of LTV Aerospace and Defense Company, discussed below (and in chapter 5).

In one case where an acquisition was allowed to proceed, the takeover of Fairchild Semiconductor by the French firm Matra, the CFIUS required that the investing firm restructure its export control system as a precondition for approval.

A particularly contentious case was the takeover of the US-controlled firm Semi-Gas Systems by the Japanese firm Nippon Sanso. Semi-Gas produces ultrapure industrial gases used in the fabrication of high-performance semiconductor microchips. It collaborated in R&D activities with the Sematech semiconductor consortium. President Bush approved the transaction, but it was reported that approval was conditioned on commitments from the new owners to restrict the dissemination of technical data held by Semi-Gas. The deal was also subjected to preliminary investigations by antitrust authorities in the US Justice Department, who operate separately from the CFIUS. However, a federal judge in early 1991 refused to block the acquisition, and the Justice Department subsequently decided to drop the case.

Many in the US Congress disapproved of the handling of the Semi-Gas case. One response was a bill, the Technology Preservation Act of 1991, introduced by Representative Cardiss Collins (D-IL) and House Majority Leader Richard A. Gephardt (D-MO), that would have required a number of changes in the way the CFIUS handled Exon-Florio cases. Although the bill was not passed, elements of it resurfaced in amendments to the Exon-Florio law in 1993, discussed below.

As noted in the previous chapter, the proposed acquisition in April 1992 of the missile division of LTV Aerospace and Defense Company by the French firm Thomson-CSF has been the most important case to date taken up by the CFIUS under Exon-Florio. Major factors in this case that weighed in favor of blockage were the following: the proposed takeover was of a large defense contractor, which produced important items of weaponry and held large amounts of classified information; the "foreign person" seeking to take the company over was a state-owned enterprise and major military contractor in its home country (France); and sentiment in Congress was clearly against allowing the transaction to proceed. Other factors, however, weighed against blockage: the parent of the targeted operation, LTV Corporation, was in bankruptcy, and significant complementarities existed between the missile division and the would-be acquiring firm (indeed, the LTV missile division sourced important components from Thomson-CSF). The transaction therefore would surely have strengthened LTV financially, and the missile division under French control might have also been strengthened technologically. However, there was considerable fear that R&D and production would have been transferred to France (on this question see Moran 1993).

As noted in chapter 5, we will never know what the outcome of the Exon-Florio investigation of this case might have been, because Thomson-CSF withdrew its bid in July 1992, just days before a recommendation was to have been made. It is conjectured (but far from established as fact) that the recommendation would have been to block the transaction and, indeed, that the near certainty of blockage was the major reason why Thomson-CSF withdrew its bid. In September 1992 a group of US investors (the Loral Corporation, the Carlyle Group, and Northrop Corporation) took over the LTV missile division and subsequently became involved in a number of legal proceedings with Thomson-CSF.

One major reason why this case is important is that it led to major amendments to Exon-Florio that went into effect in 1993. The major new provisions are the following: first, investors controlled by a foreign government are prohibited from acquiring US defense contractors who have been awarded Department of Defense or Department of Energy contracts worth more than $500 million in any one fiscal year; second, entities under foreign government control may not receive contracts involving access to information classified as "top secret" or higher, unless a waiver is granted by the Secretary of Defense; third, CFIUS investigation is mandated in all cases where an investor under the control of a foreign government seeks to acquire or merge with a US firm producing defense-related technologies (including dual-use technologies); fourth, the president's science and technology and national security advisers were added de jure to the CFIUS (as noted above, an executive order had already added the science and national security advisers, along with the president's economic adviser); fifth, detailed reports must be presented to Congress of all cases reviewed by the CFIUS; sixth, the Secretary of Defense may require that analysis of the potential for diversion of critical technology be part of a CFIUS investigation; seventh, in an investigation, the CFIUS must consider a transaction's potential impact upon US "international technological leadership in areas affecting US national security," the potential effect of the transaction upon proliferation of nuclear, chemical, and biological weapons, and the impact upon the capabilities of countries that support terrorism; eighth, and finally, the departments of Defense and Energy are required to create data bases to identify those entities controlled by foreign governments that might pose risks to national security and to report to Congress on these. The net effect is to produce a presumption against acquisition of US firms engaged in anything remotely "high-tech" by investors controlled by foreign governments (even friendly ones), and to move toward more specific criteria regarding exactly what is "national security."

In spite of these amendments, the role that the CFIUS will play in federal policy toward FDI in the United States remains to be fully defined. One fear that has been expressed (primarily within the Washington legal community) is that the direction of policy is toward ever broader definitions of national security concerns, with the result that potential foreign investors, recognizing the risk of intervention, will begin routinely to submit all proposed acquisitions to the CFIUS for approval. If that should happen, the Exon-Florio amendment will have created a de facto screening agency for FDI. A natural further development would be for potential investors to offer to negotiate with the CFIUS over the details of their investment, a process that many Washington lawyers suggest had already begun to happen under the Bush administration. If this should continue, Exon-Florio will have created a mechanism for imposing performance requirements as well.

This is an important point. Much discussion of policy toward FDI focuses on the possibility that future legislation might establish formal screening mechanisms and performance requirements. In fact the existing CFIUS structure could be used as the instrument of a highly interventionist policy *without* any further legislative action; all that would be needed is a broad interpretation of the committee's mandate. Under the Bush administration this did not happen; with the possible exception of the Hüls case, performance requirements were limited to restructuring of deals to meet existing US laws and policies affecting munitions control, technology export, and foreign ownership of activities performing classified work for the federal government.

However, the Clinton administration's approach to implementation of Exon-Florio is not really known. The policy of each new administration toward Exon-Florio is revealed only by the outcomes of actual cases, and it so happens that under the Clinton administration few cases have arisen as yet. As a result, the CFIUS's role under the Clinton administration is not yet fully defined. This could easily change.

Information Gathering

In addition to its authority to restrict FDI, the federal government plays a monitoring role. Part of that role is to collect rather detailed data pertaining to FDI in the United States. Foreign investors must report certain information about themselves and the US operations they control to the Bureau of Economic Analysis (BEA), an agency of the US Department of Commerce, at regular intervals. The aggregated information is publicly reported as part of the BEA's mission to prepare and present information pertaining to the US balance of payments and the activities of foreign multinational firms operating in the United States. Information on individual companies is submitted to the BEA on a confidential basis and is available to only a limited number of persons, mostly within the BEA. Appendix A surveys the data collected by the BEA, to whom the data are available, and how the data are used.

Information on certain types of foreign investor activity is collected by federal agencies other than the BEA, and some of this information is available to the public at the level of individual firms. For example, the Bureau of the Census, like the BEA an agency within the Commerce Department, collects extensive data on firms in the manufacturing sector, including establishments under foreign control. Until 1993 these data were not presented in a manner that segregated foreign-owned from domestically owned activities. Indeed, the Census Bureau did not know specifically which establishments it surveyed were under foreign control. Information held by the BEA could potentially have been used to identify the foreign ownership of specific establishments, but certain legal barriers prevented the interbureau cooperation required to make the identification. A bill that passed Congress late in 1990, the Foreign Direct Investment and International Financial Data Improvements Act of 1990, discussed in appendix A, both enabled and required such cooperation between the two agencies (and between them and the Bureau of Labor Statistics within the Department of Labor); the results of this "data linking" are now beginning to appear and indeed are the basis for many of the revisions in this third edition.

Also within the Commerce Department, the International Trade Administration publishes lists of publicly announced foreign investments in the United States independently of the BEA.

Outside the Commerce Department, the Department of Agriculture collects information on agricultural land owned by foreign persons. The Department of Labor gathers data on employment by establishment, and under the 1990 legislation mentioned above it is involved in an effort to improve information pertaining to US employment by foreign-controlled enterprises. Certain specific information on individual foreign-owned depository institutions is gathered by the Federal Reserve and is available to the public on request. The Internal Revenue Service extracts information on foreign investors from their tax returns, and certain aggregated data series are made public.

In addition to the above, a variety of reporting requirements set by the Securities and Exchange Commission (SEC) apply to at least some foreign investors; in general, a firm falls under these requirements if its securities are sold in interstate commerce, if it has over $1 million in assets, and if either it has more than 500 shareholders or its securities are listed on a registered national securities market. Not all foreign-controlled firms meet these requirements, and hence SEC reports are not available on anything like all foreign-owned firms. But many firms are covered, and indeed even some foreign parent firms of US subsidiaries are themselves subject to SEC reporting requirements because their stocks are listed on US securities exchanges.

A number of specialized federal regulatory agencies collect information on foreign as well as domestically controlled firms falling within their specialties. Such agencies include the Federal Communications Commission, the Federal Power Commission, and the Federal Maritime Administration.

Policy Toward Outward FDI

Policy toward inward FDI is inevitably intertwined with policy toward outward investment. The role of the United States as both the world's largest home and the world's largest host nation for multinational enterprises means that US policies play a particularly important role in shaping the worldwide rules of the international investment game. US policy toward outward direct investment has two main components: policies concerning foreign nations that host US outward investment, and policies affecting the foreign operations and affiliates of US firms.

The basic US negotiating stance on outward FDI with respect to foreign nations has been the counterpart of US policy toward inward investment. It is based on the idea that policy should be neutral regarding the nationality of a firm's owner. This means that the United States expects that foreign affiliates of US firms will be treated as domestic corporate residents of their host countries, with full right of establishment and national treatment.

US diplomatic efforts on behalf of right of establishment and national treatment of US firms abroad have taken several forms. The most important of these are US support for a series of efforts by the Organization for Economic Cooperation and Development (OECD) on behalf of liberalization of capital movements; the special agreements negotiated with Canada under the US-Canada Free Trade Agreement and, very important, the provisions regarding direct investment in chapter 11 of the North American Free Trade Agreement (NAFTA); and the measures bearing on investment in the recently completed Uruguay Round of multilateral trade negotiations under the General Agreement on Tariffs and Trade (GATT).

Within the OECD, two codes affected international investment, the Code of Liberalization of Capital Movements and the Code of Liberalization of Current Invisible Operations, have been adopted. Under these, each nation pledges to remove barriers to inward or outward investment, to allow free transfer of capital following liquidation of assets or the obtaining of finance in the form of long-term loans, and to allow current transactions (payments of dividends, interest payments, royalties, etc.) to proceed without undue hindrance. In principle these codes are binding on all OECD member nations.[4] An OECD member country must categorize any exceptions it seeks to its obligations under the two codes as "reservations" or "derogations" (long-term and temporary exceptions, respectively). The two codes also bind each member country to a "standstill" on new reservations and derogations, that is, an obligation not to enlarge its list of exceptions.[5]

Under OECD procedures the practices of each member country are regularly reviewed to determine if these obligations are being met. This review is conducted by the standing OECD Committee on Capital Movements and Invisible Transactions (CCMIT). In principle, any member country can demand that the country under review *or any other country* explain and justify any new measure that might be seen as in violation of code obligations, although in recent years countries have exhibited a reluctance to exercise the right to make such a demand.

In addition to these codes, which do not provide for full national treatment for foreign-controlled enterprises in OECD member countries, the OECD has drafted a nonbinding "National Treatment Instrument" (NTI). OECD nations choosing to adhere to the NTI (all currently do) must grant national treatment to enterprises that are controlled by investors from another member country, subject to reservations and derogations. A number of efforts have been mounted over the years to make the NTI binding and to make OECD countries subject to reviews similar to those conducted under the codes, but so far these have foundered over specifics. The OECD Committee on International Investment and Multinational Enterprise is currently considering a "Wider Investment Instrument" that would, inter alia, strengthen the national treatment provisions.

The US-Canada Free Trade Agreement (FTA) was signed in January 1988, and US implementing legislation was passed later that year. Despite its primary focus on trade, the agreement deals extensively with investment as well. It commits each nation to national treatment with respect to ownership by nationals of the other, except in a few specified industries such as energy within Canada. (In fact, so far Canada has not insisted on domestic ownership of activities within the energy industry; in particular, the Canadian government was willing to let the US firm Amoco Corp. buy

---

4. They are not, however, enforceable in national courts, which has caused some to question whether they are binding in a de facto sense.

5. The codes also commit each member nation over time to "roll back" (reduce the number and scope of) its exceptions. In fact, however, in recent years there has been very little such reduction.

the Canadian producer Dome Petroleum shortly after the agreement went into effect.) The FTA limits the extent to which Canada can screen acquisitions by US residents and firms (see the discussion of policies of other advanced nations below),[6] and it calls for free repatriation of capital and earnings. The FTA also goes well beyond preexisting multilateral agreements in several important respects: the most important of these are that both countries are precluded from imposing new performance requirements on investments that affect trade between them, and that disagreements over investment policy may be brought under the general dispute settlement mechanism that is part of the FTA.

Under the general dispute settlement mechanism, the parties may agree to binding arbitration of disputes that cannot be settled through the usual diplomatic procedures. This arbitration is not simply intergovernmental consultation continued in a different venue; in design, at least, it is more like an impartial judicial proceeding, in which parties to a dispute (or their representatives) can present their cases directly before an arbitration panel. In dispute settlement proceedings within the GATT, even as modified by the Uruguay Round, only government representatives directly participate in the settlement process. The US-Canada arrangement thus goes beyond the GATT, not simply in extending the range of issues to which the rules of the game apply, but also by making the enforcement of these rules more of a judicial and less of a diplomatic procedure.

The North American Free Trade Agreement went into effect on 1 January 1994. The NAFTA preserves most of the features of the US-Canada FTA pertaining to investment, but goes beyond the FTA in a number of important respects and backtracks on one. The backtracking is on performance requirements: NAFTA allows for some types of performance requirements that are banned under the FTA. But chapter 11 of the NAFTA provides for a dispute settlement mechanism that breaks new ground. One desirable feature is that it enables an investor of a NAFTA party (member country) directly and unilaterally to seek arbitration against another party where that party allegedly fails to meet obligations set out under part A of NAFTA chapter 11 (pertaining to investment) or articles of chapter 15 pertaining to state enterprises or state-sanctioned monopolies, and where the investor can demonstrate monetary loss resulting from this failure. (Under the US-Canada FTA both governments must agree to arbitration, although once this is agreed to, private parties can press their cases.) Under the NAFTA, only an investor, as opposed to an investment

---

6. There is considerable dispute among US business groups about the net effect of the agreement with Canada on the ultimate status of US firms there. On the one hand, the pact limits the extent of Canadian screening and performance requirements. On the other hand, it effectively accepts the principle that Canada may screen and regulate direct investment to some extent; some groups in the United States regard this as a significant concession. The fact is, however, that since the agreement has come into effect Canada has not used this authority.

(i.e., a foreign affiliate), can seek arbitration; thus the parent organization of a multinational firm can seek arbitration of a dispute with a host country (provided that both home and host countries are NAFTA members), but a subsidiary cannot. However, the parent can seek arbitration on behalf of the subsidiary.[7]

Under NAFTA chapter 11 procedures, an effort must be made to resolve a dispute by means of consultation and negotiation before arbitration may be sought. If arbitration is sought, the disputing investor may submit the claim to arbitration under the rules of the ICSID (International Centre for the Settlement of Investment Disputes) Convention within the World Bank, the Additional Facility Rules of the ICSID, or the United Nations (UNCITRAL) Arbitration Rules. Inter alia, the ICSID rules require that a judgment by an arbitral tribunal be treated as if it emanated from the highest court in the relevant nation.[8] In any of these three cases, the NAFTA modifies somewhat the arbitration procedures, the most important modification being that the government against which the dispute is lodged must be willing to submit the dispute to arbitration if the investor seeks it. Under any of these rules, a tribunal is established that can order interim measures to protect the rights of the investor and, if a breach of the NAFTA is found, can order that an award be made to the investor, including monetary (but not punitive) damages. The damages are awarded under the New York Convention on Recognition and Enforcement of Arbitral Rewards, whereby in the event of nonpayment of the damages the investor may pursue assets of the NAFTA government against which the award was made. The tribunal cannot order, however, that the offending party take measures to modify its policies and practices so as to meet its NAFTA obligations.

Use of the arbitration provisions of NAFTA chapter 11 does not preclude a disputing investor (or its investment) from seeking redress of the same dispute in the national or local judicial system of the party allegedly breaching the NAFTA obligation, if the party is Canada or the United States. In Mexico, if a dispute is brought to arbitration, proceedings involving the same dispute may not be simultaneously brought before a Mexican court. The NAFTA chapter 11 dispute settlement mechanism may not be used to contest an adverse ruling on entry or establishment by the Mexican National Commission on Foreign Investment or under the Investment Canada Act. Also, this mechanism may not be used to contest the blocking of an acquisition, takeover, or merger by the president of the United States under the Exon-Florio authority.

---

7. This distinction could be of importance, for example if the dispute were to be initiated by minority shareholders of the subsidiary.

8. At the time of the conclusion of the NAFTA negotiations, neither Canada nor Mexico subscribed to the ICSID. Both, however, plan to do so in the future.

The United States made it a priority in the Uruguay Round to include so-called trade-related investment measures (TRIMs) on the agenda. TRIMs are essentially the same as performance requirements, that is, laws or policies adopted by a host-country government that are designed to affect the conduct of local subsidiaries of foreign-controlled firms. For example, governments sometimes impose "local-content" requirements on domestic affiliates of foreign firms; that is, they require that the affiliate purchase a certain minimum percentage of its inputs from local vendors rather than import them. Another type of performance requirement is one that specifies that a specified minimum percentage of total value added of a product be produced locally. Governments also often require that some minimum percentage of the affiliate's output be exported.

Performance requirements in some countries are linked to investment incentives. Typically, in order to qualify for a direct or indirect subsidy (offered as an inducement to get the investor to locate in the country), the foreign investor has to agree to abide by certain requirements. The BEA's 1982 benchmark survey of US direct investment abroad found that 28 percent of overseas affiliates of US firms reported having received one or more incentives to invest, whereas 7.6 percent reported being subject to at least one performance requirement.[9] Performance requirements are imposed most frequently by developing nations, although there have also been numerous cases of their imposition by industrialized nations (Moran and Pearson 1988).

The position of the US government in the Uruguay Round was that TRIMs represent distortions of trade that are contrary to the spirit if not the letter of the GATT. Largely at the behest of the United States, the trade ministers of the GATT member nations, at their meeting in Montreal in December 1988, agreed to a work program within the Uruguay Round that directs negotiators to continue to examine the trade effects of TRIMs and the "relationship of the GATT articles to TRIMs," to consider where additional GATT measures might be necessary to discipline TRIMs and their trade effects, and to consider the "trade development effects" of TRIMs. This third item was put on the agenda largely at the insistence of the developing countries, which have indicated that they will resist any encroachment on their ability to control and regulate FDI and other activities of multinational firms.

The US government initially identified 13 specific practices that it believed fell into the category of trade-distorting investment measures. Alas, only two of these appeared in the final Uruguay Round agreement signed at Marrakesh in mid-1994, but at least these were the very important ones

---

9. This number seems very low. Officials at the BEA suggest that technical difficulties with the survey may have led to some confusion and hence an understatement of the prevalence of performance requirements.

of local-content requirements and export performance requirements.[10] Earlier, the United States, the European Community, and Japan had agreed on a list of seven objectionable practices, and the narrowing of the list to two apparently represents an effort to keep developing countries on board. Also, there was no agreement to impose any new discipline on the linkage of investment incentives to performance requirements.

The US position on TRIMs was crafted at a time when the United States was primarily a home rather than a host country for direct investment. As the US host position increases, there will be a growing potential conflict between US interests. Indeed, we have already noted that the enhanced oversight powers created under the 1988 trade act not only have turned the CFIUS into a potential screening agency but also raise the possibility that the United States will begin to impose performance requirements itself.

It would seem a logical corollary of the US demand for national treatment—that foreign subsidiaries of US firms be treated as domestic residents—that the US government should allow those subsidiaries to behave like domestic residents. In other words, the US government should relinquish any "extraterritorial" claims of authority over the foreign subsidiaries of US firms. Certainly what the United States expects of US affiliates of foreign firms operating within its borders is that they will not act as agents of their home-country governments. Unfortunately, the United States has not itself been consistent about this principle. It has on occasion attempted either to impose US regulations on foreign affiliates of US firms or to use those affiliates as instruments of US foreign policy. The most notable recent case was the Siberian pipeline dispute of the early 1980s, in which the US government attempted to prevent European subsidiaries of US firms from selling products or technologies to the Soviet Union, even to the extent of demanding that they break existing contracts. The United States eventually backed down, but the rules of the game were never really established. This episode is by no means the only one in which the US government sought to use overseas subsidiaries of US firms as vehicles of its foreign policy. Another major example involving France was discussed in chapter 5.

The position the United States has taken in international fora toward direct investment—for example, advocating the principles of national treatment and openness—have long been questioned by certain US constituencies, most notably organized labor. These constituencies have often

---

10. A GATT panel convened to investigate US-initiated complaints against Canada's Foreign Investment Review Agency determined in 1983 that local-content requirements such as Canada's were inconsistent with the national treatment principle; this finding was adopted by the GATT Council in 1984. An issue that remains is to what extent governments can legitimately claim exceptions to this ruling.

been concerned that US outward direct investment entails transfer of capital and technology in a manner detrimental to US economic interests—for example, that it somehow reduces US employment. These concerns have been reflected in policy debates within the Clinton administration over whether US outward direct investment should or should not be encouraged. These debates have not to date produced tangible changes in US policy, but they have fueled speculation that changes could be forthcoming. At the time of this writing, however, major change seems increasingly less likely. The test case was the NAFTA. After some initial reservations, the administration did support passage of the NAFTA, with its strong investment chapter. An issue that remains, however, is whether the administration would attempt to extend NAFTA-like arrangements into agreements with other nations or to incorporate these agreements into some worldwide agreement on direct investment. This issue is taken up in the final chapter of this book.

The problems that the United States has encountered in establishing a consistent policy toward investment abroad carry an ambiguous message for the future of policy toward inward direct investment, now that the United States has become a significant host to this investment. On the one hand, it could be argued that the United States is going to have to do a better job of honoring at home the principles it has tried to encourage host nations of US subsidiaries abroad to adopt, if the United States expects to receive the same treatment from these nations. But, as the discussion in this chapter indicates, the drift of US policy seems to be in the opposite direction, especially on the matter of national treatment. On the other hand, it can be argued that the United States' own past behavior toward US-based multinational firms suggests that such firms will always be subject to home-nation government pressures to serve the interests of that nation, and that this calls into question the principle of neutrality toward the nationality of ownership of these firms. Thus, ironically, supporters of conditional national treatment might argue that the behavior of the United States itself is the best case for less than national treatment for foreign investors in the United States!

State and Local Policies

A number of state and local governments in the United States have their own laws restricting the activities of foreign nationals (for example, New Hampshire allows mineral prospecting and mining only by US citizens), but in general their ability to regulate foreign ownership of manufacturing industries is limited by the constitutional prohibition on restriction of interstate commerce. For example, if a foreign firm establishes a subsidiary in New York, that subsidiary is legally a resident of New York, and under the Constitution, Connecticut may not discriminate against its products in favor of local producers. Also, most states actively seek manufacturing investment from all sources, as a means of fostering economic activity. As a result, there is not much economically important restriction of FDI at the state and local level in the manufacturing sector.

The service sectors are another matter. In particular, banking and insurance are heavily regulated by state governments, and some states discriminate against or ban outright the foreign ownership of banks or insurance companies. Most states, however, subject foreign-controlled entities in these sectors to the same regulations as domestically controlled firms—in other words, they apply the state equivalent of national treatment.

However, state and local policies remain an important issue in FDI because of two other areas of concern: provision of investment incentives and taxation. Numerous states and localities attempt to lure major foreign investment projects with a variety of investment incentives. These incentives take various forms, including outright subsidies, various forms of tax relief, provision of infrastructure free of charge, and provision of land free of charge. Although in principle such investment incentives are available to all firms that might locate a facility within a locality, in practice they are often targeted toward specific undertakings that local authorities perceive to be likely generators of local benefits. Very large undertakings can find themselves the objects of bidding wars among local governments. For example, it was widely reported that at least three subnational governments—the state governments of Ohio and Pennsylvania and the provincial government of Ontario—competed to attract the large Honda Motor Company facility that eventually was located in Marysville, Ohio. Similar bidding wars involving other large foreign-controlled automotive facilities, as well as certain domestically owned operations, have been reported.

Since the incentives offered by local governments are normally contingent on a promise (which may be implicit) by the foreign firm to provide certain local benefits, state and local bidding for foreign firms may often amount to a de facto performance requirement of the kind that US diplomacy on FDI has attempted to limit. Competition among local governments may also lead to a kind of "prisoner's dilemma" that benefits foreign firms at their (and the country's) expense. In order to prevent a new investment from being lured elsewhere, a state may feel compelled to offer the investor generous incentives. This prompts other states to offer similarly large inducements. The investor, meanwhile, might have been prepared to make the investment in any of the states even without the incentives, but will surely accept them if offered. The result is a transfer from the "winning" state's taxpayers to the investor, who sees the transfer as a pure windfall. For these reasons, a number of authors (see, e.g., Glickman and Woodward 1989) have suggested that it would make sense for the US government to ban state investment incentives to foreign investors, and that the states themselves would be better off under such a ban. We agree that such a ban would make sense.

The other way in which local governments in effect make policy toward FDI is through their tax policy. The issue here is how much tax a firm that operates in many states or nations should pay to the authorities of any one state or nation. As we elaborate below, determination of that liability is to some extent arbitrary; hence, under any conceivable set of rules, there is scope for a particular multinational firm to claim that it is being discriminated against relative to another firm that operates in only one jurisdiction. At its origins this is another one of those issues raised by the fact of multinationality itself, and not by the national origin of the firm in question—the complaining multinational could be either a US- or a foreign-based firm. However, the latter but not the former has grounds for claiming violation of the national treatment provisions of the OECD when it is assessed higher taxes than a "one-market" firm, which by definition is a domestic firm. The claim is arguably valid even if the foreign multinational is receiving substantially the same treatment as a US-based multinational.

The problem of taxing the profits of firms that operate in many states has long been a difficult one: it is probably meaningless and certainly impractical to ask, for example, what fraction of General Motors's profits is earned in Massachusetts as opposed to Connecticut. Most state governments have dealt with this problem by prorating the total profits of firms that operate within their borders according to a formula that takes account of the shares of in-state sales, payroll, and assets in the firm's US totals, and taxing the assigned share. Traditionally, however, this so-called three-factor formula stops at the water's edge: only US profits are taxed. Hence this formula is often called the "water's-edge unitary tax formula." A logical extension of the principle would be to apply a similar formula to the worldwide profits of a multinational firm, on the grounds that the attribution of profits to US operations is as elusive as attribution to an individual state within the United States. This extension is referred to as "worldwide unitary taxation."

Some states, including Alaska, California, Colorado, Florida, Idaho, Massachusetts, Montana, New Hampshire, New York, North Dakota, Oregon, and Utah, have attempted to extend unitary taxation on a worldwide basis. California, as with so many things, led the way by enacting worldwide unitary taxation during the 1960s. This led to widespread objections from multinational firms that claimed it would impose high administrative costs and represented an interference by state governments with international commerce. This last argument was dealt a blow in 1983, when in *Container Corporation of America v. Franchise Tax Board* (103 S.Ct. 2933) the US Supreme Court ruled in favor of California. This case, however, explicitly applied to US-based multinationals and not foreign-based ones. In spite of this loss, during the mid-1980s foreign-based multinational firms and in some cases their home governments began to lobby federal and state governments intensively to repeal worldwide unitary taxation. The California State Supreme Court upheld the worldwide unitary tax in 1992, but, responding to the international pressure, the California legislature subsequently amended the state's laws to allow companies to elect whether to apply a water's-edge three-factor formula or a worldwide three-factor formula. At least two other states, North Dakota and Montana, have California-style systems, and Alaska retains a straight worldwide unitary system. Other states have attempted or proposed worldwide unitary taxation, but all have since abandoned the idea.

In September 1991 the US Supreme Court agreed to hear a case brought by Barclays Bank that would reopen the issue of whether California had the right to tax multinational firms' profits on a worldwide unitary basis. Other groups and countries had asked that the court hear this case, including all the member countries of the European Union as well as Australia, Austria, Canada, Japan, Norway, Sweden, Switzerland, and several private business groups. The argument of the plaintiff was that a state-imposed worldwide unitary tax is a violation of the constitutional proscription of state regulation of foreign commerce. Under this argument, Barclays Bank is suing the state for restitution of what the bank claims are excess taxes paid under the worldwide unitary method. The state of California, joined by the Clinton administration, tried to argue that the 1992 amendments to California law make the case moot, but by agreeing to hear the case, the Supreme Court rejected this argument. The case that the state then pressed was that, because the US Senate did not, during negotiations over international tax treaties conducted during the 1970s and 1980s, explicitly prohibit worldwide unitary taxation, the method is permissible. This line of argumentation is that which won the day in the California Supreme Court.

Meanwhile the US Supreme Court decided to hear a similar suit filed by Colgate-Palmolive Company. Had the court decided in favor of the plaintiff, the effect would likely have been to reverse the court's 1983 decision in *Container Corporation of America v. Franchise Tax Board*. However, in June 1994 the court handed down a decision in favor of California. The court essentially accepted the state's argument summarized above. The following month the California Franchise Tax Board indicated that it might propose dropping worldwide unitary taxation altogether.

The Supreme Court ruled in this case that states could, without violating the US Constitution, implement a worldwide unitary tax method for assessing state income taxes on the local activities of multinational corporations. The court did not, of course, rule on the economic (or other) merits of this method. (For extensive commentary on that question see Hufbauer and van Rooij 1992.) Our own view is that the method has much to recommend it so long as all tax authorities apply it. The major objection to the method, as raised by multinational firms, is that if some authorities used it but others did not, the higher tax liabilities incurred by multinationals in the former jurisdictions would not be offset by lower taxes in the latter. The result could be an unintended rise in total taxes owed by multinationals. Presumably, if all jurisdictions did use the method (and if rates of taxation were comparable in all jurisdictions), there would be no net rise in total tax liabilities. Furthermore, use of worldwide unitary taxation in all jurisdictions would remove incentives to shift taxable income from high-tax to low-tax areas via transfer pricing and other accounting practices. Indeed, it was the fear that such practices were reducing tax revenues to the state that prompted California to introduce worldwide unitary taxation to begin with.

Before closing this topic we should note that the OECD Committee on International Investment and Multinational Enterprise, of which the United States is a member, indicated in a 1985 report that worldwide unitary taxes "insofar as they do not impose a greater burden on foreign-controlled corporations than that on domestic-controlled corporations" do not violate national treatment principles.

Both the incentives issue and the tax issue demonstrate that the problems posed by actions of subcentral governments may be increasingly important in the long run, as the United States adjusts to a large-scale foreign presence as a fact of life. Whatever the degree of federal commitment to neutrality of policy toward the nationality of a firm's owners, this neutrality may be offset or undermined by actions at the state and local level.

Comparisons with Other Nations

It is a common perception that the United States is much more open to FDI than other nations. Among the advanced nations, Japan, Canada, and France have legal machinery that in principle allows much more extensive screening of inward investment than anything currently possible under US law. A number of analysts (e.g., Glickman and Woodward 1989) argue that, because other governments have screening mechanisms, so should the United States. The logic of that argument aside, what these analysts miss is that since the early 1980s this machinery has rarely been used, and recent studies by both the OECD and the US Treasury Department have concluded that there is little meaningful difference among the advanced nations in their legal openness to inward FDI (OECD 1987; US Department of the Treasury 1988).

In chapter 1 we cited evidence that both Canada and France are marked by high levels of foreign ownership in their economies, in spite of their history of restriction. In both countries, in fact, the screening mechanisms have largely been dismantled as a result of dissatisfaction with the results of screening. In Canada, what used to be the Foreign Investment Review Agency (FIRA) was in 1985 renamed Investment Canada, and its mission was largely redefined away from critical screening of inward FDI and toward promoting Canada as a host nation for this investment. Canada does, however, retain the right to screen inward investment, and this right is reaffirmed in both the US-Canada Free Trade Agreement and the North American Free Trade Agreement. Under the latter, Mexico also has the right to screen inward direct investment, but in Mexico, as in Canada, this right has not been actively used for more than a decade. (In fact, during the NAFTA negotiations, Mexico apparently signaled a willingness to give up this right, if Canada would do likewise, but Canada balked.)

As also noted in chapter 1, Japan is an outlier in this trend toward more welcoming attitudes toward FDI: in spite of substantial liberalization of official Japanese policy toward inward investment since the 1970s (and especially since the 1980 repeal of the Foreign Investment Law of 1950), the foreign presence in Japan remains far below that in other advanced nations. Nor does this appear likely to change anytime soon (see Graham 1994). Although FDI flows into Japan have been much greater in the 1980s and early 1990s than previously, they remain small by comparison with flows into other advanced nations. For example, the direct investment flow into Japan in 1987, although a record high, was less than 3 percent as large as that into the United States in the same year.

We can find no evidence, however, that official screening of FDI is responsible for the low rate of such investment in Japan in recent years, except (perhaps) in a small number of defense-related industries. Thus Japan's situation with regard to direct investment is similar to its situation with regard to international trade in goods and services: the market appears relatively free of overt legal barriers yet remains very hard for foreign firms to penetrate. The explanation of this paradox presumably rests on the same kinds of cultural and industrial-organization factors that are usually cited to explain Japan's trade patterns; for example, cross-holdings of equity in firms among the *keiretsu* groups in Japan allegedly act as a barrier to acquisition of Japanese firms by foreign investors.

Evidently the differences between Japan and the other advanced nations will pose problems for any attempt to negotiate rules of the game for international investment, in the same way that they are a source of continual tension in trade policy. We return to these difficulties in our discussion of policy recommendations in chapter 7.

The Japan issue aside, the policies of the advanced nations do differ markedly in another area, namely, the provision of investment incentives and performance requirements. Incentives tied to performance requirements are in general offered more freely in other nations than in the United States. For example, the United Kingdom, which is among the most open nations with respect to FDI, has not been averse to combining investment incentives with performance requirements. A case in point is a large investment by Nissan Motor Company in the United Kingdom in the late 1980s, in which the quid pro quo for certain investment incentives, among them outright subsidies, included both a local-content target and a commitment to export to continental Europe. Incentives and performance requirements are used by other European nations as well.

On the whole, the other industrial nations do not seem to differ greatly from the United States in their policies toward FDI per se. They certainly act less differently than a number of other writers on this subject (e.g., Glickman and Woodward 1989; Rohatyn 1989; Spencer 1988; Tolchin and Tolchin 1988) have claimed. All of these authors suggest, for example, that the UK government (which they cite as being among the most liberal of foreign governments with respect to policies toward inward FDI) can screen FDI on national security grounds. The truth is that in the United Kingdom the Department of Trade and Industry can refer mergers and acquisitions to the Monopolies and Mergers Commission, which can then recommend that the transaction be blocked for national security reasons. This authority in fact is strikingly similar to that under the Exon-Florio amendment in the United States, with the exception that the UK procedure is more consistent with the principle of national treatment: whereas Exon-Florio applies only to takeovers by foreign persons, the Monopolies and Mergers Commission can recommend blockages of mergers and acquisitions referred by the Department of Trade and Industry even when they involve purely UK-owned firms, on grounds of national defense. In fact, the only recent case in which the commission recommended blockage on national security grounds involved a proposed merger between two UK firms.

Where foreign governments do differ from US government practice is in their greater willingness to trade incentives for performance requirements. This, it can be argued, reflects a greater willingness to engage in targeted industrial policy in general.

The US government maintains that investment incentives targeted toward "footloose" international direct investment and accompanying performance requirements act to distort the gains from this investment and from international trade as well. A major issue is whether the United States, either openly or through the back door (i.e., through Exon-Florio), will impose its own performance requirements. If it does, it will greatly weaken its case against other nations' practices.

Conclusions

US policy toward FDI remains based on the general principle of neutrality, qualified by considerations of national security and marred by occasional lapses of national treatment. Inward direct investment in the United States takes place with few restrictions, except in certain federally regulated industries where the ostensible justification is national security. In this regard the Exon-Florio amendment offers a wider scope for screening on the basis of national security, but we have yet to see fully how it will work in practice. In particular, we have yet to see how the Clinton administration will act with respect to controversial mergers or acquisitions.

The United States expects and attempts to negotiate corresponding treatment of its own firms abroad but has weakened its position by occasionally asserting extraterritorial claims. Such behavior conflicts with the idea that foreign affiliates of US firms should be regarded as ordinary corporate citizens of their host countries. State and local governments also sometimes take actions that conflict with national policy. In all this the United States is not very different from other advanced nations, all of which—except Japan—have long had a much larger foreign presence than the United States.

The question is whether the United States should now change its course. Does the upsurge of FDI that began in the mid-1970s mean that the United States should reconsider its policy of neutrality? We examine this matter in the next chapter.

7

Policy Alternatives

As we saw in chapter 6, the US government already has potentially quite extensive authority to screen and block foreign direct investment in the United States. In the federally regulated sectors of the economy there are significant restrictions on foreign participation, and the Exon-Florio amendment gives the president the ability to block foreign acquisitions and takeovers on national security grounds. Some laws have been passed requiring a policy of reciprocity rather than unconditional national treatment toward some types of activities under foreign control. Nevertheless, US policy remains in general terms at least as open to inward FDI as the policies of the other major industrialized countries.

Should the United States adopt a more restrictive, or at any rate more vigilant, policy toward FDI? The simple fact that such investment jumped during the 1980s, so that the extent of foreign control of US economic activity rose from near insignificance to something approaching international norms, is not by itself enough to justify such a conclusion. It would be justified only if we can conclude either that, absent special action, further increases in the foreign share of US assets and production will harm the United States, or that, absent special safeguards, foreign-owned firms will behave differently from domestic firms in a way that harms US interests. If neither of these criteria is met, restrictions on foreign investment, including disclosure requirements that could act in effect as a disincentive, will generally tend to restrict the possibilities for mutually beneficial transactions, to the detriment of the United States as well as of foreign investors.

The main conclusion of this study is that there is little evidence to support concerns about the negative effects of FDI in general. As we argued in chapter 2, the growth of FDI in the United States during the late 1980s did not represent a kind of artificial "fire sale" in which nonresidents acquired US assets at bargain prices. Instead, we saw for the most part a convergence toward levels of foreign control accepted as normal in other advanced countries; foreign firms entered the United States largely because of firm-specific advantages and other industrial-organization considerations rather than because of some financial distortion.

Equally important, foreign firms once in the United States do not generally behave as bad corporate citizens. Our analysis in chapter 3 indicates that foreign-owned firms as a group show no discernible tendency either to "keep the good jobs home" or to shift complex activities such as R&D out of the United States. Indeed, foreign firms on average pay about the same wages, generate about the same value added per worker, and engage in about the same amount of R&D as US firms in the same sectors.

There is one main exception to our general conclusion that foreign firms in the United States behave much like domestic firms: foreign firms, and especially Japanese firms, do show an apparent tendency to obtain a substantially larger quantity of their inputs abroad than do domestic firms in the same industry. Some of this difference may represent misclassifications (e.g., of foreign-owned firms that act as importers of final goods as well as manufacturers) and similar problems, and some of the remaining difference may reflect a life-cycle effect: as new foreign affiliates mature they are likely to increase the local content of their production. Nevertheless this tendency to import remains one real source of economic concern. We have argued that any trade and employment effects from the bias of foreign firms toward imported inputs have so far been minor, but the potential for future harmful effects remains, especially with respect to Japanese-owned firms.

The surge in FDI entering the United States in the 1980s led to a number of proposals for changes in US policy in the direction of greater regulation. As documented in chapter 6, some of these proposals became law during the early 1990s, ironically after the surge collapsed. The changes already in place, and further changes proposed in US policy, focus on four main types of restrictions:

- *Increased disclosure*: The argument is made that foreign firms should be required to make more extensive disclosures about their activity than domestic firms.

- *Increased screening*: A farther reaching proposal is that the United States should extend its screening of FDI to evaluate new foreign acquisitions and establishments on general "national interest" grounds rather than simply on grounds of national security.

- *Reciprocity*: As detailed in the previous chapter, the US government has moved to apply to some categories of foreign-controlled entities in some instances a legal standard based on the principle of reciprocity (or, equivalently, conditional national treatment), by which a firm controlled by a parent company in another country would be subject to the same treatment that US-controlled firms receive in that country, rather than on the principle of national treatment. Pending legislation would extend the principle of reciprocity into new areas, and some influential Americans have called for further extensions.

- *Performance requirements*: A number of governments have demanded as a condition for allowing foreign investment, or for granting certain incentives, that the investor meet certain performance goals that are considered to be in the local interest. Although there has not been strong vocal advocacy of such performance requirements at the US federal level to date, there could be mounting pressure in the future for this form of regulation. Some such advocacy is already coming from the Office of Technology Assessment of the US Congress.

In this chapter we critically evaluate each of these proposals. We then put forward some proposals of our own for the direction of future policy. These include limited steps that the United States should take unilaterally in the interest of national security. As will be apparent, however, we believe that the more constructive path leads to cooperation among governments on direct investment issues, and not to unilateral action on the part of any one government, including that of the United States.

First, however, we might note that the overall thrust of US policy at present is not unlike that of other countries, such as Brazil, Canada, France, and Mexico, at times when they experienced a rapid rise in foreign control of their domestic economies. Yet the case of the United States is not really parallel to that of any of these countries: the United States is bigger and less dependent upon foreign firms for virtually anything than are any of these four nations. Indeed, the competitiveness of US business enterprises in the world economy remains relatively strong, as suggested by the fact that, even as inward direct investment in the United States expanded, so did the overseas activities of US-based firms (further evidence is the fact, as detailed in chapter 1, that following the end of the inward FDI surge in 1990, US outward direct investment began to accelerate, so that today the United States is a strong net creditor on direct investment account). What is remarkable, then, is that in spite of this position of strength, the policy response of the United States to inward FDI often has resembled that of a relatively small and weak economy under siege.

There are two elements of irony in this. The first is that the four countries just mentioned, which experienced rapid rises in foreign control and, initially at least, reacted in somewhat the way that the United States has done, have all since reevaluated their policies. All have come to recognize that foreign-controlled operations in their economies act to the benefit of the economy rather than to its detriment, and, hence, all have largely abandoned policies designed to restrict and regulate FDI and have indeed moved to adopt policies to encourage it. All of these nations, being smaller and more vulnerable than the United States, probably had more reason to fear FDI than the United States ever has had.

The second element of irony is that the more the United States implements policies that deviate from national treatment, the greater the rationale for other countries to do likewise. If this were to happen, all would be losers. As we emphasize later in this chapter, the goal of the United States should be for all nations to adopt policies based on the principle of national treatment, and this is not likely to be achieved if the United States itself continues to backslide from this principle.

Proposals for Changes in US Policy That Are Unsound

Increasing Disclosure Requirements

Foreign firms operating in the United States are already required, for statistical purposes, to reveal fairly elaborate information about their operations to the Bureau of Economic Analysis (BEA) of the US Department of Commerce. In addition, US subsidiaries of foreign firms submit detailed information to the Internal Revenue Service on their annual tax returns. As noted in appendix A, this information is not made available on an individual-firm basis to the general public or even to Congress or other executive agencies. Instead the information is sequestered in the same way that proprietary information supplied by domestic firms is held for statistical purposes only.

A proposed amendment to the Omnibus Trade and Competitiveness Act of 1988 sponsored by Representative John C. Bryant (D-TX) would have required that foreign investors in the United States register with the US government and provide information that, unlike the current BEA data, would be open to public scrutiny at the individual-firm level. The Bryant amendment was supported by labor unions that had experienced difficulty in obtaining financial information relevant to collective bargaining with foreign-controlled firms. The Reagan administration opposed the amendment, and it was dropped from the trade bill; however, a modified version, which would expand access to the information only to certain government officials, was reintroduced into legislation in 1989 as H.R. 5. Then–Speaker of the House Jim Wright, Jr. (D-TX), attempted to bring this bill to the House floor early in 1989 without passing it through the normal hearing process. The effort was withdrawn in March of that year, however, and as of mid-1994 the bill has not been reintroduced. But sentiment remains among some congressional Democrats in favor of such a measure.

We believe that passage of the Bryant amendment or similar legislation would be unwise and unnecessary, for the following reasons. First, it would largely duplicate an existing mandatory program for data collection that has generally worked quite well. Few serious policy analysts have found that the limitations on disclosure of BEA data at the individual-firm level present major problems in the use of the data. Those academic researchers who need firm-level data have usually been able to get access to it, albeit only after a fairly lengthy process. Indeed, a 1988 report on FDI in the Group of Five nations issued by the Royal Institute of International Affairs in London (Julius and Thomsen 1988) praises the BEA data on foreign investment in the United States as being more open and detailed than those published by other nations. What problems exist instead involve the collection, presentation, and timeliness of the data. There are a number of ways in which collection and presentation of BEA and other US government data are being improved to make them more useful for analytical purposes, most notable in this regard are the data-linking efforts of the BEA, the Census Bureau, and the Bureau of Labor Statistics, which have produced some of the data used in this third edition of this book. Other improvements undoubtedly could be made.

Second, since the United States already has relatively good information on FDI, the main consequence of the Bryant amendment would be to remove the screen of privacy. This could actually worsen the information by providing an incentive for misreporting.

Our main objection to the Bryant amendment, however, is not that it would force greater disclosure but that it would discriminate against foreign-controlled firms. The requirement to disclose more information than competing domestic firms must disclose would place foreign firms at some strategic disadvantage. In this way, and perhaps also by signaling an increased likelihood of future restrictions, the Bryant amendment could act to deter FDI. If, as we have argued, FDI is largely beneficial to the US economy, it ought not to be especially discouraged in this way.

In practice, it is not so clear whether the disclosure requirements under the Bryant amendment would put foreign-controlled firms at any disadvantage relative to their domestic competitors. On the one hand, domestically owned firms whose stocks are publicly traded must file annually the Securities and Exchange Commission's form 10-K, which is available for public scrutiny and contains more detailed financial and operating data than would have to be disclosed under the Bryant amendment. The 10-K filing requirement also holds for any firm, foreign or domestic, whose common stock is listed on a US stock exchange or that meets certain other reporting requirements. However, cases where this requirement applies to foreign firms or their affiliates are rare; for most foreign-owned firms with US operations there is no 10-K reporting requirement. On the other hand, there are a number of major domestically owned firms whose stock is not publicly traded (and which do not meet other Securities and Exchange

Commission reporting criteria) and which therefore likewise do not file 10-K forms. Detailed financial and operating information often is not available to the public for such firms from any other source. The international asymmetries in reporting requirements probably have no greater (and no less) impact than this domestic asymmetry.

There is a case to be made that information of the sort now made public via form 10-K for all firms listed on US stock exchanges should also be available for all nonlisted firms with operations in the United States exceeding a certain size threshold. Like most economists, we believe that markets, including capital markets, work best when participants are well informed. The important point is that this reasoning surely would apply to domestically controlled "closely held" (nonlisted) firms as well as to foreign-controlled ones. There is no compelling reason why a nonlisted firm should be subject to reporting requirements simply because it is controlled by foreigners, when nonlisted US-controlled firms of similar size and engaged in similar activities are not subject to similar requirements. If the number of firms required to file a 10-K form is to be enlarged, it should be done on a national treatment basis.

An extension of this argument is that there should be a set of minimal worldwide reporting and disclosure requirements for all firms above a certain size, including multinational firms. Such requirements, however, should not—indeed, could not—be set unilaterally by a nation to apply only to foreign-controlled firms. Rather, a set of minimum reporting requirements should be established as part of an international accord on investment. We return to this matter later in this chapter.

The most important point about the Bryant amendment (and any similar bills that might be introduced in the future) is that, although mild in its current form, it would mark a broad departure of US policy from neutrality regarding nationality of ownership. It would impose on all foreign-owned firms a set of reporting requirements purely because they are foreign. Such a step could be viewed by other countries as a precedent to justify similar discriminatory treatment of local affiliates of US firms.

Screening

Much stronger controls on foreign investment have been proposed in the press and by certain scholars, although none of these proposals has actually resulted in legislation being introduced. Norman Glickman and Douglas Woodward (1989), New York investment banker Felix Rohatyn (1988), popular columnist Jack Anderson (1989), and current US Secretary of Labor Robert B. Reich (1991) are among those who have called for some form of generalized screening process under which foreign acquisitions and establishments of US businesses would be evaluated by a governmental body to determine the effects on national security and the economy.

The screening agency presumably would have the power to block the proposed acquisition or establishment, or the president would have that power upon the recommendation of the screening agency.

National security concerns arising from FDI are already addressed by the Exon-Florio amendment (see chapter 6), which charges a government agency, the Committee on Foreign Investment in the United States (CFIUS), with reviewing proposed foreign acquisitions (but not new establishments) for potential hazards to national security, and gives the president the power to block acquisitions deemed a threat to national security. With national security issues thus already covered, any new screening mechanism would necessarily focus on economic criteria. Also, implied in the power to block is the power to demand changes before granting acceptance, so screening by any government agency would inevitably imply the possibility of imposing performance requirements as well. We noted in chapter 6 that Exon-Florio reviews of acquisitions of US firms by foreign investors may have already resulted in the de facto imposition of performance requirements.

Such a screening process would be comparable to those legally in place, but now largely unused, to screen investment in a number of countries, including Mexico, Japan, France, and Canada. It would move US policy toward FDI completely away from the ideal of neutrality with respect to nationality of ownership, replacing it with a de facto industrial policy for foreign-controlled firms. It is not accidental that the majority of screening mechanisms of this type were implemented precisely in those G-7 nations that in the 1960s and 1970s attempted to pursue strategies of industrial targeting, nor is it accidental that the use of these mechanisms to restrict direct investment has declined as these same nations have turned to more market-oriented economic strategies.

In evaluating the merits of proposed screening procedures, two questions immediately present themselves. First, to the extent that a supervisory role for the government is deemed necessary to prevent firms from making investments that are harmful to the national interest, why should this oversight be restricted to foreign firms? Such discrimination against foreign firms might be justified if it were demonstrated that they systematically behave differently from domestically owned firms in ways that are less than beneficial to the US economy. As we have seen, however, there is little evidence for this proposition.

Second, what are the screening criteria to be used? The problem of setting criteria is the same as that of setting general principles for an interventionist industrial policy: aside from a general proposition that free-market outcomes are innocent until proven guilty, there are no simple criteria for determining which privately undertaken activities are more desirable than others. Much popular discussion seems to presume that a professional bureaucracy could apply some set of accepted, objective criteria to the evaluation of proposed foreign investments. The fact is that no such criteria exist. In their absence, any US government screening process would either become highly politicized or turn into a largely irrelevant rubber stamp. Foreign experience with screening has shown that both outcomes can occur—often in sequence or even in alternation. The dangers and costs of a highly politicized screening agency, which would be likely to turn into an anticompetitive captive of special-interest groups, are apparent.

We noted in chapter 6 that an activist administration could in fact use Exon-Florio as a mechanism for full-blown screening of acquisitions of US firms by foreign investors, even without new legislation. The expanded role given to the CFIUS under Exon-Florio turns that agency into a potential general screening agency, and a broad interpretation of national security under this amendment could thus establish a de facto US policy of screening FDI. Thus, the issue of screening is not a hypothetical one.

Under the Bush administration the CFIUS defined national security quite narrowly and took seriously its charge to block an investment only if, in the words of the Exon-Florio amendment itself, "there is credible evidence that leads the President to believe that the foreign interest exercising control might take action that threatens to impair the national security." Whether the Clinton administration might change this approach is, even after 18 months in office, unknown, because no major cases have thus far been reviewed. However, we believe that the narrow interpretation should be maintained. Congress was correct to have dropped the "essential commerce" clause from the Exon-Florio amendment, and economic criteria should not enter into Exon-Florio evaluations.

Reciprocity

We have seen in chapter 6 that conditional national treatment (or reciprocity) has already been introduced into US law to cover certain activities under foreign control, and that there is legislation pending that would inject this principle into other activities. Clyde V. Prestowitz, Jr. (1988), among others, has proposed that all Japanese-controlled activity in the United States be subject to strict reciprocity. This would mean that foreign-controlled firms in the United States would be subject to the same treatment under US law that US-controlled firms receive in the home country of the ultimate beneficial owner of the foreign-controlled firm. For example, under such a policy US affiliates of Japanese financial firms could not act as primary dealers for US government bonds in the United States if Japanese affiliates of US financial firms were forbidden from playing the same role for Government of Japan bonds in Tokyo.

Interestingly, one recent major international dispute over reciprocity in treatment of direct investors arose not from US demands for equal treatment abroad but from foreign demands for equal treatment in the United

States. During 1988 and early 1989 the European Commission floated proposals for a reciprocity standard to be applied to the operations of foreign-controlled banks in Europe. It appeared to the United States that, under such a standard, the operations of US banks in Europe would be fettered as a result of provisions in the US International Banking Act of 1978. Under this act, foreign-owned bank operations in the United States are subject to US restrictions on interstate banking which, although substantially the same restrictions apply to domestic banks, are more stringent than those applied to US banks in Europe. Under pressure from the United States, the Commission indicated in the spring of 1989 that it would apply a national treatment standard (under which foreign-controlled firms are not subject to requirements that do not apply to domestically controlled firms in like circumstances) rather than a reciprocity standard for US banks operating in Europe.

This example highlights a problem that would accompany adoption of a reciprocity standard for FDI in the United States. If reciprocity were applied literally and consistently on both sides, certain types of foreign investors would actually receive *more* favorable treatment under US law than would their domestically controlled competitors. To continue the example of the banking industry, either European-controlled banks operating in the United States would be freed from the constraints on their activities imposed by the International Banking Act, or US banks in Europe would not benefit from the European Union's Second Banking Directive and other measures that liberalize banking activities that cross intra-EU borders. Likewise, under a strict interpretation of reciprocity, either European-owned banks in the United States would be exempt from the requirement under the Glass-Steagall Act that commercial and investment banking functions be kept separate, or US banks operating in Europe would not be granted the right, which other banks in Europe would have, to combine their commercial and investment banking functions.

Presumably, however, advocates of reciprocity have something different in mind: FDI in the United States would be subject to reciprocity only if US firms in the investors' home country face more restrictions than these same firms do in the US home market; otherwise the foreign-controlled firm would be subject in the United States to something like national treatment.

It is clear that such selective reciprocity would discriminate against foreign-controlled firms, and that this discrimination would violate the principle of national treatment with respect to nation of ownership that the United States has long advocated and, indeed, is bound to in both the US-Canada Free Trade Agreement and the North American Free Trade Agreement (NAFTA) and voluntarily subscribes to in the Organization for Economic Cooperation and Development (OECD). Abandonment of this principle would be justifiable only if it were determined that the United States was both exceptionally open to foreign firms and was suffering losses as a result of its differential openness. In fact, neither condition appears to hold: other advanced nations are today similar to the United States with respect to their openness to foreign investment (with the apparent exception of Japan), and, as noted above, we find no evidence that foreign firms operating in the United States (Japanese firms included) are predators on the US economy. It is therefore difficult to see why the United States should suddenly abandon a principle that it has long supported, especially given the still-massive US role as a direct investor in other countries.

Indeed, we are concerned that such proposals as the Manton amendment (discussed in chapter 6) not only violate a principle that the United States has long advocated, but have the potential to cause active damage to US economic interests as well. The intent of this amendment is to deny firms under foreign control the benefits of technologies that might be developed under certain government programs; at a simple (and fairly crude) level the justification for this denial is that US taxpayers should not be assisting the fortunes of the shareholders of foreign-owned firms (who, it is presumed, are not US citizens, even though in practice sometimes they are). But the same amendment could also have the effect of denying foreign-controlled firms the opportunity to contribute to the development of technologies that ultimately benefit US citizens by raising their standards of living. For example, suppose that a program to develop much cleaner automobiles were initiated and were covered by the Manton amendment, and that Japanese automobile producers held certain technologies that could contribute to these goals and domestically owned firms did not. If it were deemed that Japan did not meet reciprocity tests, would it make sense to keep the Japanese firms out of the program if it meant the program's failure, or if success then could only be achieved at substantially higher cost than if the Japanese-controlled firms were allowed in?

Certain thoughtful analysts who are not convinced of the merits of foreign ownership have nevertheless considered the issue posed above and concluded that the answer lies in allowing foreign-controlled firms to participate in programs covered by the Manton amendment but subjecting these firms to performance requirements (see, e.g., US Congress Office of Technology Assessment 1994). As we elaborate below, we are not convinced that this is the way to go either.

Performance Requirements

Performance requirements are governmentally imposed stipulations that firms meet certain specified goals with respect to their operations within the government's jurisdiction. Such goals can include minimum local content or value added, employment goals, or trade goals (e.g., to export a certain percentage of output), among others. The United States differs from a number of other advanced nations in the absence of programs at the federal level that offer firms investment incentives in exchange for acceptance of performance requirements. As noted in chapter 6, the United States sought within the context of the Uruguay Round multilateral trade negotiations to amend the international trade rules to limit the imposition of performance requirements and bring them under the purview of world trade law. Yet the US Congress in the recent past has actively considered legislation to impose performance requirements at the federal level, most notably in the local-content bill for automobiles that was introduced in the Congress during the early 1980s. And, as just noted, there has been some discussion within government agencies about replacing conditional national treatment provisions in proposed legislation (e.g., the Manton amendment) with performance requirements.

We would argue that continued US abstention from performance requirements is justified (with some exceptions in the national security area, discussed below) for several reasons. First, as US trade negotiators have often pointed out, performance requirements amount to international trade distortions imposed by governments. Thus all of the arguments that can be marshaled against protectionism can be brought to bear on performance requirements: they are likely to lead to inefficient allocation of resources, and in particular they give rise to the danger that resources will be allocated away from industries in which the nation imposing them has comparative advantage, and toward industries in which local production is relatively inefficient. In the extreme, performance requirements could deter beneficial foreign investment.

To the extent that there is a case for performance requirements, it is a subset of the general case for industrial policy and subject to the same problems, discussed above in the context of screening. There are no simple criteria that can be used to prescribe performance criteria that are actually in the public interest. As a result, efforts to impose performance requirements will inevitably become more of a political than an economic exercise.

We take particularly strong exception to the recommendation by Glickman and Woodward (1989) that state governments impose performance requirements on firms receiving investment incentives. The problem with performance requirements at the state level is that they would often have beggar-thy-neighbor effects, where the neighbor being beggared is more likely to be another state or region within the United States than a foreign country. The real problem with state-level investment incentives is not the absence of offsetting performance requirements, but rather the inherent tendency of state-versus-state competition to transfer economic rents from the United States to foreign firms. Performance requirements that make investment incentives appear a more attractive option for individual states would only aggravate this problem. Indeed, performance requirements could increase the willingness of state officials to expand investment incentives, thus magnifying the distortions.

An additional reason to oppose state-level performance requirements is that, if successful, they would tend to undermine any US effort to achieve international rules to regulate performance requirements by other nations or to strengthen the national treatment instrument of the OECD. It is reasonable to hope that state-level requirements, if attempted, would ultimately be ruled in violation of the constitutional prohibition against state regulation of interstate commerce. Given that one state's investment incentive can drive other states to match the incentive, but that this process doesn't work in reverse, it might also make sense for the federal government to ban investment incentives. Such a ban could be based on this same constitutional prohibition and would work to the best interest of the individual states.

At the federal level, Prestowitz (1988) has called for performance requirements aimed specifically at Japanese firms. The essence of his argument is that, without coercion, Japanese investors are unlikely to take the steps necessary for the United States to realize the potential economic benefit from their investments. Gastner (1992) has made a similar proposal, arguing that European nations have imposed such requirements on Japanese firms and, as a result, received more benefit from Japanese FDI than has the United States. We regard Prestowitz's economic case as greatly overstated: as we showed in chapter 3, Japanese firms do not exhibit any tendency to withhold high-value-added activities or R&D from the United States. They do tend to obtain a large share of their production inputs from outside the United States, and this tendency will continue to be a source of tension if there is not a substantial shift to greater local content as the Japanese presence in the US economy grows. At present, however, the economic costs, if any, to the United States resulting from Japanese sourcing practices are quite small. Likewise, Gastner's claim that European nations, through performance requirements, have been able to extract more benefits from Japanese FDI than has the United States is just that: a claim, which Gastner offers no evidence whatsoever to support.[1]

Japanese private analysts claim, and the Japanese government predicts, that Japanese firms will become much less distinctive in their import behavior as their investments mature (Nomura Research Institute 1989, Ministry of International Trade and Industry 1994). If this does not happen, however, a "Japan problem" with respect to US foreign direct investment policy could eventually arise. To call for an immediate radical shift in policy on this basis, however, is premature.

---

1. Indeed, what little evidence has been brought to bear on the issue suggests that the facts might be the opposite of what Gastner claims. See Gittelman and Graham (1994).

Finally, even though no federal legislation imposing performance requirements is on the immediate horizon (unless such a measure were to be substituted for the Manton amendment, something that has been discussed but not formally proposed at the time of this writing), the same question arises that we have noted with respect to screening: will the CFIUS in effect become an agency that imposes performance requirements as well as screening? Commitments reportedly requested by the CFIUS with respect to the Hüls AG takeover of the silicon wafer operations of Monsanto (discussed in chapter 6 in the context of the Exon-Florio amendment) amount to performance requirements, albeit with a narrowly defined national security focus. Was this a unique special case, as the Bush administration claimed, or could it be seen as a precedent when and if a major case comes up for review under the Clinton administration? Only time will tell.

An Agenda for US Policy on FDI

The main thrust of this discussion of policy has been to arrive at a set of things that should *not* be done, even though they are popular in current discussion. We now proceed to an agenda of positive actions that the United States should take. This agenda can be divided into three parts: actions the US government should take to strengthen existing policies affecting foreign-controlled operations in the United States; actions that the United States should take with respect to these operations and national security; and actions that should be initiated on a multilateral basis.

Strengthening Existing Policies

Certain actions of foreign-controlled firms should be regulated as part of general US policy toward all business operations. For example, there undoubtedly have been foreign acquisitions of US enterprises that should have been subject to severe scrutiny, and possibly should have been blocked, on antitrust grounds. The reason is not that the acquiring firms were foreign controlled, but rather that there exists a strong general economic case against monopolization or excessive concentration in an industry. Otherwise put, there is a case for greater scrutiny and regulation of *all* mergers and acquisitions than we saw during the Reagan and Bush years, when proponents of the "Chicago school" of antitrust reigned supreme. Such an increase in scrutiny would surely have affected a number of foreign takeovers of US entities. The Clinton administration has indicated that it will adopt a more activist antitrust policy, but merger and acquisition activity by foreign investors has been slow during the first two years of the Clinton administration, and no cases have arisen that put the administration's rhetoric to the test.

In other areas, however, there may be a case for further deregulation. For example, US restrictions on interstate banking effectively hamper interregional competition more than do the corresponding regulations in the European Union, and this is likely to remain a source of tension as European banks continue to demand reciprocity. There is a good case for further liberalization of US banking law. The case rests primarily on arguments that demonstrate banking deregulation to be in the US interest, although deregulation would also serve to defuse a potential source of international conflict.

FDI and National Security

The United States will also need to alter its ways of doing business so as to accommodate a larger share of foreign ownership in other sectors of the economy. The most important changes fall in the domain of defense. As we noted in chapter 5, regulations affecting foreign-controlled firms involved in US defense contracting still presume that reliance on foreign-owned firms for technology is rare. This presumption is no longer true. It will almost surely become necessary to reform defense contracting so as to make better use of foreign-owned firms; the alternative, maintenance of a wholly US-owned defense industrial base, is a virtual impossibility. The difficulties associated with maintaining a wholly domestic, wholly self-sufficient defense industrial base are likely to increase in the future, as more countries outside the United States become sources of important new technologies.

The US Department of Defense to some extent does recognize these realities and has taken considerable steps toward internationalizing its procurement during the past several years. Also, the various agencies involved with export controls have taken steps to deregulate the sales of those dual-use technologies (i.e., technologies developed primarily for the civilian sector, but with important military applications) that are widely available from non-US sources. Such trends should continue, as it would be counterproductive to retreat from this path in the name of maintaining the national industrial base.

In this spirit, we question certain measures that have been announced or taken by the Department of Defense and other agencies under the Clinton administration. These include statements by senior Defense Department officials to the effect that the United States must maintain a domestic capability, under domestic ownership, to develop and produce every technology of military significance, including those in the dual-use category, such as flat panel displays. The implications of this would be to exclude participation by US subsidiaries of foreign-controlled firms in government-organized partnerships and consortia to develop and maintain certain technological capabilities within the United States. But the exclusion of foreign-controlled firms could do more to keep foreign-developed technology out of US hands than to contain any leakage of US-developed technologies to other countries. It might be better, even from a narrow defense perspective, to admit strong foreign competitors to the consortia than to exclude them, and to take other steps to ensure that their participation leads to a two-way exchange of technical know-how. One such measure is compulsory licensing, discussed below.

There are a number of other measures that the United States should take with respect to national security and FDI. Some go beyond the FDI issue per se and address the more general problem of international sourcing of goods and services required for the defense effort.

We recommended in chapter 5 that the United States explicitly identify what activities and technologies (especially dual-use technologies) should, in the interest of national security, be maintained under domestic ownership and control. The identification should be made by professionals with requisite technical qualifications and close knowledge of defense-related affairs.

What would be the criteria for inclusion on the list of activities that should remain under domestic control? We do not consider ourselves qualified to set precise criteria, much less to spell out what specific activities might appear on the list. Two general criteria were suggested in chapter 5: the military importance of the activity (taking into account the availability of substitutes) and the number and diversity of potential suppliers. We suspect that under these two criteria the list would be relatively short.

What should happen once an activity or technology is placed on the list? If the activity or technology is already under domestic control, its presence on the list would signal to the CFIUS that a foreign takeover might be undesirable. If the domestic firm or firms controlling the activity find themselves in financial difficulty, presence of the activity on the list might trigger consideration of government subsidy, although we hope that subsidization would only occur after investigation of other alternatives to put the activity on a firmer financial footing. One such alternative would be to allow the foreign takeover to proceed, but to impose certain requirements on the activity to safeguard the national security. These are discussed below. If, on the other hand, the activity or technology is controlled by foreigners and there are no viable domestically controlled alternative suppliers, more drastic action might be warranted. We discuss below what that action might be.

We also argued in chapter 5 that the United States should never become dependent upon a foreign-controlled monopoly for any good or service vital to the national defense. Indeed, the security of the United States should never depend upon any monopoly producer, whether foreign- or domestically controlled. Monopolization of a product or service is already illegal under the Sherman Antitrust Act, but it is questionable whether this law is strong enough to deal with all the sorts of monopolies that might arise in defense contracting. In antitrust cases the courts have typically taken a broader view of what constitutes the "relevant market" than is appropriate for militarily critical goods.

One option might be to amend the Sherman Act to narrow the definition of "monopolization" as it applies to goods or services listed as critical to the national defense (perhaps the same list of goods and services proposed above). Monopolization might be defined for these purposes as a threshold market share held by one producer or by a family of producers under common control. We do not know exactly what the threshold level should be: it would surely be less than 100 percent but probably more than 25 percent. Whatever the criterion, defense-related activities meeting the criterion would then be subject to more stringent antitrust provisions than non-defense-related ones. We emphasize that these criteria should apply to domestically controlled as well as foreign-controlled firms.

In some countries the relevant authorities already have the power to apply special criteria to antitrust cases involving national security. For example, in the United Kingdom the Monopolies and Mergers Commission has this power. Indeed, during the mid-1980s a proposed merger between two UK firms (Plessey and GEC) was blocked by the commission precisely because the merger would have created a monopoly within the United Kingdom for the provision of certain defense-related systems.[2]

If an activity or service (we define "service" to include the capability to develop a specific new technology) that is vital to the national defense is monopolized by a foreign supplier, including through the acquisition of a financially troubled US firm, what are the possible remedies?

As we suggested in chapter 5, one remedy would be compulsory licensing: the foreign monopolist would be required to license to a domestic producer the capability to provide the good or service. The US government clearly has the power to take intellectual property for its own use, and compulsory licensing of this type is consistent with the Paris Convention (an international agreement on the regulation of patent protection) so long as it is applied on a national treatment basis. In fact, under US law (28 USC 1498) the Defense Department routinely uses ("works") patents, or has them used by contractors, on a compulsory basis. The patent holder is compensated under these circumstances, as is consistent with the Fifth Amendment to the US Constitution. Because many militarily important technologies fall into the dual-use category, compulsory licensing might

---

2. Details of this case and of Monopolies and Mergers Commission procedures and policies are contained in Graham and Ebert (1991).

be required as a precondition for participation in civilian markets as well as in military markets.

A practical problem that arises with compulsory licensing is that although the government can legally "work" a patent that is held by a private party, the government cannot force the holder to surrender knowhow that might be necessary to use the patent. An alternative remedy that might be more cost-effective in such cases is mandatory foreign investment coupled with local-content requirements. These requirements could include provisions that R&D capabilities be maintained in laboratories and pilot plants located within the United States and that these facilities employ US nationals. Although such provisions would constitute performance requirements, which we generally oppose (see the discussion earlier in this chapter), they may at times be warranted in the interest of national security. Performance requirements of this sort, which would allow firms to maintain control of their intellectual properties, might well produce less international friction than compulsory licensing. Indeed, mandatory foreign investment would allow the innovative firm to maintain a large degree of managerial control over technologies that it considers proprietary. This would be consistent with the principle embodied in US patent law that the innovator of a new technology should have a temporary monopoly right to exploit its commercial applications. At the same time, mandatory investment and performance requirements would ensure that the capability to deliver the goods needed by the military would be located on US soil. Such requirements, as discussed previously, were apparently imposed by the CFIUS upon Hüls AG, in the matter of the takeover of certain operations of Monsanto. We believe that these measures made good sense, and we are somewhat baffled by the CFIUS's apparent reluctance to use similar measures in subsequent cases.

Mandatory investment within the United States has already been stipulated by the US government as a condition for participation by foreign firms in certain US defense contracts. For example, Robert B. Costello, Under Secretary of Defense for Acquisitions in the Carter administration, has indicated that while in office he required the French-owned tire and rubber manufacturer Michelin to set up "advanced manufacturing facilities in the United States" as a condition for supplying advanced radial aircraft tires to the military (Eckhouse 1991). One reason for seeking US production, as we have already noted, is that US subsidiaries of foreign firms are subject to the defense priorities and allocations provisions of the Defense Production Act of 1950 (see chapter 5), whereby in the event of shortage of supply of a critical item, defense needs would get priority.

We have already indicated that the United States should never become dependent upon a monopoly producer for a good or technology critical to the national defense. How do we reconcile this with our willingness to allow foreign investors to maintain monopoly control over certain technologies under our proposal for mandatory FDI? An easy reconciliation follows from the observation that the "no dependence" requirement applies only to certain very critical products and technologies. Thus, the only activities that would be subject to compulsory licensing would be those included in the list we proposed earlier in this section.

There are, however, cases where pragmatic considerations suggest the mandatory FDI alternative over compulsory licensing, even for activities that do fall on the list. For example, a foreign firm that controls an important technology might choose to withdraw from the US market altogether rather than subject itself to compulsory licensing. In such a case, it might be preferable to allow that firm to operate on US soil while maintaining control over the technology rather than see the firm withdraw. Under such circumstances the United States might also do well to encourage domestic entry into the activity.

Suppose, however, that a firm holding monopoly control of a militarily vital activity were headquartered in a country that at some point became hostile to the United States. What options would then be available? If the activity involved a US subsidiary, an extreme solution would be forced divestiture of the subsidiary to bring the activity under domestic control. However, as we pointed out in chapter 5, it is likely that the subsidiary would not be capable of producing the needed goods, or of producing them at peak efficiency, when cut off from the parent. Large federal subsidies might be required to resuscitate the operation. Forced spinoffs of activities critical to the national defense are not well advised if they are going to be dead on arrival. For this reason we consider forced divestiture a policy alternative that should be undertaken only under emergency conditions.

Under the International Emergency Economic Powers Act (IEEPA, discussed in chapter 5), in a dire emergency short of war the US government can seize the assets of a foreign national but cannot take title to them. Exactly what this power implies for the takeover of a foreign-controlled subsidiary remains somewhat ambiguous, but the 1991 Persian Gulf war clarified some issues. During that war, under the authority of the IEEPA, President George Bush effectively shut down US firms under Iraqi control but allowed US firms under Kuwaiti control to continue to operate under existing management. But what if in the future the US government should want to allow a US subsidiary of a hostile nation to continue to operate but under new management? Can it seize such a subsidiary and place it under the control of a domestically controlled firm? Can the government itself temporarily manage the subsidiary as a state-controlled (but not state-owned) enterprise? These matters will require some clarification and perhaps modification of the IEEPA.

Overall, on pragmatic grounds we tend to favor mandatory local investment coupled with appropriate performance requirements as the remedy for foreign monopoly control of an activity vital to the national security. Such investment is overwhelmingly likely to originate in friendly nations, and our example of Ford Motor Company in the United Kingdom (chapter 5) shows that a subsidiary of a firm headquartered in a friendly nation can contribute greatly to the military needs of the host nation. In the event of a national emergency, however, it is highly desirable that the militarily vital activity actually be located on host-nation soil and that the activity be capable of standing on its own if cut off from its parent. For these reasons we believe that national security can constitute an acceptable reason for the imposition of strong performance requirements.

A bill introduced in Congress in 1991 by Representative Philip R. Sharp (D-IN), H.R. 2631, would have amended the Exon-Florio authority to enable some of these ideas to be implemented. Existing Hart-Scott-Rodino requirements for prenotification of a merger or acquisition would have been modified so that any such transactions likely to have national security applications would be notified. A special office within the Department of Justice would review the notifications and refer those with security implications to the CFIUS under a modified Exon-Florio process. Under this process the president would have explicit authority to seek "assurances" (i.e., performance requirements) as a condition of approval of the transaction. These transactions would then be simultaneously reviewed on antitrust grounds by the Department of Justice or the Federal Trade Commission, and the effect of the transaction on competition within the industry would be one factor explicitly considered by the CFIUS. Representative Sharp's bill did not explicitly require the CFIUS or the president to develop lists of critical technologies; however, implementation of the bill would surely require that some such list exist (but not necessarily that it be made public). This bill died with the 102nd Congress.

Another option when foreign-controlled firms monopolize the supply of a militarily vital technology is for the Defense Department to promote the entry or development of a domestic supplier. Indeed, this approach is currently being attempted by the Clinton administration in the matter of flat panel displays, which we discuss below. How far in general such promotion should go is a matter of controversy. For example, to switch all procurement to an unproven "national champion" could result in dependence on an unreliable or technologically inferior supplier. On the other hand, to switch some procurement to a domestic entrant as a second source of supply could make sense. Clearly, the correct course of action will depend on the specifics of the case. One such case is flat panel displays, to which we now turn.

Flat panel displays (FPDs) are semiconductor devices that allow images like those generated by the cathode ray tube of an ordinary television set to be displayed on a thin, flat surface (an example of an FPD is the screen on a laptop computer). There is little doubt that FPDs have become a critical military item, and that they embody a dual-use technology (indeed, military applications, according to the Department of Defense, account for less than 5 percent of world demand for FPDs). Japanese firms account for about 95 percent of world output of FPDs, and one Japanese firm, Sharp Corporation, is the clear market leader, with over 40 percent of the world market of active matrix liquid crystal diodes (AMLCDs). AMLCDs are the current technology of choice of FPD users because of their faster response times and greater clarity. There is no US domestic capacity to produce FPDs on a commercial scale. FPDs therefore do seem to meet our criteria as a technology that should be subject to some sort of special policy in the interests of national security.

The question is, Which of the options posed above is the correct one? The Department of Defense, through its Advanced Research Projects Agency (ARPA, formerly DARPA), has already invested upward of $300 million in developing a US source and claims some "technological success" from this investment. But ARPA's previous support has not created any US domestic production capacity beyond the pilot plant stage. The Clinton administration proposes to invest about $600 million over five years to create such capacity; the producers who benefit from the subsidies will be allowed to compete in civilian markets as well as supply the military, on the grounds that to achieve static and dynamic scale economies (including moving down "learning curves") it would not be sufficient for a producer to sell to the military alone. In principle at least, foreign firms could participate in the ARPA-sponsored programs, although past experience suggests that this might be difficult in practice: the DARPA-backed Sematech consortium, for example, excluded foreign firms; this exclusion was claimed to have been instituted solely by the private-sector participants, but in fact it almost surely reflected DARPA preferences.

Is this all a good idea? Several points to the contrary can be raised. First, although FPDs are almost without question militarily important devices and their production is monopolized by one nation (but not by one firm), they may be entering a phase of their product life cycle where they will become commodity items and where entry barriers will fall. Two Korean firms, for example, are entering the business. Some semiconductor industry specialists argue that competition in FPD production will grow and that the dominant Japanese position will rapidly erode. Even so, however, the case can be made that the United States needs domestic production capability and not simply a more internationally diversified production base.

Perhaps more fundamentally, even though $600 million over five years does not seem to be an inordinately large amount, at least by the standards of defense expenditure, one wonders whether subsidization is the most cost-efficient way of obtaining domestic production capability. Would a performance requirement to get the large Japanese firms to locate facilities in the United States be a viable alternative? The Department of Defense claims that Sharp and the other Japanese firms have an "allergy" with respect to supplying the US military.[3] But some analysts aren't so sure that this "allergy" isn't more in the Department of Defense itself than in the Japanese suppliers—in other words, the department may be simply reasserting its historic preference for US ownership and control.[4] Also, there is the case to be made that US entry into this market would happen even without government support. A joint venture between Motorola, Inc., and In Focus Systems, Inc. (the latter is a small high-technology firm based in Oregon), will produce FPDs, but not AMLCDs. (The technology will be an active-addressing passive matrix LCD, a new technology designed to upgrade the capability of passive matrix LCDs.) Raytheon Company, under French license, will build yet another type of FPD, one based on conventional cathode ray tube technology. Both of these technologies have at least the potential to challenge the technological superiority of AMLCDs and might prove to be lower cost technologies as well.

Whatever the case for and against ARPA support of FPDs, ARPA (with the full backing of the Clinton administration) does seem determined to go ahead with the program. Thus, one thing that can definitely be said is that FPDs will become a useful test case. Critical issues to be assessed after the program has run its course are the following: Did the programs actually succeed? That is, was domestic capacity to produce FPDs, of the quality needed by the Defense Department and at something like competitive costs, actually achieved? Did the costs remain in line with the projections? Most important, could as favorable an outcome (or, especially if the outcome is less than as desired, a more favorable outcome), in retrospect, have been achieved more cost-effectively through other policy options?

In brief, we feel that FPDs are a borderline case in terms of the desirability of using government backing to build a domestic manufacturing capability under domestic control. Given that the Clinton administration intends to go ahead with it, it will if nothing else serve as a useful laboratory experiment in how such programs pan out in practice.

Multilateral Policy Actions

The rising role of foreign-owned firms in the United States raises the potential for future political conflict. Just as the United States has on occasion attempted to meet national objectives by means of extraterritorial application of its laws and policies to the overseas activities of US-headquartered firms, other governments might someday attempt to do the

---

3. Oral presentation by Kenneth Flamm, Principal Deputy Assistant Secretary of Defense, at the National Academy of Sciences, July 1994.

4. Oral presentation by Claude Barfield of the American Enterprise Institute at the National Academy of Sciences, July 1994.

same with respect to the US subsidiaries of firms based in their countries. There almost surely is no effective way for the United States to stop these efforts unilaterally through domestic laws or regulations. What are needed instead are some sort of internationally agreed-upon rules regarding FDI, including a dispute settlement mechanism through which deviations from these rules can be redressed.[5]

The most fruitful approach is likely to be an accord on investment and multinational enterprise among the world's largest industrial nations. To involve a larger number of nations in setting the rules would be both impractical and unnecessary. It would be impractical because the potentially common goals among the major industrial nations and certain of the developing nations with respect to FDI differ markedly from the goals of other developing nations, making agreement on a common set of rules difficult or impossible. (However, as noted previously, many developing countries are revising their policy goals, and one result is greater openness toward direct investment.) It would be unnecessary because the vast bulk of FDI at present takes place among a relatively small number of industrially advanced and rapidly industrializing nations. Nonetheless, it should be made possible for nations outside the core group eventually to sign the FDI accord as well.

There would be some procedural problems to be worked out with any such accord. For example, the European nations might have to enter the agreement via the European Union. If so, the interests of some of the smaller and poorer members of the Community would have to be taken into account.

Such an accord is more feasible now than at any time in the recent past, for a number of reasons. First, the United States, for the first time in this century, possesses a large and visible foreign-controlled sector within its domestic economy; therefore the United States must consider the implications of its own policies with respect to outward FDI upon inward FDI, and vice versa, whereas until quite recently US policy toward FDI was almost solely determined by the outward component. Second, the EU nations are moving toward common policies to govern both intra-European direct investment and direct investment across EU borders in both directions. Third, the US-Canada Free Trade Agreement and now the NAFTA have created new precedents for international rules regarding direct investment, including rules establishing dispute settlement procedures. Fourth, Japan has exhibited at least a rhetorical commitment to more-open investment policies. And, fifth, through much of the world a major reassessment of attitudes and policies toward direct investment and multinational enterprises is taking place, with many countries that during

---

5. The proposals contained in this section are more fully developed in Bergsten and Graham (forthcoming).

the 1970s shunned direct investment activities of multinational enterprises now welcoming them.

None of these factors ensures that an effective accord could actually be reached, yet none of them even existed fifteen years ago. We have noted already that among the major industrial countries there is now more convergence of national policies regarding FDI than at any time in the recent past. In a word, if the time for a new international initiative in this domain is not now, it is not far off.

It is possible to sketch out some of the elements such an accord should include. One is some formal declaration of the basic rights and responsibilities of home nations, host nations, and multinational enterprises. This should not be a long list. Host-nation responsibilities would include the granting of right of establishment and national treatment to local subsidiaries of foreign parentage. Acceptable deviations from these principles would also have to be enumerated in a transparent manner.

Home-nation rights and responsibilities should also be spelled out. In general, home nations should have the right to take appropriate action to protect the domestic property rights of their citizens, including those of locally based multinational corporations, and to protect their rights with respect to property held in foreign nations. This right must, however, be delimited. It is not appropriate for a home government to attempt to use the property rights of its citizens who own overseas subsidiaries as vehicles for extending home-nation policies or laws abroad, especially when these conflict with host-country policies or laws. Thus, for example, it would be appropriate for a home government to attempt to guarantee that one of its multinational firms facing expropriation of properties abroad was treated in a nondiscriminatory manner. But it would not be appropriate for the home government to insist that its own standards be applied to the expropriation process.

What this does and does not imply for the conduct of multinational firms and their home nations can be illustrated by a further example. Suppose that a US subsidiary of a Japanese firm decided to hire a former high-level US official to represent it in its dealings with the federal government. So long as a US firm engaged in comparable business could legally hire the same official for the same purposes, there would be no problem with respect to national treatment. Indeed, any US law specifically forbidding such hiring by foreign-controlled firms only would be a violation of the national treatment principle, and the Japanese government could legitimately complain that Japanese investors were subject to discriminatory procedures. However, if the subsidiary were to respond to parent-company orders that were in turn a response to instructions from the Japanese Ministry of International Trade and Industry (MITI), this would be an abuse of home-country rights as defined above. Direct countermeasures by the US government would then not necessarily violate the principle of national treatment, although a better US response might be an appeal to the dispute settlement mechanism referred to below.

Responsibilities of multinational firms would include a commitment not to compel their overseas subsidiaries to disobey the laws of the jurisdictions in which they are located. An important extension of this principle, consistent with the home-nation government responsibilities outlined above, would be to ensure that if the subsidiary's efforts to obey local laws should conflict with directives from the parent company (perhaps to comply with laws or policies of the home government), the local laws take precedence.

Other responsibilities of firms under an international accord could include compliance with requirements for public disclosure of certain current financial and operating information. In other words, there is a case for something like a Bryant amendment at the international level. However, any such provision should not force multinational firms to disclose publicly more information than is required of locally controlled firms operating in the same locality and industry. One option would be a set of common standards for disclosure and reporting that would apply to all business enterprises exceeding a specified size threshold.

The accord should include restrictions on the use of performance requirements. The US-Canada Free Trade Agreement provides a model for such restrictions:[6] new performance requirements that affect international trade are proscribed, although others are grandfathered. A multilateral extension of this proscription would be desirable, and indeed we see an accord among a limited group of nations as a more practical basis for such a proscription than the agreement on trade-related investment measures negotiated as part of the Uruguay Round. A useful approach here would be, first, to develop a list of practices deemed to distort international commerce and therefore to be banned or avoided; second, to develop a list of specific practices now in place that are to be grandfathered, and another list of practices to be phased out; third, to develop a list of acceptable categories of performance requirements (we have in mind requirements deemed necessary for reasons of national security, as discussed earlier in this chapter, but we cannot exclude that other acceptable categories might emerge); and fourth, to establish a mechanism for monitoring and regulating the use of these requirements.

A further desirable extension would be some limitation on the use of investment incentives. Under such a limitation, the United States would have to ensure that the individual states comply. As we have suggested, limitation of these incentives would be in the states' own best overall interest.

There are numerous domains in which problems posed by the existence of multinational corporations would be best resolved by consultation and

---

6. Unfortunately, as noted in chapter 6, the NAFTA backtracked on this issue.

agreement among the relevant national governmental agencies. Examples include questions of taxation, antitrust and control of restrictive business practices, pollution and environmental standards, export controls for national security purposes, product safety and liability standards, and other areas where public regulation of private enterprise is deemed necessary. It is entirely possible that different institutional mechanisms will be brought to bear in different domains. For example, jurisprudential mechanisms, including perhaps some that have not yet been created (e.g., an international tribunal to adjudicate cases involving anticompetitive practices), might well figure heavily in antitrust matters, whereas in the domain of taxation the primary mechanism would remain national tax authorities whose functions are linked via a network of tax treaties.

Thus we do not in general believe that our proposed accord should initially include specific "codes" to deal with these domains. Rather, it should provide a framework within which relevant national authorities might consult and, where appropriate, cooperate among themselves. Modes of cooperation might vary from domain to domain. For example, in one domain explicit rules might be embodied in the form of a code, whereas in another the cooperation might be limited to formal avenues of consultation.

To some degree the Organization for Economic Cooperation and Development already provides such a framework. The OECD has, for example, been very successful in fostering a series of treaties bearing on the taxation of multinational enterprises and mechanisms of cooperation among national tax authorities to administer the treaties. The existing framework is, however, very informal, and its effectiveness is spotty. What is needed is an enlargement of this framework.

An essential ingredient of such an enlargement is an effective dispute settlement mechanism. Here the NAFTA provides an effective model. The dispute mechanism for investment established under NAFTA chapter 11, part B, breaks new ground (see chapter 6), and a similar mechanism should be carried forward into our proposed international accord on investment.

For an effective accord to come about, both the Congress and the president must recognize that there is a substantial potential for nations to harm one another through unilateral actions in the domain of international investment. Such harm can be prevented only by international rules to govern international investment and home and host nations' policies affecting that investment.

Conclusions

The role of foreign-owned firms in the US economy increased sharply in the 1980s, and although the rate of expansion of this role fell just as sharply during the early 1990s, it could pick up again as Japan and Europe come out of recession. We hope that we have shown satisfactorily that there is nothing sinister about this increased role, and that indeed its general economic effect is beneficial. Thus there is no need from an economic perspective for new unilateral laws or policies specifically targeted toward greater regulation of foreign-controlled activities in the United States. This does not imply that in a fast-changing world there is no need for a continual rethinking of the ideas upon which policies rest. There is, and in some cases the outcome might be more regulation affecting FDI (e.g., stronger enforcement of certain of the antitrust laws) and in other cases less (e.g., in banking and defense).

The rapid growth of FDI in the United States will, of course, continue to generate political tensions. In particular, it remains a probability that the United States will face a "Japan problem" in its international investment policy, just as it does in its international trade policy. Japan remains an outlier both in terms of the penetration of its economy by foreign firms and in terms of the behavior of Japanese-based firms in the United States. A significant further opening of Japan to inward direct investment would do much to reduce future investment-related stress.

If anything, Japan is even more of an outlier in terms of the low level of foreign control of its economy than it is in terms of its low propensity to import manufactured goods. As in the case of trade in manufactures, however, Japan's difference from other advanced nations in this respect seems to owe little to differences in current government policy, which is roughly as open to direct investment as that in other advanced nations. Instead, there appear to be differences in the structure of Japan's economy that make it difficult for foreign firms to penetrate.[7] Although there are reasons to hope that Japan will eventually become more open both to imports and to direct investment, Japan's outlier status will be a source of tension for a long time to come.

To this must be added the apparent difference in import behavior exhibited by Japanese firms in the United States. It is important not to overstate this difference and accuse Japanese firms of antisocial behavior. In most respects Japanese firms in the United States look quite normal. For example, the widespread belief that Japanese firms keep high-value-added activities or research and development at home is not borne out by the data. Japanese firms in the United States do, however, import considerably more per employee even in comparable activities than do other foreign direct investors, and much more than do domestically owned firms. Japanese firms and Japanese government officials argue that this is a transitional phenomenon reflecting the newness of their direct investment here.

---

7. Some of this, however, is doubtless a legacy of Japan's restrictive policies of the past. On this question see Mason (1992). See also Encarnation (1992) and Wakasugi (1994).

We hope that this turns out to be the case; otherwise a rethinking of US openness to direct investment will become difficult to avoid.

We reiterate, however, that on economic grounds the case in favor of an open policy toward FDI, including investment from Japan, remains strong. Even where the case against direct investment is strongest, on the import issue, the maximum possible cost is small, and it is quite possible that there is in fact a gain, in that direct investment may displace imports of finished goods. In our view, the evidence does not shake the presumption that FDI in general makes a significant positive contribution to the US economy.

Indeed, the major threat to US welfare comes not from the growing foreign presence but from the potential for an "investment war" in which governments attempt unilaterally to capture greater benefits from foreign investment through such measures as performance requirements, or attempt to use multinationals headquartered in their territories to further their own foreign policy interests at the possible expense of nations that are hosts to subsidiaries of these enterprises. (For an early delineation of the dangers of investment wars, see Bergsten 1974.)

Cooperative action is essential if investment wars are to be avoided. The United States must avoid hysteria; like the citizens of other advanced nations that have experienced waves of inward direct investment, Americans will eventually realize that on the whole the process is highly beneficial. But other players, especially Japan, must also make efforts to ensure that their own behavior is conducive to a liberal world climate for direct investment. And we should take seriously the possibility that an explicit multilateral agreement on direct investment can be reached. Like the GATT, such an agreement will not solve all our problems, but also like the GATT, it could do us all a lot of good.

Appendices

US Data on Foreign Direct Investment

This appendix consists of two parts. The first part consists of the version of this appendix that appeared in the first edition of this book, in 1989. At that time there was much controversy in the US Congress and elsewhere regarding whether data on US inward FDI collected by the Bureau of Economic Analysis (BEA) of the US Department of Commerce were adequate for policymaking purposes or not. The first edition appendix represented our own best efforts to address this issue, and it has been credited with helping to motivate some of the reforms that have come since.

The second part assesses the changes that have occurred in the collection and analysis of the data by the BEA and other relevant US government agencies since the first edition was published. The bottom line of this assessment is that things mostly have been moving in a positive direction, but some problem areas remain.

The State of US Government FDI Data Collection and Analysis: 1989

One of the more contentious issues in the debate over foreign direct investment in the United States is the adequacy of data on this investment collected by the US government. Several federal agencies collect data on various aspects of FDI, but the Bureau of Economic Analysis, an agency of the US Department of Commerce, has the major role. In this appendix we survey the nature of the information the BEA gathers and assess its adequacy for policy analysis.

The BEA is the federal agency responsible for the preparation of the US national income and product accounts, the balance of payments accounts, and a number of other important data series. The BEA publishes these data in its monthly *Survey of Current Business* and in greater detail in separate volumes. For most of its data the BEA relies on information supplied by other government bureaus and agencies; relatively few source data are collected by the BEA itself directly from private-sector sources. However, among the data that the BEA does collect directly are those on inward and outward FDI.

The BEA is a small agency by federal government standards, with a total 1988 budget of $32.1 million. The BEA's budget was reduced sharply during the Reagan years. By one estimate, the cut amounted to 8 percent annually in real terms from 1981 to 1988. In 1988 the total staff of the BEA consisted of 391 persons, compared with 455 in 1980.

Nature and Collection of BEA Data

The BEA's collection of data on inward FDI is conducted under the authority of the International Investment and Trade in Services Survey Act. This law was passed in 1976 largely in response to congressional fears that investors from member nations of the Organization of Petroleum Exporting Countries (OPEC) were acquiring too large a stake in the US economy. The act was amended in 1984 to include data on services. The BEA collected data on the activities of US affiliates of foreign companies before the passage of the Survey Act, but the act increased the scope of the information gathered.

Compliance with the BEA surveys of US affiliates of foreign companies is mandatory; that is, the affilates are required by law to furnish the requested information. However, the BEA treats records for individual affiliates and their parent companies as confidential. Access is restricted to BEA staff, certain consultants and contractors to the BEA, and a limited number of other government officials specifically designated to perform certain functions under the Survey Act. Persons with access to the records may not disclose to the public information that would identify the company furnishing the information. The records are closed to Congress and to other executive officials not specifically granted access under the act. The data may be used for statistical and analytical purposes only; in particular, they may not be used for purposes of investigation or regulation or to determine tax liability. For reporting purposes, a US affiliate of a foreign company is defined as a US business enterprise in which a foreign person (actual or corporate) owns, directly or indirectly, at least 10 percent of the voting equity (or the equivalent if the enterprise is unincorporated). Under the law, it is the responsibility of any affiliate meeting these criteria to identify itself to the BEA and to provide the required information.

The BEA collects and publishes two types of data on FDI: balance of payments data and financial and operating data. Balance of payments information gathered by the BEA includes data on the value of current holdings (positions) of foreign direct investors as well as transactions between US affiliates and their foreign parents. This information is needed to calculate the US balance of payments and the national income and products accounts as well as the international investment position of the United States. The transactions information includes equity and interfirm debt flows between the affiliates and their parents; income flows, royalties, and license fees; and other services transactions. Information on the international investment position of the United States includes the stocks of foreign parents' equity in and net outstanding loans to their US affiliates. Detailed tabulations are published by industry of US affiliate and by country of foreign parent.

Financial and operating data collected by the BEA cover the overall financial structure and operations of US affiliates of foreign firms. Much of this information consists of general income and balance sheet information. Certain items of specific interest that might not be carried on the firms' income statements and balance sheets are also collected, such as the value of affiliates' US merchandise exports and imports; property, plant, and equipment expenditures; number of workers employed and their compensation; and research and development expenditures. Detailed tabulations are published by industry of US affiliate, by country of ultimate beneficial owner, and (for selected items) by state.

It is important to distinguish clearly between the balance of payments data and the financial and operating data. We have seen critics of the BEA data confuse, for example, total assets of US affiliates of foreign firms with the total stock of FDI in the United States on a balance of payments basis. The latter consists essentially of the net equity and interfirm debt claims of foreign parents on their US affiliates and is therefore quite different from total assets. It is entirely possible (and indeed likely) that these two series will grow at different rates. For example, if a large foreign parent firm increases its equity in its US affiliate from 50 to 100 percent, then all else being equal, the total stock of FDI in the United States will grow by the amount of the additional equity, yet the transaction will have no effect on the total assets of US affiliates of foreign firms.

The BEA collects its data by three means: the comprehensive but relatively infrequent benchmark survey, yearly and quarterly sample surveys, and a yearly survey of US businesses newly acquired or established by foreign direct investors.

The BEA considers the benchmark survey to be the foundation of its reporting system. Normally this survey is conducted at least once every five years. The most recent surveys, however, were those for 1987 and 1980. The seven-year lag in this case was exceptional; its purpose was to have the benchmark survey coincide with the economic censuses performed by the Bureau of the Census so that data from the two agencies could be related and combined.

The benchmark survey is more comprehensive than the other surveys in terms of both the amount of information gathered from each reporting affiliate and the number of affiliates surveyed. In the 1987 survey, all foreign affiliates having assets, sales, or net income in excess of $20 million were requested to submit full balance sheets and income statesments, as well as all of the following information: reconciliation of retained earnings; sales data by industry; sales data by goods versus services; employee compensation information; the number of employees in each industry in which the affilate had sales; the number of employees whose compensation was subject to collective bargaining; the composition of external debt by where carried on the balance sheet; depreciation and depletion charges; plant and equipment expenditures by type of expenditure; interest receipts and payments; taxes; research and development expenditures; US merchandise exports and imports by product, country of destination or origin, and (for imports) intended use; and detail by states for total employment and manufacturing employment, acres of land owned, acres of mineral rights owned or leased, and the gross book value of land, plant, and equipment by use.

These affiliates also had to provide the name (unless the owner was an individual), country, and industry of the first foreign parent and the ultimate beneficial owner, the affiliate's ownership structure, and the existence of any foreign government ownership of 5 percent or more. Detailed information on transactions and positions between the affiliate and its foreign parent and other members of the foreign parent group was also required. Affiliates not meeting the $20 million criteria but whose assets, sales, or net income were above $1 million had to report a smaller amount of information, and affiliates not meeting the $1 million criterion were required to provide data on assets, sales, and income only.

The results of each benchmark survey are contained in a volume published by the BEA. Highlights of the surveys appear in the *Survey of Current Business*.

The sample surveys include quarterly surveys of balance of payments data. The sample is selected to cover about 90 percent of the universe in value terms. Items from these surveys that are also part of the balance of payments accounts appear in the March, June, September, and December issues of the *Survey of Current Business*. An estimate of the international direct investment position of the United States appears in the June issue, and more detailed estimates of this position as well as balance of payments items appear in the August issue. Selected financial and operating data are surveyed annually; sample coverage is 92 to 93 percent in value terms. Highlights of this survey are also reported in the *Survey of Current Business*, and more detailed information is published in a separate volume.

All US businesses newly acquired or established by foreign owners must be reported to the BEA within 45 days of the transaction; the reporting must include a limited amount of financial and operating data as well as information on the foreign parent, the ultimate beneficial owner, and the cost of the acquisition or establishment. Information from these filings is summarized annually in the *Survey of Current Business*.

Adequacy of the BEA Data

Critics of the BEA have alleged that the agency misses a significant share of FDI; that inconsistencies in the data cast doubt on the validity of the numbers; that not enough information is collected; that there is systematic mismeasurement of the industrial composition of foreign holdings; and that the limits on reporting imposed by the commitment to confidentiality are excessive. We consider each of these criticisms in turn.

Noncompliance

The question of whether substantial foreign holdings of US assets go unreported to the BEA is addressed in chapter 1. Interviews with BEA personnel have convinced us that the BEA does an adequate job of monitoring compliance with the filing requirement of firms meeting the 10 percent ownership criterion. Within the Commerce Department, for example, the International Trade Administration compiles a list of all foreign acquisitions of US enterprises reported in the press; the BEA uses this list to cross-check its filings and follows up wherever it appears that an enterprise that should have filed has not done so. As with many other types of government reporting (e.g., the filing of income tax returns), the accuracy of the information filed with the BEA depends largely on voluntary compliance. That is, although accurate filing is mandatory, the forms are generally not audited unless discrepancies are observed or errors suspected. All forms are reviewed for internal consistency and completeness, and reviews are conducted to ensure consistency across reports and with related data filed elsewhere with the government.

Under a system of "mandatory voluntary" compliance there is always some room for abuse. However, there is little incentive to falsify data on FDI submitted to the BEA, since the information is confidential and cannot be used for investigative or regulatory purposes. We therefore have no reason to believe that any significant degree of misreporting takes place. At any rate, the alternative to mandatory voluntary reporting would be a policing system that could prove oppressive as well as costly.

Inconsistencies

Critics have noted several apparent discrepancies that appear to indicate flaws in the BEA data. Discrepancies have been alleged to occur within the

US data themselves, and data gathered by certain foreign governments relating to their residents' direct investment in the United States have been found not to reconcile with the corresponding US data. For example, Canadian data on Canadian direct investment in the United States show more such investment than do the US data.

We have been able to find no discrepancies within the US data. One reason such discrepancies are perceived is that, as we have noted, analysts often misinterpret the data. Part of the blame for confusion does, however, rest with the BEA. The distinctions between different data series might not be clear to many users of the data, and no layperson's guide to the data exists. Descriptions of methodologies are provided in the benchmark publications and in articles in the *Survey of Current Business*, which has also published articles explaining the differences in the data series. However, these explanations are often quite technical and make for difficult reading for persons not trained in balance of payments or financial accounting. Our understanding is that the BEA is now preparing a written guide to the FDI data aimed at persons with nontechnical backgrounds. We have also found that BEA personnel were quite willing and able to provide us with satisfactory explanations of the data when asked.

The observed cross-national discrepancies partly result from differences in definitions and standards applied. For example, Canada classifies as outward direct investment some holdings that the United States classifies as inward portfolio investment. The BEA reports that it has cross-checked its data on inward FDI from Canada with the data collected by the government of Canada and, after adjusting for differences in definitions and standards, found the two series to be over 95 percent reconcilable.

It would be desirable for all governments to work toward harmonizing their definitions and standards concerning FDI and how it is reported. This would facilitate international comparisons and thus make the task of the researcher much easier. Such a harmonization could be undertaken within the context of the Committee on Investment and Multinational Enterprise of the Organization for Economic Cooperation and Development (OECD), or perhaps through the United Nations Center on Transnational Corporations. Until then, differences in definitions and standards will remain a fact of life with which analysts must live.

Insufficient Information

There are evident limitations on the range of questions that can be answered using BEA data. For example, there is no way to use the data to produce an exact accounting of the sources of growth in the assets of foreign firms. Such data would be useful, but we are assured that it would be close to impossible to collect them. However, the fact that there are useful data not being collected by the BEA does not imply that the BEA data that exist are useless. In fact, as we have shown, the data can be used to get a quite good picture of trends in the US direct investment position. By international standards the US data are actually quite good: a recent report by the British Royal Institute for International Affairs indicates that US data on FDI are more detailed than those published by any of the other Group of Five nations.

One possible approach to improving data collection would be to convene a group of researchers who have used the BEA data, along with BEA personnel themselves, to identify the holes that do exist. The BEA has already convened such a group to examine the information collected on outward FDI. A similar group for inward FDI would be desirable.

Expansion of the BEA's data collection would require augmenting the agency's limited resources. In addition, under the Paperwork Reduction Act, the Office of Management and Budget would have to permit the expansion. Reporting companies would also have to devote additional resources to fulfilling the reporting requirements, and this could adversely affect their willingness to comply. The question that must be asked is whether the marginal value of any additional information is greater than the marginal cost of generating it.

Misclassification

In the BEA's published data series, all investment by any one enterprise is classified by the principal industry of that enterprise. This can cause obvious problems when the activities of the enterprise are in fact diversified across industries. Thus, for example, the US manufacturing operations of certain Japanese automotive firms are classified under the major industry of their US affiliates and therefore listed under wholesale trade rather than manufacturing.

One answer to this problem would be to augment the data on consolidated enterprises with data collected at the "establishment" level—that is, data that pertain to individual facilities within a consolidated enterprise, such as manufacturing plants. Such a compilation is technically possible using raw data already being collected by the Census Bureau. As we have noted, the most recent benchmark survey of inward FDI was postponed for two years precisely to allow cross-referencing of Census and BEA data. Some cross-referencing has already been accomplished on a pilot basis, and efforts are under way to extend this compilation.

Another approach would be for the BEA itself to collect data at the establishment level. In fact, beginning with the 1987 benchmark survey the BEA will have data on sales and employment by industry of sales. These data will approximate data collected at the enterprise level, although the correlation will not be perfect.

There are some legal, budgetary, and possibly bureaucratic problems associated with the effort to link BEA and Census data. We believe, nonetheless, that much potentially important policy analysis depends upon such an effort. For example, comparisons of the relative performance of foreign-controlled and domestically controlled operations in particular industries can be meaningfully accomplished only when this linking is complete. Only then will it be possible to answer such questions as whether US affiliates of Japanese automobile firms achieve higher labor productivities than do domestically controlled operations, and whether foreign-controlled semiconductor manufacturing facilities are mere "screwdriver" (i.e., assembly only) operations compared with US-controlled ones. We therefore commend that the US government attach a high level of priority to this linkage effort, and that legislation be introduced if needed to break legal barriers that might impede its progress. Elements of a bill introduced in Congress by Senator Frank H. Murkowski (R-AK) are designed to do just that.

We also believe that the type of policy analysis we have described will require that industry-specific data be more finely disaggregated than they are at present. In some cases, publication of the disaggregated data might conflict with company-specific confidentiality requirements. We address this matter in the next section.

Limitations Due to Confidentiality

Because of the requirement of confidentiality, company-level data collected by the BEA are not generally available to persons outside the agency either for research or for policy formulation (although consultants to the BEA and contractors performing research for the BEA can have access under some circumstances). This restriction is not arbitrary; confidentiality serves to ensure that the information submitted to the BEA is accurate, because there is little incentive for a reporting enterprise to submit false or inaccurate data. Most policy analysis does not require that researchers or policymakers have access to specific company-level data.

Nonetheless, we believe that the extent of confidentiality presently observed in BEA data gathering is in some respects overdone. We would see no harm, for example, in allowing the reporting firms themselves to decide whether their submissions will be open to the public. In Japan, information on inward direct investment by individual companies is open for public scrutiny unless the company requests that it not be; if the company does so request, its wishes are observed scrupulously. It is also easy to envisage a multitiered level of confidentiality, wherein certain types of company-specific information would be open to the public while more sensitive information would remain closed. These two ideas could be combined: companies could elect which tiers would be open and which closed. Such an arrangement would surely not have a chilling effect on FDI. One could also envisage a time limit on confidentiality, whereby after some specified period company records would become open to the public.

Critics of the BEA also note that its records cannot be scrutinized by high government officials for investigative purposes even in times of national emergency, even though other files normally kept confidential (Internal Revenue Service 1040 forms, for example) can be released to certain officials for emergency national security purposes. There has been no known abuse of these provisions to date. Arguably, the BEA records should also be subject to some sort of national-emergency provision. Such a provision, were it deemed desirable, would require a legislative change.

We have already indicated that linkage of BEA and Census data could make possible some useful policy analysis that cannot now be accomplished. One requirement for meaningful intraindustry comparisons of foreign- and domestically controlled operations will be access to data at a disaggregated level. There is no reason, however, why the researchers must have access to company-specific information. BEA and Census personnel could combine company-specific records into aggregated data files that do not divulge confidential information, and these files could then be provided to the researcher.

This sort of service is already provided by the BEA and the Census Bureau on a limited basis. The researcher must reimburse the agencies for the cost of the data preparation. Some users of this data report that it is difficult and costly to gain access to this type of service. The Census Bureau in particular has been cited as difficult to work with, and there is some feeling that the price charged to users for "customized" data from the Census Bureau is excessive. Since research based on census information is in at least some respects a public good, pricing the service above its marginal cost could be misguided policy. This issue notwithstanding, fruitful research using both BEA and Census data has been accomplished. The present study is an example of research done largely on the basis of data readily available from the BEA and other government sources.

Update for the Third Edition

Since the first edition was published, changes have been made in the way in which BEA and other relevant agencies collect and analyze data on FDI. Here we assess these changes and comment on other developments that have occurred in the interim. We follow the format of the first edition's section titled "Adequacy of the BEA Data," reexamining each of the five criticisms that have been leveled against the BEA and its data collection.

Noncompliance

The BEA now openly admits that there has been some underreporting of new FDI in the United States. This admission was prompted by the fact that in recent years there have been a number of significant errors and omissions in the capital account of the US balance of payments, suggesting that either capital flows in the United States are being understated or that the current account deficit has been overstated. Since the latter seems unlikely, the prime suspect is the former. The BEA believes that most of the likely underreporting falls within accounts other than those for direct investment, but the possibility of errors in the inward direct investment accounts is not ruled out. The most likely reasons for such errors are failure of new investors to file mandatory reports with the BEA or, in some cases, the fact that investors are exempt from the requirements. To correct for this, the BEA now includes in the balance of payments–based data on FDI estimates of delinquent or exempt reporters.

At the same time, the 1987 benchmark survey of FDI in the United States revealed some overreporting of existing stocks of FDI. The reason for this was that some operations once under foreign control had been closed or sold to domestic owners but were still being carried in the data base as under foreign control. The consequent changes in the estimates of FDI stocks are presented in the June 1991 issue of the *Survey of Current Business*.

Certain definitional changes have been introduced into the accounting standards to bring these more in line both with national income and product accounting (NIPA) standards for calculating GNP and its components and with International Monetary Fund standards regarding treatment of royalties and fees. The most significant change in the first category is that the net income of foreign-controlled firms is now reported on a basis consistent with NIPA standards.

An effort has also been made to improve compliance with the mandatory reporting requirements. However, investigation of alleged cases of significant underreporting consistently reveal that noncompliance is not a major problem.

Inconsistencies

In the five years since the first edition was published, we have been able to find no new evidence of inconsistencies in the BEA data. The agency has implemented a number of procedures aimed at preventing inconsistency, for example, using the new data linkage with the Census Bureau (see below) to double-check employment figures. The Census figures, on the basis of a separate and independent reporting, are typically within 1 percent of the BEA figures when account is made of differences in the timing of the reports.

Insufficient Information

Major changes that bear upon this issue are covered in the next section.

Misclassifications

In the fall of 1990 Congress passed and President Bush signed into law the Foreign Direct Investment and International Financial Data Improvements Act, which, inter alia, permits the data linkage between the BEA and the Bureau of the Census recommended in the original version of this appendix. This law was a synthesis of bills introduced separately by Senator J. James Exon (D-NE) and Representatives Philip R. Sharp (D-IN) and Norman F. Lent (R-NY). We are gratified to note that the first edition of this book was cited in the letter circulated to House members announcing the introduction of the Sharp bill. The new law also enables data sharing with the Bureau of Labor Statistics, the statistical division of the US Department of Labor. The first effort was to create a data series on employment in foreign affiliates by industry of establishment. Later efforts have produced series for other operating data of the sort presented in chapter 3 of this book. Data for these series have been created only back to 1987, and hence time series analysis is presently limited to this relatively short eight-year period. However, with the passage of time this time line will grow, and such analyses will become more robust.

Some conclusions about the behavior of foreign-owned affiliates are already made possible by the new operating data resulting from the data interlinkage. For example, in the manufacturing sector, the data show that foreign-owned firms operate larger plants on average than their US-owned counterparts. This conclusion holds even after adjusting for industry mix; that is, the result is not an artifact of foreign-owned plants being concentrated in industries with larger than average plants overall.

The operations of foreign-owned firms are of greater capital intensity, exhibit higher average labor productivity, and pay higher hourly wages than their US counterparts. However, all three of these findings do seem largely to be the result of industry mix; that is, foreign-owned plants are concentrated in industries where capital intensity, productivity, and wages are higher than in the manufacturing sector overall. After adjusting for this factor, the differences between foreign-owned and US-owned establishments largely disappear.

The BEA has also released data on employment in foreign affiliates by industry of sales. This series, as we explained in the first edition, is useful because it helps to eliminate industry classification distortions present in the data series classified by industry of affiliate. We used the new series, for example, in the second edition to confirm something we had suspected (but were unable to confirm) in the first edition, namely, that the relative underrepresentation of Japanese FDI in manufacturing was more an artifact of the method of industry classification than a real phenomenon. We reconfirm that finding in this edition (see chapter 1).

A further criticism of BEA data has been that the numbers are very slow in being released. We find that the overall problem persists, although the main problem we identified in earlier editions—the very slow release of data on the gross product (value added) of affiliates under foreign control—has been corrected. These very useful data are now released at the same time as other operating data. But the release of the operating data themselves remains slow. Officials of the BEA inform us that the main problem lies with the reporting firms, whose mandatory submissions to the BEA are often incomplete or inaccurate. The BEA follows up with each firm whose report is missing requested data or contains discernibly inaccurate data, and the whole process takes time. Because the reporting companies and not the agency are responsible for most of the delay, BEA officials do not believe that the process could be significantly speeded up by allocating more resources to the task.

There are a number of other efforts under way to improve the data available on FDI. These include a reworking of BEA's reports, both in the *Survey of Current Business* and in the separately published volumes, to make them less descriptive and more analytical. Mainframe computers have been replaced with a more user-friendly, personal computer–based local area network, used for both data storage and analysis. The data bases themselves have been made more user-friendly by making them compatible with software used widely in PC applications. Some data from the data linkage effort are now available on the Census Bureau's longitudinal data base, which should enable researchers to track the sources of growth of FDI more accurately.

The Census Bureau is in the process of creating a data base from Customs data that will allow researchers to track the establishment (i.e., individual plant) to which imports are destined or from which exports originate. In the past it has been possible only to determine which port the products were exported from or imported through. The new data base will enable much more precise analysis of the import and export activities of all firms in the United States. It is planned to link this data base with the BEA's FDI data, so that much more precise analysis can be done of the import and export activities of foreign-owned firms.

Problem areas persist. Outside researchers still have limited access to BEA data, although more researchers have been accommodated in recent years than in the past. The BEA claims its limited resources are the major reason it cannot satisfy all requests. Also, confidentiality requirements still require that certain data at the level of individual industries not be disclosed, but for employment data the agency now provides data ranges rather than completely suppressing the information.

Overall, we find that the data generation activities of the US government have improved markedly since the first edition of this book appeared. There is more to be done, to be sure, but things seem to be on track.

Industrial-Organization Explanations of Foreign Direct Investment

In this appendix we survey some of the main themes that fall into the general category of industrial-organization explanations of foreign direct investment. Some of these are based upon the classical theory of industrial organization, whereas others are based on newer, game-theoretic approaches. This appendix is not meant to be an exhaustive review of the relevant literature. The interested reader is referred to the sources listed in the bibliography for more complete reviews of the literature. Perhaps the most detailed review is provided in Caves (1982), although this reference does not cover work done during recent years. An excellent and up-to-date, but shorter and less comprehensive survey is provided in Cantwell (1991).

Generally, industrial-organization theories of FDI can be divided into two categories: those that focus on the internal characteristics of multinational firms, and those that focus on rivalry among such firms. A number of theories rely on arguments from both categories, and hence the two categories are not wholly disjoint. Nonetheless, they do provide some basis for a taxonomical treatment of the subject.

Internal Characteristics

The work most often cited as seminal in creating this basis is the 1959 doctoral dissertation of Stephen Hymer, published posthumously in 1976. Hymer first articulated the now widely accepted notion that a firm whose operations cross national boundaries faces costs that a firm whose operations are limited to one nation does not. These extra costs include those of managing geographically widespread operations and those of dealing with different languages, cultures, technical standards, and customer preferences. Hymer argued that for a firm to overcome the handicaps posed by these extra costs, it must possess internal, firm-specific advantages over its rivals. He speculated that these advantages largely took the form of economies of scale or of superior product technology.

A second very influential early work was that by John Dunning (1958). This work was largely empirical in nature. Dunning examined manufacturing operations in the United Kingdom controlled by US–based firms. He found that these operations generally paid higher wages and were characterized by higher rates of labor productivity and new product innovation than their UK–controlled rivals. Dunning's work, although done quite independently of that of Hymer, seemed to confirm many of Hymer's speculations.

Much of the work since Hymer and Dunning has attempted to pin down the firm-specific advantages that drive FDI. Aharoni (1966) noted the importance of imperfect information about markets as a determinant of FDI flows; Vernon (1968, 1974) pointed out the linkage between the product cycle in technology and the shift from exports to direct investment among US firms; Kindleberger (1969) noted the role of firm-specific advantages other than technology, such as organizational and marketing skills. Caves (1971) summarized these developments by noting that the advantages possessed by multinational enterprises can include any of a number of intangible assets, including organizational and marketing skills and product and process technologies.

Buckley and Casson (1976) suggested a still broader interpretation of the motivations for FDI that has since become more or less the standard point of departure. They observed that for the multinational enterprise to service non-home-nation markets via direct investment rather than alternative modes of doing business (e.g., exporting or licensing) there must exist some "internalization" advantage for the firm to do so. That is, there must be economies associated with a firm exploiting a market opportunity through internal operations rather than through arm's-length transactions such as the sale of rights to the firm's intangible assets to other firms. These economies might be associated with costs (including opportunity costs) of contract enforcement or maintenance of quality or other standards. Buckley and Casson noted that, where these costs are absent, firms very often do use licensing or franchising as a means of serving international markets. For example, Coca-Cola franchises the right to market its products in many nations where contract enforcement is not a problem, but the firm directly controls operations in nations where enforcement is a problem.

Dunning (1988) has emphasized that the advantages of internalization must interact with both firm-specific advanatages and locational advantages to explain FDI. He also suggests that the reasons for FDI are diverse and thus that no one theory can account for all such investment.

The effort to define the advantages of internalization is ultimately part of the theory of why firms exist. This effort has generated a large literature, which is surveyed by Rugman (1986).

More recent developments have been the attempt to embed theories of FDI in formal models of international trade (see, for example, Helpman and Krugman 1985) and technological accumulation theory. The latter postulates that firms have different technological histories, which may critically influence the ability of an individual firm to apply a new technology. This theory helps explain why, for example, a small high-technology firm seeking to be acquired can have greater value to one acquiring firm than to another. This, in turn, can explain why in some cases foreign investors are apparently willing to pay premium prices for such acquisitions (see Cantwell 1990 for details of this theory).

Intraindustry Rivalry

The possibility that rivalry among firms operating in the same industry, but not necessarily in the same country or countries, can affect FDI behavior was suggested by Hymer both in his doctoral dissertation and in some later work (see, e.g. Hymer and Rowthorne 1970). To some extent rivalry drives FDI in Raymond Vernon's work (e.g., 1968) as well. The same idea appears in an influential book by Seev Hirsch (1967).

Knickerbocker (1973) noted a "follow the leader" pattern in the timing of FDI by US firms. He interpreted this phenomenon as a rational response to oligopolistic rivalry. Other studies have detected similar patterns in the overseas activities of non–US firms (Flowers 1976). Also, detailed studies of certain industries have confirmed Knickerbocker's findings for US firms (e.g., Yu and Ito 1988). Finally, Graham (1978, 1990) suggests that intraindustry FDI may take place as an "exchange of threat," in which firms invade each others' home markets as part of an oligopolistic rivalry. This model is similar in construction to the "reciprocal dumping models" that have characterized recent strategic trade theory (see, e.g., Brander and Krugman 1983 and Krugman 1990b).

References

Aharoni, Yair. 1966. *The Foreign Investment Decision Process*. Boston: Harvard University Graduate School of Business Administration.

Anderson, Jack. 1989. "Is America For Sale?" *Parade* (16 April).

Bacow, Lawrence. 1987. "Understanding Foreign Investment in Real Estate." *Working Papers* 12. Cambridge, MA: Massachusetts Institute of Technology Center for Real Estate Development.

Bacow, Lawrence. 1988. "The Internationalization of the U.S. Real Estate Industry." *Working Papers* 16. Cambridge, MA: Massachusetts Institute of Technology Center for Real Estate Development.

Becker, Michael. 1989. *Myths About Foreign Investment*. Washington: Citizens for a Sound Economy Foundation.

Bergsten, C. Fred. 1974. "Coming Investment Wars?" *Foreign Affairs* 53 (October):135–52.

Bergsten, C. Fred, and Edward M. Graham. *The Globalization of Industry and National Governments*. Washington: Institute for International Economics (forthcoming).

Bergsten, C. Fred, Thomas Horst, and Theodore H. Moran. 1978. *American Multinationals and American Interests*. Washington: Brookings Institution.

Bob, Daniel E. 1990. *Japanese Companies in American Communities*. New York: The Japan Society.

Brander, James A., and Barbara J. Spencer. 1985. "Export Subsidies and Market Share Rivalry." *Journal of International Economics* 18, no. 1/2 (February):83–100.

Brecher, Richard A., and Carlos F. Díaz-Alejandro. 1977. "Tariffs, Foreign Capital, and Immiserizing Growth." *Journal of International Economics* 7, no. 4 (November):317–22.

Buckley, Peter J., and Mark C. Casson. 1976. *The Future of Multinational Enterprise*. London: Macmillan.

Burstein, Daniel. 1988. *Yen: Japan's New Financial Empire and Its Threat to America*. New York: Simon and Schuster.

Cantwell, John. 1989. *Technological Innovation and Multinational Corporations*. London: Blackwell.

Cantwell, John, ed. 1992. *Multinational Investment and Modern Europe: Strategic Interaction in the Integrated Communit*. Aldershot, UK: Edward Elgar.

Carter, Barry E. 1988. *International Economic Sanctions: Improving the Haphazard U.S. Legal Regime.* Cambridge, England: Cambridge University Press.

Caves, Richard E. 1971. "International Corporations: The Industrial Economics of Foreign Investment." *Economica* 38, no. 141:1–27.

Caves, Richard E. 1982. *Multinational Enterprise and Economic Analysis.* Cambridge, England: Cambridge University Press.

Cline, William R. 1989. *United States External Adjustment and the World Economy.* Washington: Institute for International Economics.

Dalton, Donald H., and Manuel G. Serapio, Jr. 1993. *U.S. Research Facilities of Foreign Companies.* Washington: US Department of Commerce.

Dunning, John H. 1958. *American Investment in British Manufacturing Industry.* London: George Allen & Unwin.

Dunning, John H. 1988. "The Eclectic Paradigm of International Production: A Restatement and Some Possible Extensions." *Journal of International Business Studies* 19, no. 1:1–31.

Eckhouse, John. 1991. "Japan Firms Reportedly Stalled US War Supplies." *San Francisco Chronicle* (30 April): A1.

Eisner, Robert, and Paul J. Piper. 1991. "Real Foreign Investment in Perspective." *Annals of the American Academy of Political and Social Science* 516:22–35.

Emmott, Bill. 1994. *Japanophobia: Myth of the Invincible Japanese.* New York: Times Books.

Encarnation, Dennis. 1992. *Rivals Beyond Trade: America versus Japan in Global Competition.* Ithaca, NY: Cornell University Press.

Flowers, Ed B. 1976. "Oligopolistic Reactions in European and Canadian Direct Investment in the United States." *Journal of International Business Studies* 7, no. 3:43–55.

Forbes, Malcolm S. 1988. "Before Japan Buys Too Much of the U.S.A." *Forbes* (25 January): 17.

Frankel, Jeffrey A. 1992. "Japanese Finance: A Survey." In Paul R. Krugman, *The United States and Japan: Trade and Investment in the 1990s.* Cambridge, MA: National Bureau of Economic Research.

Frankel, Jeffrey A. 1993. "The Evolving Japanese Financial System and the Cost of Capital." In Ingo Walton and Tahato Hirahi, *Restructuring Japan's Financial Markets.* Homewood, IL: Business One Irwin.

Franko, Lawrence G. 1976. *The European Multinationals.* London: Harper and Row.

Frantz, Douglas, and Catherine Collins. 1989. *Selling Out: How We Are Letting Japan Buy Our Land, Our Industries, Our Financial Institutions, and Our Future.* Chicago: Contemporary Books.

Froot, Kenneth, and Jeremy C. Stein. 1991. "Exchange Rates and Foreign Direct Investment: An Imperfect Capital Markets Approach." *Quarterly Journal of Economics* 106: 1191–1217

Gastner, Robin. 1992. "Protectionism with Purpose: Guiding Foreign Investment." *Foreign Policy* 88: 91–106.

Gittelman, Michelle, and John H. Dunning. 1990. "Japanese Multinationals in Europe and the United States: Exporting Cars, Computers, and Comparative Advantage Through Foreign Direct Investment." Paper prepared for a conference at the American Institute for Contemporary German Studies, Washington (4 September).

Gittelman, Michelle, and Edward M. Graham. 1994. "The Performance and Structure of Japanese Affiliates in the European Community." In Mark Mason and Dennis Encarnation, *Does Ownership Matter? Japanese Multinationals in Europe.* Oxford and New York: Oxford University Press.

Glickman, Norman, and Douglas Woodward. 1989. *The New Competitors: How Foreign Investors Are Changing the U.S. Economy.* New York: Basic Books.

Goldfinger, Nat. 1971. "A Labor View of Foreign Investment and Trade Issues." In Commission on International Trade and Investment Policy, *United States International Economic Policy in an Interdependent World.* Washington: Government Printing Office.

Graham, Edward M. 1978. "Transatlantic Investment by Multinational Firms: A Rivalistic Phenomenon?" *Journal of Post Keynesian Economics* 1, no. 1:82–99.

Graham, Edward M. 1989. "Strategic Interaction Among Multinational Firms and International Direct Investment." In C. N. Pitelis and R. Sugden, *The Nature of the Transnational Firm*. London: Routledge, Chapman and Hall.

Graham, Edward M. 1992a. "Government Policies Towards Inward Foreign Direct Investment: Effects on Producers and Consumers." In P. J. Buckley and M. C. Casson, *Multinational Enterprises in the World Economy: Essays in Honor of John Dunning*. Cheltenham, United Kingdom: Edward Elgar.

Graham, Edward M. 1992b. "Japanese Control of R&D Activities in the United States: Is This Cause for Concern?" In Thomas S. Arrison, C. Fred Bergsten, Edward M. Graham, and Martha C. Harris, *Japan's Growing Technological Capability: Implications for the U.S. Economy*. Washington: National Research Council.

Graham, Edward M. 1994. "What Can the Theory of Foreign Direct Investment Tell Us About the Low Level of Foreign Firm Participation in the Japanese Economy?" Paper presented at the Wharton School, University of Pennsylvania (7 October).

Graham, Edward M., and Michael E. Ebert. 1991. "Foreign Direct Investment and National Security: Fixing the Exon-Florio Process." *The World Economy* 14, no. 3 (September).

Graham, Edward M., and Paul R. Krugman. 1990. "Trade-Related Investment Measures." In Jeffrey J. Schott, *Completing the Uruguay Round: A Results-Oriented Approach to the GATT Trade Negotiations*. Washington: Institute for International Economics.

Grubert, Harry, Timothy Goodspeed, and Deborah Swenson. 1991. "Explaining the Low Taxable Income of Foreign-Controlled Companies in the United States." Paper presented at a conference at the National Bureau of Economic Research, Cambridge, MA (August).

Haber, L. F. 1971. *The Chemical Industry, 1900–1930*. Oxford, England: Oxford University Press.

Hastings, Max. 1984. *Overlord and the Battle for Normandy*. New York: Simon and Schuster.

Helpman, Elhanan, and Paul R. Krugman. 1985. *Market Structure and Foreign Trade*. Cambridge, MA: MIT Press.

Helpman, Elhanan, and Paul R. Krugman. 1989. *Trade Policy and Market Structure*. Cambridge, MA: MIT Press.

Hirsch, Seev. 1967. *Location of Industry and International Competitiveness*. Oxford, England: Oxford University Press.

Hooper, Peter, and Catherine L. Mann. 1987. *The U.S. External Deficit: Its Causes and Persistence*. International Finance Discussion Papers 316. Washington: Board of Governors of the Federal Reserve (November).

Hufbauer, G. C., and F. M. Adler. 1968. *Overseas Manufacturing Investment and the Balance of Payments*. US Department of the Treasury Tax Policy Research Studies 1. Washington: Government Printing Office.

Hufbauer, Gary Clyde, and Kimberly Ann Elliott. 1994. *Measuring the Costs of Protection in the United States*. Washington: Institute for International Economics.

Hufbauer, Gary Clyde, assisted by Joanna M. van Rooij. 1992. *U.S. Taxation of International Income: Blueprint for Reform*. Washington: Institute for International Economics.

Hufbauer, Gary Clyde, Jeffrey J. Schott, and Kimberly Ann Elliott. 1990. *Economic Sanctions Reconsidered*, 2nd ed. Washington: Institute for International Economics.

Hull, Cordell. 1948. *Memoirs* (2 vols.). New York: Macmillan.

Hymer, Stephen H. 1976. *The International Operations of National Firms*. Cambridge, MA: MIT Press (originally Ph.D. dissertation, Massachusetts Institute of Technology, accepted 1959).

Hymer, Stephen H., and Robert Rowthorne. 1970. "Multinational Firms and International Oligopoly: The Non-American Challenge." In Charles P. Kindleberger, *The International Corporation: A Symposium*. Cambridge, MA: MIT Press.

Industry Canada. 1994. *Investment Barriers in the G-7 Nations*. Ottawa: Industry Canada.

Jackson, John H. 1977. *Legal Problems of International Economic Relations*. St Paul, MN: West.

Jackson, James K. 1987. *Japan: Increasing Investment in the United States*. Report #87-747E. Washington: Congressional Research Service.

Jahnke, Art. 1989. "Six Flags Over Boston." *Boston* (May).

Julius, DeAnne. 1990. *Global Companies and Public Policy*. London: Royal Institute for International Affairs, and New York: Council on Foreign Relations Press.

Julius, DeAnne, and Stephen Thomsen. 1988. "Foreign-owned Firms, Trade, and Economic Integration." In *Tokyo Club Papers* 2. London: Royal Institute for International Affairs.

Kester, W. C., and P. Luehrman. 1991. "Cross-Country Differences in the Cost of Capital: A Survey and Evaluation of Recent Empirical Studies." *Working Paper* 92-011. Boston: Harvard Business School (August).

Kindleberger, Charles P. 1969. *American Business Abroad: Six Lectures on Foreign Direct Investment*. New Haven, CT: Yale University Press.

Klein, Michael W., and Eric Rosengren. 1994. "Determinants of Foreign Direct Investment in the United States." Medford, MA: Fletcher School of Law and Dipomacy, Tufts University (photocopy).

Knickerbocker, Frederick T. 1973. *Oligopolistic Reaction and Multinational Enterprise*. Boston: Harvard University Graduate School of Business Administration.

Krugman, Paul R. 1990. *The Age of Diminished Expectations: U.S. Economic Policy in the 1990s*. Cambridge, MA: MIT Press.

Lawrence, Robert Z. 1990. *Foreign Affiliated Automakers in the United States*. Washington: author.

Lewis, Jordan D. 1982. "Technology, Enterprise, and American Economic Growth." *Science* 215:1204–11.

Lipsey, Robert E. 1991. "Foreign Direct Investment in the United States and US Trade." *Annals of the American Academy of Political and Social Science* 516:76–90.

Long, William F., and David J. Ravenscroft. 1994. "Financial Performance of Cross-Border Acquisitions." Paper presented at a conference of the Strategic Management Society, Paris, September.

Magaziner, Ira C., and Robert B. Reich. 1982. *Minding America's Business: The Decline and Rise of the American Economy*. New York: Vintage.

Mann, Catherine L. 1989. *Determinants of Japanese Direct Investment in U.S. Manufacturing Industries*. International Finance Discussion Papers 362. Washington: Board of Governors of the Federal Reserve System (September).

Mason, Mark. 1992. *American Multinationals and Japan: The Political Economy of Japanese Capital Controls 1899–1990*. Cambridge, MA: Harvard University Press.

Mason, Mark, and Dennis Encarnation. 1994. *Does Ownership Matter? Japanese Multinationals in Europe*. Oxford and New York: Oxford University Press.

McCulloch, Rachel. 1991. "Why Foreign Corporations Are Buying into US Business." *Annals of the American Academy of Political and Social Science* 516:169–82.

Ministry of International Trade and Industry, Government of Japan. 1990. *Third Basic Survey on Japanese Business Activities Abroad* (in Japanese). Tokyo: Ministry of International Trade and Industry.

Ministry of International Trade and Industry, Government of Japan. 1994. *White Paper on International Trade*. Tokyo: Ministry of International Trade and Industry.

Moran, Theodore H. 1990. "The Globalization of the Defense Industry." *International Security* 15 (Summer):57–100.

Moran, Theodore H. 1993. *American Economic Policy and National Security*. New York: Council on Foreign Relations.

Moran, Theodore H., and Charles S. Pearson. 1988. "Tread Carefully in the Field of TRIP Measures." *The World Economy* 11, no. 1, 119–34.

Morgan Guaranty Trust Company. 1989. "Foreign Direct Investment in the United States." *World Financial Markets* 2 (29 June):1–11.

Mundell, Robert. 1987. "A New Deal on Exchange Rates." Paper presented at the Japan–United States Symposium on Exchange Rates and Macroeconomics, Tokyo (29–30 January).

Niskanen, William A. 1991. "The Determinants of U.S. Capital Imports." *Annals of the American Academy of Political and Social Science* 516:36–49.

Nomura Research Institute. 1989. *Nomura Medium-Term Outlook for Japan and the World.* Tokyo: Nomura Research Institute.

Office of Industrial Resource Allocation, International Trade Administration, US Department of Commerce. 1984. *The Defense Priorities and Allocations System.* Washington: Government Printing Office.

Organization for Economic Cooperation and Development. 1987. *Controls and Impediments Affecting Inward Direct Investment in OECD Member Countries.* Paris: Organization for Economic Cooperation and Development.

Orr, James. 1990. *Foreign Direct Investment in U.S. Manufacturing: Effects on the Trade Balance.* Working Papers 9032. New York: Federal Reserve Bank of New York.

Peterson, Peter G. 1989. "Japanese Mergers and Acquisitions in the United States: The Deals and the Dealmakers." Paper presented at a conference of the same name sponsored by the Japan Society, New York (13 July).

Prestowitz, Clyde V., Jr. 1988. *Trading Places: How We Allowed the Japanese to Take the Lead.* New York: Basic Books.

Reich, Robert B. 1990. "Who Is Us?" *Harvard Business Review* (January-February).

Reich, Robert B. 1991. "Who Is 'Them'?" *Harvard Business Review* (March-April): 77–88.

Rohatyn, Felix. 1989. "America's Economic Dependence." *Foreign Affairs* 68, no. 1:53–65.

Rugman, Alan M. 1986. "New Theories of Multinational Enterprises: An Assessment of Internalisation Theory." *Bulletin of Economic Research* 38, no. 2 (May):101–18.

Scholes, Myron, and Mark Wolfson. 1988. "The Effects of Changes in Tax Laws on Corporate Reorganization Activity." Stanford, CA: Stanford University (mimeographed).

Shapiro, Carl, and Joseph E. Stiglitz. 1984. "Equilibrium Unemployment as a Worker Discipline Device." *American Economic Review* 74, no. 3 (June):433–44.

Slemrod, Joel. 1989. "Tax Effects on Foreign Direct Investment in the U.S: Evidence from a Cross-Country Comparison." Paper presented at the National Bureau of Economic Research Conference on International Aspects of Taxation, Cambridge, MA (February). Spencer, Linda M. 1988. *American Assets: An Examination of Foreign Investment in the United States.* Arlington, VA: Congressional Economic Leadership Institute.

Spencer, Linda M. 1991. *Foreign Investment in the United States: Unencumbered Access.* Washington: Economic Strategy Institute.

Stekler, Lois E., and Guy V. G. Stevens. 1991. *The Adequacy of US Direct Investment Data.* International Finance Discussion Papers 401. Washington: Board of Governors of the Federal Reserve System (June).

Swenson, Deborah L. 1991. "The Determinants of FDI in the United States." Unpublished doctoral dissertation, Massachusetts Institute of Technology.

Tanzi, Vito, and Isaias Coelho. 1991. "Barriers to Foreign Investment in the U.S. and Other Nations." *Annals of the American Academy of Political and Social Science* 516:154–68.

Terrell, Henry S., Robert S. Dohner, and Barbara Lowrey. 1989. *The U.S. and U.K. Activities of Japanese Banks.* International Finance Discussion Papers 316. Washington: Board of Governors of the Federal Reserve System (September).

Thomsen, Stephen, and Phedon Nicolaides. 1991. *The Evolution of Japanese Direct Investment in Europe.* New York: Harvester Wheatsheaf.

Thomsen, Stephen, and Stephen Woolcock. 1993. *Direct Investment and European Integration.* London: Royal Institute for International Affairs.

Tolchin, Martin, and Susan Tolchin. 1988. *Buying Into America: How Foreign Money Is Changing the Face of Our Nation.* New York: Times Books.

Ulan, Michael. 1991. "Should the U.S. Restrict Foreign Investment?" *Annals of the American Academy of Political and Social Science* 516:117–25.

Ulan, Michael, and William G. Dewald. 1989. "The U.S. Net International Investment Position: Misstated and Misunderstood." In James A. Dorn and William A. Niskanen, *Dollars, Deficits, and Trade.* Boston: Kluwer Academic Publishers.

United Nations Centre on Transnational Corporations. 1991. *World Investment Report: The Triad in Foreign Direct Investment.* New York: United Nations.

US Congress. House. Committee on Banking, Finance, and Urban Affairs. 1991. *Banca Nazionale del Lavoro Scandal,* hearings, 102nd Cong., 1st sess.

US Congress. House. Committee on Strategic and Military Affairs. 1939. *Strategic and Critical Raw Materials,* hearings, 76th Cong., 1st sess.

US Congress. Joint Economic Committee. 1981. *International Competition in Advanced Industrial Sectors: Trade and Development in the Semiconductor Industry.* Report prepared by Michael Borrus, James Millstein, and John Zysman, 97th Cong., 2nd sess.

US Congress. Office of Technology Assessment. *Multinationals and the US Technology Base.* OTA-JTE-612. Washington: Government Printing Office.

US Congress. Senate. Committee on Military Affairs. 1944. *Economic and Political Aspects of International Cartels.* Report prepared by Corwin Edwards, Subcommittee on War Mobilization Monographs 1, 78th Cong., 2nd sess.

US Congress. Senate. Special Committee Investigating Petroleum Resources. 1946. *American Petroleum Interests in Foreign Countries,* hearings, 79th Cong., 1st sess.

US Department of the Treasury. 1988. "Survey of G-7 Laws and Regulations on Foreign Direct Investment." Washington: US Department of the Treasury (internal memorandum available on request from the Office of Foreign Investment).

US Department of the Treasury. 1991. "31 CFR Part 800: Regulations Pertaining to Mergers, Acquisitions, and Takeovers by Foreign Persons: Final Rule." *Federal Register* 56, no. 225 (21 November): 58774–88.

US General Accounting Office. 1988. *Foreign Investment: Growing Japanese Presence in U.S. Auto Industry* (GAO/NSIAD-88-111, March). Washington: Government Printing Office.

US General Accounting Office. 1991. *Foreign Investment: Concerns in the U.S. Real Estate Sector During the 1980s* (GAO/NSIAD-91-140, June). Washington: Government Printing Office.

Vernon, Raymond. 1966. "International Investment and International Trade in the Product Cycle." *Quarterly Journal of Economics* 83, no. 1:190–207.

Vernon, Raymond. 1971. "Multinational Enterprise and National Security." *Adelphi Papers* 74. London: Institute for Strategic Studies.

Vernon, Raymond. 1974. "The Location of Economic Activity." In John H. Dunning, *Economic Analysis and the Multinational Enterprise.* London: George Allen & Unwin.

Wakasugi, Ryuhei. 1994. "Why Is FDI in Japan so Small? An Examination of the Entry of Foreign Firms into Japan." Paper presented at the 21st Pacific Trade and Development Conference, Hong Kong (1–3 June).

Warner, Mark A. A., and Alan M. Rugman. 1994. "Competitiveness: An Emerging Strategy of Discrimination in U.S. Antitrust and R.P.D. Policy?" *Law and Policy in International Business* 25:945–82.

Wilkins, Mira. 1970. *The Emergence of Multinational Enterprise: American Business Abroad from the Colonial Era to 1914.* Cambridge, MA: Harvard University Press.

Wilkins, Mira. 1974. *The Maturing of Multinational Enterprise: American Business Abroad from 1914 to 1970.* Cambridge, MA: Harvard University Press.

Wilkins, Mira. 1989. *The History of Foreign Investment in the United States.* Cambridge, MA: Harvard University Press.

Wilkins, Mira, and Frank Earnest Hill. 1964. *American Business Abroad: Ford on Six Continents.* Detroit: Wayne State University Press.

Womack, James P., Daniel T. Jones, and Daniel Roos. 1990. *The Machine That Changed the World.* Greenwich, CT: Rawson Associates.

Yu, Chwo-Ming J., and Kiyohiko Ito. 1988. "Oligopolistic Reaction and Foreign Direct Investment: The Case of the U.S. Tire and Textile Industries." *Journal of International Business Studies* 19, no. 3:449–60.

Zilg, Gerard C. 1974. *Du Pont: Behind the Nylon Curtain.* Englewood Cliffs, NJ: Prentice-Hall.

Index

data-linking exercise of, 6, 71, 133, 153, 185–86
disclosure requirements of, 11, 29–30, 180, 183, 187–88
incompleteness of data of, 184–85
methods of data collection of, 181–83
misclassifications in data of, 185–86
role in government information gathering of, 132–33, 179–80
slowness in releasing data of, 189–90
types of data of, 181
Bureau of Labor Statistics, 133, 153, 189
Bureau of the Census, 133, 153, 187, 189, 190
Bush, George, and administration of, 107, 156, 166
Business cycle, impact on FDI flows of, 50–51

California, 142–44
Canada, 21–22, 44, 135–37, 139, 144–45, 184
Capital-intensive industries, concentration of FDI in, 19, 20, 71
Capital structure of foreign affiliates, 10, 11
Casson, Mark C., 192
Caves, Richard E., 191, 192
Census Bureau, US, 133, 153, 187, 189, 190
Chemical industry, 75, 103. *See also names of companies*
China National Aero-Technology Import and Export Corporation, 129
Classification and measurement problems, 7–11, 68, 75, 77, 185–86, 189
Cline, William R., 70
Clinton, Bill, and administration of
    policy on outward US FDI of, 140
    policy toward foreign participation in defense contracting of, 114, 117
    promise to limit transfer pricing abuses of, 82
    role of CFIUS under, 132
    R&D policy of, 73, 86, 167–68
Code of Liberalization of Capital Movements (OECD), 134
Code of Liberalization of Current Invisible Operations (OECD), 134
Colgate-Palmolive Company, 143
Collins amendment, 125
Collins, Rep. Cardiss, 130
Collins, Rep. Michael, 125
Color televisions, 51–53, 79
Commerce, US Department of, 9. *See also* Bureau of the Census; Bureau of Economic Analysis
Committee on Capital Movements and Invisible Transactions (OECD), 135
Committee on Foreign Investment in the United States (CFIUS), 127–32, 156, 161
Committee on International Investment and Multinational Enterprise (OECD), 135, 144, 184

Communications Satellite Corporation (COMSAT), 123
Compensation. *See* Wages paid by foreign affiliates
Compliance with US disclosure requirements, 11, 29–30, 180, 183, 187–88
Compulsory direct investment, 104, 165–66
Compulsory licensing, 104, 164–65
Conditional national treatment. *See* Reciprocity,
Confidentiality of BEA data, 10, 133, 152, 180, 186–87, 190
Consortia, R&D, participation of foreign affiliates in, 124, 162–63, 168
Consultative framework, in proposed international investment accord, 173
Container Corporation of America v. Franchise Tax Board, 142
Control of assets, problems in determining, 9–11
Convergence of United States toward "normal" levels of FDI, 31–32, 55
Cost-benefit analysis of FDI policy, 86–88
Cost-of-capital explanation of FDI, 3, 36–38
Costello, Robert B., 165
Costs, economic, of FDI, 59–67
Critical technologies lists, 167
Current account deficit, US, FDI inflows and, 3, 20, 33, 38, 54, 55, 80

Data collection and analysis. *See* Bureau of Economic Analysis, *names of other agencies*
Data-linking exercise, interagency, 6, 71, 133, 153, 185–86, 188, 189
Debt, US, relation to FDI inflows of, 38–39. *See also* Current account deficit, US, FDI inflows and
Decline, relative US economic, role of FDI in, 41–42
Defense contracting
    Clinton administration policy on, 114, 117
    need to avoid foreign monopoly in, 104, 111, 120, 163, 165
    participation of foreign affiliates in, 111–20
    proposals for reform of, 162–69
Defense conversion, 124
Defense industrial base, shrinkage of, 5, 112–19, 162
Defense Production Act of 1950, 105–06, 126, 165
Defense Science Board, 104, 108
Defense, US Department of, 108, 109, 162
Dexcel, 118
Dingell, John D., 7
Disclosure by foreign affiliates
    compliance problems in, 11, 29–30, 183, 187–88
    national security considerations in, 108–10
    proposed amendment on (Bryant amendment), 7, 108, 152–54, 172

Ministry of International Trade and Industry (MITI), 118

Misclassification of FDI. *See* Bureau of Economic Analysis; Measurement and classification problems,

MIT Center for Real Estate Development, 31

Mitsubishi Estate Co., 31

Mobil Corp., 101

Monopolies and Mergers Commission (UK), 146, 164

Monopoly, need to avoid foreign, in key defense technologies, 104, 111, 120, 163, 165. *See also* Antitrust

Monsanto Company, 129, 161, 165

Motorola, Inc., 52, 169

Multinational firms. *See also* Foreign affiliates
  alleged tendency to hold back newest technologies of, 119–20
  and bargaining power of US labor, 60
  as facilitating device for trade, 58
  internal characteristics of, 191–93
  location of R&D operations by, 66
  political influence of, 88–90
  problems in determining nationality of, 8–9
  reasons for engaging in FDI of, 3, 36–38, 58, 79–80, 191–93
  taxation of, 47–49, 83, 142–44

Mundell, Robert, 80

Murkowski, Frank H., 186

National Association of Realtors, 30

"National champion," promotion of, 167

National Competitiveness Act, 125

National Cooperative Productions Act, 124

National emergencies, restrictions on FDI in, 96–111

National Emergencies Act of 1975, 107

National security. *See also* Defense contracting
  antitrust and, 163
  blockage of foreign acquisitions for purposes of, 126–32
  breaking of parent-subsidiary links as threat to, 103–04, 110
  compulsory licensing of activities critical to, 164–65
  erosion of defense industrial base as threat to, 115–19
  FDI as potential fifth-column threat to, 98–102
  investment incentives for activities vital to, 163
  mandatory foreign investment for purposes of, 165–67
  performance requirements for purposes of, 105, 163, 165, 167
  policy toward FDI during war or national emergency, 105–11
  promotion of "national champion" for purposes of, 167

proscribing foreign control for reasons of, 112–15

National treatment. *See also* Reciprocity
  definition of, 93, 122
  in proposed international investment accord, 171
  in taxation, 142–44
  US advocacy of, 93
  under US-Canada Free Trade Agreement, 135
  for US outward FDI, 134

National Treatment Instrument (OECD), 135

Nationality of a firm, determining, 8–9

Net US international investment position, 13, 39, 41

Netherlands, 21–22, 44

Netherlands Antilles, 96

Neutrality of US policy toward FDI, 93, 122, 134, 146, 154

New York Convention on Recognition and Enforcement of Arbitral Rewards, 137

Nippon Sanso, 130

Nissan Motor Company, 79, 83, 145

Nonaccelerating-inflation rate of unemployment (NAIRU), impact of FDI on, 61–62

Nonvoting trust, 117

North American Free Trade Agreement (NAFTA), 136, 137, 145, 170, 173

Norton, 130

Nuclear energy, 122

Office of Technology Assessment, 151

Oil companies, 100–01. *See also* Petroleum refining; *names of companies*

Omnibus Trade and Competitiveness Act of 1988, 126

Organization for Economic Cooperation and Development, 134–35, 173, 184

Organized labor, 60, 139, 152

Outward FDI, US policy toward, 93, 97–98, 100—01, 134–40

Performance requirements,
  arguments against, 159
  CFIUS imposition of, 132
  definition of, 158
  in Hüls-Monsanto case, 129
  investment incentives and, 138, 145–46, 159–60, 168
  in NAFTA, 136
  for national security purposes, 105, 163, 165, 167
  proposal to impose on Japanese firms, 160
  in proposed international investment accord, 172
  state and local, 141, 159–60
  in Uruguay Round, 138
  in US-Canada Free Trade Agreement, 172

Persian Gulf war, 107–08, 166

Petroleum refining, 16, 75
Political effects of FDI, 4, 85–93
Political geography of FDI in United States, 96
Portfolio investment, 9, 31, 36—37, 39
President, powers to restrict FDI of, 106–08, 113, 126–32
Prestowitz, Clyde V., 156, 160
Protectionism, effect on FDI flows of, 49–50

Quality of employment in foreign affiliates, 62–63

Rated orders, 105–06
Ravenscroft, David J., 82
Raytheon Company, 169
Reagan, Ronald, and administration of, 122, 126, 152
Real estate, 9–10, 28–31, 33
Reciprocity
    in banking, 157
    as condition for participation in R&D consortia, 124
    defined, 123
    proposals for US policy regarding, 156–58
    selective, 157
Redistributional effects of FDI, 85–92
Refining industry, 16, 75
Registration of FDI. *See* Disclosure by foreign affiliates
Reich, Robert B., 63, 154
Research and development
    applications-oriented versus basic, 73
    in automobile industry, 125
    by foreign affiliates generally, 65–66, 73–74
    by Japanese affiliates, 84
    participation of foreign affiliates in US, 124, 125, 162–63, 168
    US policy on, 73, 86
Right of establishment, 93, 122, 134, 171
Rockefeller Center, 31
Rohatyn, Felix, 43, 80–82, 154
Royal Dutch/Shell, 20, 101
Royal Institute of International Affairs, 153

Santa Fe Industries, 108
Scholes, Myron, 48
Screening of FDI
    arguments against, 154–56
    CFIUS as potential agency for, 132
    in other countries, 144–45, 146
Sectoral composition of FDI in United States, 40, 75
Securities and Exchange Commission, 133, 153
Sematech, 123, 168
Semiconductors, 116, 123
Semi-Gas, 130
Sharp, Rep. Philip R., 167, 189
Sharp (Japanese electronics firm), 168
Shell, 20, 101
Sherman Antitrust Act, 164

Siberian pipeline dispute, 139
Slemrod, Joel, 49
Slowdown of US inward FDI in early 1990s, 2, 12, 20–21, 39
Sophisticated cost-of-capital argument for FDI, 37
Special security arrangements, 117
Standard Oil of New Jersey. *See* Exxon Corp.
Stanvac, 101
State and local governments
    competition for FDI among, 89–90, 141
    performance requirements imposed by, 141, 159–60
    regulation of banking and finance by, 141
    taxation by, 142–44
Statistics, US government, on FDI. *See* Bureau of Economic Analysis, *names of other agencies*
Stein, Jeremy C., 46
Stevenson-Wydler Technology Innovation Act of 1980, 124
Strategic trade, 66–67, 193
Subnational governments. *See* State and local governments
Subsidies. *See* Investment incentives
Swenson, Deborah L., 49
Switzerland, 96

Tachonics, 130
Taxation
    avoidance by foreign affiliates of, 82–84
    effect on FDI flows of, 47–49, 56
    in Japan, 83
    national treatment in, 142–44
    in proposed international investment accord, 173
    state and local, 142–44
    territorial corporate, 48
    water's-edge formula for, 142
    worldwide corporate, 48, 142–44
Technology Preservation Act of 1991, 130
Telecommunications, 123
Televisions, 51–53, 79
"Territorial" corporate taxation, 48
Texaco, 101
Thomson-CSF, 112–13, 130–31
Tokuyama Soda, 130
Toshiba Corp., 120
Toyota Motor Corp., 89
Trade balance effects of FDI, 63–65, 68–71. *See also* Current account deficit, US, FDI inflows and
Trade-related investment measures (TRIMs). *See* Performance requirements
Trading with the Enemy Act, 103, 106
Transfer pricing abuses, 82–84
Transplants. *See* Foreign affiliates
Transportation Appropriations Act, 122

UNCITRAL Arbitration Rules, 137

United Kingdom, 21–22, 33, 40, 44, 75, 101, 145, 164
United Nations Centre on Transnational Corporations, 32
United States, government of. *See also names of federal departments and agencies*
  ability to identify potential fifth columns of, 108–10
  advocacy of national treatment by, 93
  emergency powers of, 106–08
  imposition of performance requirements by, 129, 132, 158–61
  official neutrality toward FDI of, 93, 122, 134, 146, 154
  policy on foreign participation in defense contracting of, 111–20
  policy toward high-technology industries of, 123, 167–68
  policy toward outward FDI of, 93, 97–98, 100–01, 134–40
  position on performance requirements of, 138
  powers to block foreign acquisitions of US firms of, 126–32

  reciprocity policy of, 123–25, 156–58
  R&D policy of, 73, 86
  screening of FDI by, 154–56
  trade policy for automobiles of, 91
  welfare effects of FDI policy of, 85–93
Uruguay Round, 138
US-Canada Free Trade Agreement, 135–36, 145, 170, 172
USAir Group, 123

Value added by foreign affiliates, 2, 19–20, 33, 71, 72, 78, 84
Van Rooij, Joanna, 143
Vernon, Raymond, 192, 193

Wages paid by foreign affiliates, 71, 72, 78, 84
Water's-edge unitary tax formula, 142
Wealth effects, 46
Welfare effects of US FDI policy, 85–93
Wolfson, Mark, 48
Woodward, Douglas, 60, 141, 144, 154, 159
Worldwide corporate taxation, 48, 142–44

Zenith Electronics Corp., 52, 53

Other Publications from the
Institute for International Economics

POLICY ANALYSES IN INTERNATIONAL ECONOMICS Series

BOOKS

Trade Protection in the United States: 31 Case Studies
Gary Clyde Hufbauer, Diane E. Berliner, and Kimberly Ann Elliott/1986
ISBN paper 0-88132-040-4   371 pp.

Toward Renewed Economic Growth in Latin America
Bela Balassa, Gerardo M. Bueno, Pedro-Pablo Kuczynski,
and Mario Henrique Simonsen/1986
(out of stock)   ISBN paper 0-88132-045-5   205 pp.

Capital Flight and Third World Debt
Donald R. Lessard and John Williamson, editors/1987
(out of print)   ISBN paper 0-88132-053-6   270 pp.

The Canada-United States Free Trade Agreement:
The Global Impact
Jeffrey J. Schott and Murray G. Smith, editors/1988
ISBN paper 0-88132-073-0   211 pp.

World Agricultural Trade: Building a Consensus
William M. Miner and Dale E. Hathaway, editors/1988
ISBN paper 0-88132-071-3   226 pp.

Japan in the World Economy
Bela Balassa and Marcus Noland/1988
ISBN paper 0-88132-041-2   306 pp.

America in the World Economy: A Strategy for the 1990s
C. Fred Bergsten/1988
ISBN cloth 0-88132-089-7   235 pp.
ISBN paper 0-88132-082-X   235 pp.

Managing the Dollar: From the Plaza to the Louvre
Yoichi Funabashi/1988, 2d ed. 1989
ISBN paper 0-88132-097-8   307 pp.

United States External Adjustment and the World Economy
William R. Cline/May 1989
ISBN paper 0-88132-048-X   392 pp.

Free Trade Areas and U.S. Trade Policy
Jeffrey J. Schott, editor/May 1989
ISBN paper 0-88132-094-3   400 pp.

Dollar Politics: Exchange Rate Policymaking in the United States
I. M. Destler and C. Randall Henning/September 1989
ISBN paper 0-88132-079-X   192 pp.

Latin American Adjustment: How Much Has Happened?
John Williamson, editor/April 1990
ISBN paper 0-88132-125-7   480 pp.

The Future of World Trade in Textiles and Apparel
William R. Cline/1987, 2d ed. June 1990
ISBN paper 0-88132-110-9   344 pp.

Completing the Uruguay Round: A Results-Oriented Approach
to the GATT Trade Negotiations
Jeffrey J. Schott, editor/September 1990
ISBN paper 0-88132-130-3   256 pp.

Economic Sanctions Reconsidered (in two volumes)
Economic Sanctions Reconsidered: Supplemental Case Histories
Gary Clyde Hufbauer, Jeffrey J. Schott, and Kimberly Ann Elliott/*1985, 2d ed.*
December 1990

ISBN cloth 0-88132-115-X	928 pp.
ISBN paper 0-88132-105-2	928 pp.

Economic Sanctions Reconsidered: History and Current Policy
Gary Clyde Hufbauer, Jeffrey J. Schott, and Kimberly Ann Elliott/*December 1990*

ISBN cloth 0-88132-136-2	288 pp.
ISBN paper 0-88132-140-0	288 pp.

Pacific Basin Developing Countries: Prospects for the Future
Marcus Noland/*January 1991*

ISBN cloth 0-88132-141-9	250 pp.
ISBN paper 0-88132-081-1	250 pp.

Currency Convertibility in Eastern Europe
John Williamson, editor/*October 1991*

ISBN cloth 0-88132-144-3	396 pp.
ISBN paper 0-88132-128-1	396 pp.

Foreign Direct Investment in the United States
Edward M. Graham and Paul R. Krugman/*1989, 2d ed. October 1991*

ISBN paper 0-88132-139-7	200 pp.

International Adjustment and Financing: The Lessons of 1985-1991
C. Fred Bergsten, editor/*January 1992*

ISBN paper 0-88132-112-5	336 pp.

North American Free Trade: Issues and Recommendations
Gary Clyde Hufbauer and Jeffrey J. Schott/*April 1992*

ISBN cloth 0-88132-145-1	392 pp.
ISBN paper 0-88132-120-6	392 pp.

American Trade Politics
I. M. Destler/*1986, 2d ed. June 1992*

ISBN cloth 0-88132-164-8	400 pp.
ISBN paper 0-88132-188-5	400 pp.

Narrowing the U.S. Current Account Deficit
Allen J. Lenz/*June 1992*

ISBN cloth 0-88132-148-6	640 pp.
ISBN paper 0-88132-103-6	640 pp.

The Economics of Global Warming
William R. Cline/*June 1992*

ISBN cloth 0-88132-150-8	416 pp.
ISBN paper 0-88132-132-X	416 pp.

U.S. Taxation of International Income: Blueprint for Reform
Gary Clyde Hufbauer, assisted by Joanna M. van Rooij/*October 1992*

ISBN cloth 0-88132-178-8	304 pp.
ISBN paper 0-88132-134-6	304 pp.

Who's Bashing Whom? Trade Conflict in High-Technology Industries
Laura D'Andrea Tyson/*November 1992*

ISBN cloth 0-88132-151-6	352 pp.
ISBN paper 0-88132-106-0	352 pp.

Estimating Equilibrium Exchange Rates
John Williamson, editor/*September 1994*
ISBN paper 0-88132-076-5   320 pp.

Managing the World Economy: Fifty Years After Bretton Woods
Peter B. Kenen, editor/*September 1994*
ISBN paper 0-88132-212-1   448 pp.

Reciprocity and Retaliation in U.S. Trade Policy
Thomas O. Bayard and Kimberly Ann Elliott/*September 1994*
ISBN paper 0-88132-084-6   528 pp.

The Uruguay Round: An Assessment
Jeffrey J. Schott, assisted by Johanna W. Buurman/*November 1994*
ISBN paper 0-88132-206-7   240 pp.

Measuring the Costs of Protection in Japan
Yoko Sazanami, Shujiro Urata, and Hiroki Kawai/*January 1995*
ISBN paper 0-88132-211-3   96 pp.

Foreign Direct Investment in the United States, Third Edition
Edward M. Graham and Paul R. Krugman/*January 1995*
ISBN paper 0-88132-204-0   232 pp.

SPECIAL REPORTS

1 Promoting World Recovery: A Statement on Global Economic Strategy
   by Twenty-six Economists from Fourteen Countries/*December 1982*
   (out of print)   ISBN paper 0-88132-013-7   45 pp.

2 Prospects for Adjustment in Argentina, Brazil, and Mexico:
   Responding to the Debt Crisis
   John Williamson, editor/*June 1983*
   (out of print)   ISBN paper 0-88132-016-1   71 pp.

3 Inflation and Indexation: Argentina, Brazil, and Israel
   John Williamson, editor/*March 1985*
   ISBN paper 0-88132-037-4   191 pp.

4 Global Economic Imbalances
   C. Fred Bergsten, editor/*March 1986*
   ISBN cloth 0-88132-038-2   126 pp.
   ISBN paper 0-88132-042-0   126 pp.

5 African Debt and Financing
   Carol Lancaster and John Williamson, editors/*May 1986*
   (out of print)   ISBN paper 0-88132-044-7   229 pp.

6 Resolving the Global Economic Crisis: After Wall Street
   Thirty-three Economists from Thirteen Countries/*December 1987*
   ISBN paper 0-88132-070-6   30 pp.

7 World Economic Problems
   Kimberly Ann Elliott and John Williamson, editors/*April 1988*
   ISBN paper 0-88132-055-2   298 pp.

   Reforming World Agricultural Trade
   Twenty-nine Professionals from Seventeen Countries/*1988*
   ISBN paper 0-88132-088-9   42 pp.

8 Economic Relations Between the United States and Korea:
   Conflict or Cooperation?
   Thomas O. Bayard and Soo-Gil Young, editors/*January 1989*
   ISBN paper 0-88132-068-4   192 pp.

FORTHCOMING

The Globalization of Industry and National Governments
C. Fred Bergsten and Edward M. Graham

The Political Economy of Korea–United States Cooperation
C. Fred Bergsten and Il SaKong, editors

International Debt Reexamined
William R. Cline

Trade, Jobs, and Income Distribution
William R. Cline

American Trade Politics, Third Edition
I. M. Destler

Environment in the New World Order
Daniel C. Esty

Overseeing Global Capital Markets
Morris Goldstein and Peter Garber

Global Competition Policy
Edward M. Graham and J. David Richardson

Toward a Pacific Economic Community?
Gary Clyde Hufbauer and Jeffrey J. Schott

The Economics of Korean Unification
Marcus Noland

The Case for Trade: A Modern Reconsideration
J. David Richardson

The Future of the World Trading System
John Whalley, in collaboration with Colleen Hamilton

For orders outside the US and Canada please contact:
Longman Group UK Ltd.
PO Box 88
Fourth Avenue
Harlow, Essex CM 19 5SR
UK

Telephone Orders: 0279 623923
Fax: 0279 453450
Telex: 81259

Canadian customers can order from the Institute or from either:

RENOUF BOOKSTORE	LA LIBERTÉ
1294 Algoma Road	3020 chemin Sainte-Foy
Ottawa, Ontario K1B 3W8	Quebec G1X 3V6
Telephone: (613) 741-4333	Telephone: (418) 658-3763
Fax: (613) 741-5439	Fax: (800) 567-5449